# HOPE UNDER NEOLIBERAL AUSTERITY

## Responses from Civil Society and Civic Universities

Edited by
Mel Steer, Simin Davoudi, Mark Shucksmith
and Liz Todd

Foreword by
Lord Kerslake

First published in Great Britain in 2021 by

Policy Press, an imprint of
Bristol University Press
University of Bristol
1–9 Old Park Hill
Bristol
BS2 8BB
UK
t: +44 (0)117 954 5940
e: bup-info@bristol.ac.uk

Details of international sales and distribution partners are available at
policy.bristoluniversitypress.co.uk

British Library Cataloguing in Publication Data
A catalogue record for this book is available from the British Library

ISBN 978-1-4473-5682-0 hardcover
ISBN 978-1-4473-5685-1 ePub
ISBN 978-1-4473-5684-4 ePdf

The right of Mel Steer, Simin Davoudi, Mark Shucksmith and Liz Todd to be identified as
editors of this work has been asserted by them in accordance with the Copyright, Designs and
Patents Act 1988.

Every reasonable effort has been made to obtain permission to reproduce copyrighted
material. If, however, anyone knows of an oversight, please contact the publisher.

The statements and opinions contained within this publication are solely those of the editors
and contributors and not of the University of Bristol or Bristol University Press. The
University of Bristol and Bristol University Press disclaim responsibility for any injury to
persons or property resulting from any material published in this publication.

Bristol University Press and Policy Press work to counter discrimination on grounds of
gender, race, disability, age and sexuality.

Cover design: Clifford Hayes
Front cover image: https://pxhere.com/en/photo/967739
Bristol University Press and Policy Press use environmentally responsible
print partners.
Printed and bound in the UK by CPI Group (UK) Ltd, Croydon, CR0 4YY

FSC
www.fsc.org
MIX
Paper from
responsible sources
FSC® C013604

# Contents

# List of tables, figures and boxes

## Tables

## Figures

## Boxes

# Notes on contributors

**Dominic Aitken** is a research associate in environmental gerontology who joined Newcastle University in 2017 following a post at Northumbria University. With a background in medical sciences and urban regeneration, Dominic's work focuses on the contribution better housing can make to health, most recently, home adaptations.

**Paul Benneworth** was Professor of Innovation and Regional Development at the Department of Business Administration at the Western Norway University of Applied Sciences. His research focused on better conceptualising the connections between higher education and society, and the implications this raised for policy and practice.

**Elizabeth Brooks** is a research associate at the School of Architecture, Planning and Landscape, Newcastle University, specialising in social and environmental justice. She has worked in research for almost 25 years and is currently employed by two European Union studies, RELOCAL and BEMINE, exploring, respectively, community development and levels of governance.

**Sara Bryson** is a community organiser for Tyne and Wear Citizens. Citizens UK organises communities to act together for power, social justice and the common good. Launched by Citizens UK in 2001, the living wage campaign has won over £210 million of additional wages, lifting over 70,000 families out of working poverty.

**Lizzie Coles-Kemp** is a qualitative researcher at Royal Holloway University of London. She uses creative engagement methods to research the intersections between human security and digital security. Lizzie is currently an Economic and Physical Sciences Research Council (EPSRC) research fellow and coordinates the 'Digital Security for All' theme as part of the UK Research and Innovation NetworkPlus Not-Equal.

**Clara Crivellaro** is a Human–Computer Interaction researcher at Newcastle University's Open Lab. She explores the design of social technologies to support democracy, social innovation and socio-economic justice. Clara is currently leading the UK Research and Innovation NetworkPlus Not-Equal, 'Social Justice through the Digital Economy'.

**Simin Davoudi** is Professor of Environment and Planning, and Director of the Global Urban Research Unit, at Newcastle University. She is past President of the Association of European Schools of Planning, and Fellow of the Royal Town Planning Institute, Academy of Social Sciences and Royal Society of Arts. Her research focuses on governance, power, knowledge, justice and democracy.

**Anne de A'Echevarria** works as a freelance creative learning consultant and writer, directing her own consultancy, Thinkwell. She has worked with many teams within the education, media and health sectors – any group that is interested in exploring how best to develop a culture of enquiry, creativity and creative learning within their organisation.

**Ben Dickenson** was Executive Producer of City of Dreams, appointed by NewcastleGateshead Cultural Venues, from 2017 until the end of 2020. His career has involved community arts, writing for stage and screen, filmmaking, teaching, and managing supported housing, youth citizenship and children and young people's programmes. He has written two critically acclaimed books and, since 2014, has led Alphabetti Theatre's literary development.

**Caroline Emmerson** is based in Newcastle. For 40 years, she has worked in various community and youth work settings, including 11 years at the CHAT (Churches Acting Together) Trust. Her key areas of expertise are empowering people and bringing together diverse community groups to build community resilience.

**Lindy Gilliland** is Project Manager of Common Ground in Sacred Space. She previously led the redevelopment of the Great North Museum and the Hatton Gallery (Newcastle University) while working at Tyne and Wear Archives and Museums. She is an experienced museum professional formerly working in university and local authority sectors.

**Rose Gilroy** is Professor of Ageing, Planning and Policy at Newcastle University. She has published extensively on the city, neighbourhood and housing as arenas for ageing well. She founded the Future Homes Alliance community interest company that will build innovative housing in Newcastle.

**John Goddard OBE** is Emeritus Professor of Regional Development Studies at Newcastle University and formerly Deputy Vice Chancellor responsible for the university's civic engagement. In that role, he was appointed a member of the Council of St Nicholas's Cathedral and subsequently chaired the board for its Common Ground in Sacred Space project. He was Vice Chair of the Civic University Commission.

**Jill Haley** is Chief Executive of Byker Community Trust, Housing Association, Newcastle. She is a demonstrated and experienced professional with a long history of working in the civil and social organisation industry, also attaining private sector practice. She has strategic housing, community development, finance, governance, business development and risk management skills. She is a qualified coach, passionate about excellence in leadership, empowerment and customer excellence.

**Annette Hastings** is Professor of Urban Studies in the School of Social and Political Sciences at the University of Glasgow. Annette's research and teaching focuses on the drivers of urban inequality and approaches to tackling this, with a particular focus on the role of public services.

**Kirsty Hayward** is STEM Engagement Manager at Success4All, a small educational charity based in the North East of England. Success4All supports children and young people in community centres and schools where it is needed most. Success4All believes that young people learn best from each other and embeds open-ended, young person-led learning throughout all its services.

**Patsy Healey** (an elected trustee of Glendale Gateway Trust) is Professor Emeritus in the School of Architecture, Planning and Landscape at Newcastle University. She has qualifications in geography and planning, and is a specialist in planning theory and practice. She was Chair of the Glendale Gateway Trust from 2012 to 2015.

**Tom Johnston** is the Chief Executive and a founder trustee of Glendale Gateway Trust, and active community volunteer. Tom became a paid member of staff for the trust and has been employed by them since 2000, championing community enterprise and ownership projects, including local housing, refurbished retail units and a community resource centre.

**Louise Kempton** is a researcher in the Centre for Urban and Regional Development Studies at Newcastle University. Her main interest is the role of universities in local/regional economic growth and innovation.

In 2019, Louise was appointed Associate Dean for Research and Innovation in the Faculty of Humanities and Social Sciences.

**David Leat** is Professor of Curriculum Innovation at Newcastle University and the University of South East Norway. His original research interest in thinking skills has developed over the last 20 years, through projects on metacognition, Learning2Learn and innovative coaching, to focus on 'enquiry-based learning' and 'community curriculum making'.

**Daniel Mallo** is an architect and lecturer in architecture at Newcastle University. His practice-led research focuses on socially engaged spatial practice and design activism. In recent years, Daniel has led projects in both the UK and Europe with institutions including KU Leuven (Belgium), Creative Partnerships and Economic and Social Research Council Impact Acceleration Account-funded projects.

**Frank Mansfield** is an elected trustee of Glendale Gateway Trust. Frank was a broadcast journalist (mainly with the BBC), also teaching part-time at Sheffield University. Having lived in Tyneside, London, Sheffield and Liverpool, he bought a bungalow in Wooler in 1996 and moved there permanently in 2004. He was Chair of the Glendale Gateway Trust from 2015 to 2018.

**David Marlow** is a development economist and place-making strategist who runs Third Life Economics and is Visiting Professor of Practice at the Centre for Urban and Regional Development Studies, Newcastle University. After a 25-year senior public service career – eight as chief executive – David currently works on supporting local growth, devolution and place-based strategy in England and overseas.

**Jane Midgley** is Reader in Urban Social and Economic Practice at Newcastle University. Jane's research explores responsibility and vulnerability within communities, and specifically the food system, leading to her specific focus on surplus food redistribution and the practices of industry and charitable actors in this process.

**Philip Miller** is a senior architect at Ryder Architecture. He joined the practice in 2013 and has been involved in a number of key national healthcare projects, including the Emergency Care Centre, Dumfries and Galloway Royal Infirmary and The Children's Heart Unit. He studied at Sheffield and Newcastle Universities.

**Mark Pardoe** is a Fenham resident with a young family. In 2015, after compulsory redundancy, Mark got involved with the DIY Streets project on Fenham Hall Drive. Mark established a constitution for the group and is secretary. Mark has been a Sustrans supporter since 1996.

**John Pendlebury** is Professor of Urban Conservation at Newcastle University. John is a town planner and urban conservationist, with ten years' practice experience in local government, central government and consultancy before re-entering academia. He has had many university roles, including serving as head of school. John teaches and undertakes research on heritage, conservation and planning.

**Venda Louise Pollock** is Dean of Culture and Creative Arts, and Professor of Public Art, at Newcastle University. She works to catalyse initiatives contributing to research and wider economic, cultural and societal benefit. Her broader research relates to the relationship between art and the urban environment.

**Mark Shucksmith OBE** is Professor of Planning, former Director of Newcastle University's Institute for Social Renewal and Trustee of Carnegie UK Trust and Action with Communities in Rural England. Mark's research addresses social exclusion in rural areas and rural development. He chaired the Committee of Inquiry into Crofting and engages actively in policy and practice.

**Sam Slatcher** is a community music practitioner and the director of Citizen Songwriters, a social enterprise that encourages social harmony through songwriting. At the time of writing, Sam was the refugee volunteer coordinator at REᴱUSE. He has a PhD in human geography on encounters in creative community engagement projects in West Yorkshire.

**Mel Steer** is Vice Chancellor's Fellow at Northumbria University and previously worked as a researcher at Newcastle University. Her research interests include social policy, social justice, reducing poverty and disadvantage, health and social inequality, and the public and voluntary sectors.

**Marion Talbot** has worked in a variety of jobs in the statutory, voluntary and private sectors, and has a range of experience at senior management level. She recently stepped down after seven years as a Newcastle City councillor representing West Fenham ward. As a ward councillor Marion was involved in a number of initiatives to improve the environment, health and well-being of residents, especially those who are socially isolated.

**Armelle Tardiveau** is a lecturer in architecture at Newcastle University, design practitioner, educator and researcher in the disciplines of architecture and urban design. Her multidisciplinary research, involving artists, landscape architects and ethnographers, focuses on participatory design, design activism and co-production in the public realm.

**Ulrike Thomas** is a research associate in the Centre for Learning and Teaching at Newcastle University. Formerly a primary school teacher, her research interest focuses on curriculum and pedagogic innovation. She is currently working with teachers and community partners to develop projects and resources underpinned by the principles of enquiry/project-based learning.

**Liz Todd** is Professor of Educational Inclusion at Newcastle University. Liz engages in research with a strong social justice agenda, being known for her work on the interaction between communities and schools, the engagement of young people in development and research, and respectful democratic approaches to change (personal and organisational).

**Michael Walker** drives Gateshead's anti-poverty approach, working with strategic partners and businesses. He has worked for Gateshead Council for 13 years, including as financial inclusion lead and employment support manager, and is passionate about tackling poverty in the place where he lives and works, aiming to make Gateshead a place where everyone thrives.

**David Webb** is Senior Lecturer in Planning and also Director of Engagement at the School of Architecture, Planning and Landscape, Newcastle University. His work centres on the government of people and places, and the way this unfolds over time to reflect pressures exerted socially and geographically.

**Karen Wood** has worked in the community for over 20 years supporting those most vulnerable. She is a voice for those who need to be heard. As the Manager of Pallion Action Group, a charity based in Sunderland, Karen has now become a local councillor to help influence decision-making.

# Acknowledgements

This book originated from a series of discussions in 2016, prompted by a suggestion from the Advisory Board of the Newcastle University Institute for Social Renewal (NISR), which led to a project exploring 'Social Renewal in the North East of England', funded by NISR in 2017. From the outset, our aim was to work with our non-academic partners from organisations in the voluntary, community and social enterprise, public, and private sectors to co-produce the research and the contributions in this volume. We are grateful for the support given by the NISR throughout this time. We also owe special thanks to Derek Bell (Professor of Environmental Political Theory at Newcastle University) for his invaluable and thoughtful inputs into the early stages of the research.

The book project itself was launched on 2 November 2017 in a workshop on 'Social Justice and Social Renewal in the North East: The Role of Non-Governmental Organisations'. This included a series of thought-provoking speeches by Jo Curry (Changing Lives), Alison Dunn (Citizens Advice Gateshead) and Professor Emeritus Susan Fainstein (Harvard Graduate School of Design), who also presented a public lecture at Newcastle University organised by the School of Architecture, Planning and Landscape. The launch was followed by two more authors' workshops on 24 January and 16 September 2019, in which the structure and content of the book were co-produced. We are grateful to all speakers and participants for their active engagements in the debates and in shaping the production of this volume.

We also owe thanks to those with whom we had insightful conversations during the planning stages of the book: Jo Curry (Changing Lives), Mark Pierce (The Community Foundation), Nitin Shukla (Office of the Police and Crime Commissioner Northumbria), Jane Hartley (Voluntary Organisations Network North East), Steve Forster (Together Newcastle), Abu Tayeb Khairdeen (Islamic Diversity Centre), Lindsay Cross (West End Refugee Service), Sally Young (Newcastle Council for Voluntary Service), Sara Bryson (Tyne and Wear Citizens), Helen Dickinson (Newcastle City Council), Deborah Harrison (North East Child Poverty Commission) and Alison Dunn (Citizens Advice Gateshead).

Our special gratitude goes to Dr Faith Goodfellow, whose editorial assistance and support has been crucial in enabling us to deliver the book on time. As a committed voluntary worker and supporter of civil society actions, Faith has also been a valuable contributor to the debates in the workshops and beyond. We are also grateful to Stuart Hand and Alex Robson from Newcastle University's Institute for Social Science for their administrative support, and to Emily Watt and Caroline Astley from Policy Press for their support throughout this project.

Just before the book reached the production stage, we heard the tragic and shocking news that Professor Paul Benneworth had sadly passed away. Paul generously supported our book by agreeing to write a reflective chapter on the role of civic universities. We are saddened by his sudden death and feel privileged to have worked with him on what was probably his last piece of writing in a prolific and acclaimed academic career.

Finally, the opinions expressed in the chapters are entirely the responsibility of the authors and do not necessarily reflect the views of the editors, the funding organisations or those who have taken part in interviews and workshops.

# Foreword

*Lord Kerslake*

The 'austerity decade' between 2010 and 2020 was a unique period in British economic, political and social history. Prior to that, public spending had continued to grow steadily with the development of the state's role in protecting and promoting the well-being of its citizens, albeit with periodic reining in during economic crises. Even in the Thatcher government, the cuts were borne most by capital expenditure, notably, housing investment, rather than day-to-day spending on services.

The austerity programme introduced by the Conservative–Liberal Democrat Coalition in 2010 represented a sharp reversal of that trend. It was born out of the financial crisis of 2008 – essentially a banking crisis – the cost of responding to which had seriously impacted the country's finances. This was common to most developed nations but was particularly significant in the UK due to the high proportion the financial services sector made up of its economy.

For the then Chancellor George Osborne, austerity was both a political and an economic agenda. The sense of crisis and urgency created – we had 'maxed out' on our credit cards and were heading towards becoming another Greece – served to underline a political argument that the previous Labour government had left the country in a financial mess and were not to be trusted on the economy. The reality was more complex than this, of course, but the political argument stuck.

There is an irony that, ten years on, the need to respond to another global crisis – this time, a health one – has resulted in ballooning deficits and total debt exceeding £2 trillion, compared to £1.2 trillion in 2010. Austerity temporarily reduced the rate of growth of our debt rather than paying it down.

The economic impact of austerity was arguably self defeating. In a period when demand and confidence in the global economy was low, severely reducing public spending simultaneously across the developed world added to the challenge of low growth and reduced government revenues. The 'expansionary fiscal contraction' vaunted by the Chancellor turned out to be a recipe for economic stagnation and led to an easing of austerity and an extension of the timescales to reduce the deficit.

Some, including former Prime Minister David Cameron, have argued that the scale of the spending reductions was not that great and the impact of austerity has been overstated. There is no doubting, though, the massive impact on local authority spending, which fell by a quarter, and the impact that this had on local communities. The reduction was even more acutely felt because of the growing demands on the adult and children's care budgets, which together make up over half of local authority spending. The consequential impact on other services – leisure, the public realm, early years and so on – was proportionately much greater.

Deprived communities suffered a triple whammy. Being more dependent on government grant meant that the scale of the cuts was even greater. At the same time, their economies were much slower to recover from the effects of the Great Depression than other, more affluent areas. The significant reductions to benefits also had a disproportionate effect.

This timely and important book tells the story of austerity from the perspective of a particular place. There is much to learn from this comprehensive and rigorous piece of work. While the story is a tough one, there are also great positives in the way that the community responded to this enormous challenge. Particularly positive is the role of the university, which fully lived up to its civic role. Universities were fortunate to be spared the full impact of austerity – this was visited on their students in the form of significantly higher fees and loans. That story has still to be played out. Some universities took this as a sign of their intrinsic importance and invested the additional funding generated solely in themselves. Others, such as Newcastle, who were more enlightened, recognised the importance of maintaining the fabric of their local communities and invested in supporting them. I was very pleased to chair the Civic University Commission in 2019, which explored this vital civic role. Professor John Goddard was my deputy and a very valued contributor.

The timeliness of this book lies in the choices confronting the current government in dealing with the cost of COVID-19. The Prime Minister has set his face against another round of austerity but there are powerful political voices on his own side calling for just this instead of the tax rises being mooted by his Chancellor Rishi Sunak. The key decision-makers in government would do well to read this book before making their final decisions.

# 1

# Islands of hope in a sea of despair: civil society in an age of austerity

*Simin Davoudi, Mel Steer, Mark Shucksmith and Liz Todd*

## Introduction

> It was the best of times, it was the worst of times ... it was the season of Light, it was the season of Darkness, it was the spring of hope, it was the winter of despair. (Dickens, 1859: 1)

Charles Dickens opens his most political novel, *A Tale of Two Cities*, with these words. Nearly two centuries later, we cannot but agree with his suggestion that, 'In short, the period was ... like the present period' (Dickens, 1859: 1). Such entangling of hope and despair not only defines our everyday life experiences; it is also echoed in the intellectual dilemma that is at the heart of this book. From the outset, we were searching for 'hope in the dark' (Solnit, 2004), with the 'dark' being austerity policies and their implications for people and places, and 'hope' being civil society's responses to them. By the time the manuscript was ready for submission (in spring 2020), the coronavirus (COVID-19) pandemic was in full swing. While a full analysis of its effects is premature and beyond the scope of this chapter, we cannot but reflect on it where appropriate, especially in the conclusion. The juxtaposing of hope and despair does not suggest that hope is an unqualified positive attribute. On the contrary, as Ernst Block (1986 [1954–59]: 56) suggests, 'fraudulent hope is one of the malefactors, even enervators, of the human race, concretely genuine hope is its most dedicated benefactor', defining the latter as 'informed discontent' with the status quo and a call for action. So, for us, hope is that which allows us to imagine an alternative future and strive to achieve it. This is particularly apt in relation to the COVID-19 crisis and the limited preparedness for tackling it. The aim of this chapter is to engage with a number of critical questions that arise from the interplay of hope and despair, such as:

- Should we celebrate the growing contributions from voluntary sector and charitable organisations as the best of times for a flourishing civil society, or should we reproach the decline of public services as the worst of times for a diminishing welfare state?
- Should we embrace civil society initiatives as a mark of resistance to neoliberal policies, or should we repel them for mopping up the consequences of such policies?
- Do civil society responses to austerity offer genuine or false hope?
- Will the flames of their actions burn strongly enough to withstand the harsh winds of neoliberal austerity and the effects of the COVID-19 pandemic?

In engaging with these questions, the chapter unpacks two core concepts that run throughout: austerity and civil society. In doing so, particular attention is paid to the North East of England in the context of the pre-COVID-19 policy landscape in the UK. This focus provides both an illustrative example of the implications of austerity measures and civil society roles, and the contextual setting (along with Chapter 2: 'The North East of England') for the case-study chapters in this volume.

## Neoliberal austerity as 'the worst of times'

The collapse of Lehman Brothers in 2007 paved the way for the largest, widest and deepest financial crisis in living memory. It revealed the inherent contradictions in the global capitalist economy, as well as the drastic consequences of excessive deregulation of the financial markets for social equality and political democracy. The financial crash was followed by the bailing out of the failing banks with a huge amount of public money, and one of the worst economic recessions in Britain. The then Labour government's response was to introduce a set of fiscal stimuli, which was promptly withdrawn by the subsequent Conservative–Liberal Democrat Coalition government in 2010 and replaced with a wave of drastic austerity policies that continued until 2020, when it was, perhaps temporarily, suspended by the Conservative government, mainly in response to the pandemic and its economic contagions.

The dictionary definition of 'austerity' refers to the 'difficult economic conditions created by government measures to reduce public expenditure' (Oxford English Dictionary). In this definition, reducing public expenditure is invoked as the only 'natural' solution to economic problems. Other economic solutions such as increasing corporate taxes are not considered. The definition, maybe inadvertently, depoliticises austerity as an economic necessity rather than a neoliberal political choice (Mattie and Salour, 2019) – a choice based on an economic rationality that has recently been further boosted by highly acclaimed economists (notably, Alberto Alesino). They suggest that by cutting welfare spending, taxes will go down, leading to an increase in the money available to private investors, whose increased wealth will eventually trickle down and reach everyone else. So, those who have disproportionately suffered from the cuts simply need to be patient. According to these economic rationalities, what matters is the effect of austerity on aggregate gross domestic product (GDP)[1] figures rather than the differential impact on different social groups. While they ask the question of when austerity works and when it does not, they shy away from asking for whom austerity works.

David Kynaston (2010) makes an intriguing comparison between post-2010 and post-Second World War austerity, and argues that 'austerity was a hard sell in the 40s. Today it's harder still.' He argues that the four conditions that enabled popular assent to post-Second World War austerity are not present in the contemporary political climate. These conditions are: 'shared purpose', 'hope', 'confidence in the political class' and 'equity of sacrifice'. While recognising the contextual differences between now and the 1950s, we argue that the presence or absence of these conditions is largely the manifestation of different ideological approaches to austerity. These conditions are discussed one by one, with reflections also made regarding the post-COVID-19 implications.

The post-war sense of 'shared purpose' was invoked by the necessity of fighting off fascism and collectively responding to the devastations and destructions of the war. Today, as Kynaston (2010) suggests, there is no similar 'historic feelgood victory to look back on'. The vacuum has been filled by 'a moralistic good housekeeping, live-within-our-means of future redemption' narrative that is not only at odds with the dominant culture of consumption, but also an advocacy of neoliberal morality about individualisation of responsibility, privatisation of social risks and self-reliant resiliency (Bohland et al, 2018). The latter has been applied not only to individuals, but also to institutions, notably, local authorities (John, 2014). The responsibilisation agenda ignores the effects of structural inequalities and considers social problems such as low educational attainment, poor housing, low income, morbidity and premature death as consequences of personal choices and individual failings (Barry, 2005). Imposing stringent austerity measures offers the potential for a neoliberal government to sermonise on the follies of a nanny state, on individual failings and on a 'broken society', as the Coalition government claimed. Failure of government to meet citizens' needs in the face of austerity is presented as a failure of the nanny state and the inherent problems associated with it, not a failure of (re)distribution and underfunding. People are vilified as being victims of their own irresponsibility rather than the collapse of the social contract. In many ways, health and economic crises resulting from COVID-19 have been exacerbated by decades of underinvestment in areas such as health, social care and social benefits in the name of austerity.

Post-war Britain was a time of grief, and also a time of 'hope'. Based on egalitarian ideals, the state could legitimately intervene in the free market and redistribute national wealth socially and spatially. It was also expected to share with citizens the responsibility for social risks. Hope was founded on this social contract and its manifestation in the provision of free education, social housing, the national health system and lifetime social security, all of which cultivated a hopeful prospect for social mobility. According to neoliberal ideology, however, state intervention in the market is not only inefficient and ineffective, but also morally dangerous because it is claimed that providing welfare cultivates a culture of dependency and eradicates self-reliance (Davoudi and Madanipour, 2015). Former Conservative Prime Minister David Cameron's notion of a 'Big Society' was indeed an advocacy of civil society assuming greater responsibility for societal problems, though without any accompanying transfer of resources. These assumptions have been called into question in response to the COVID-19 crisis, whereby the state has had to step in to provide safeguards for those affected by its economic consequences.

The 'trust and confidence' that was enjoyed by the post-war state and its political institutions has since been eroded. While key post-war political figures 'attained almost surreal levels of personal popularity' (Kynaston, 2010), the level of trust in political elites has dropped significantly, as shown in a British Social Attitudes Survey (BSAS, 2013: 16): 'The last 30 years have seen a number of important institutions fall from grace very publicly … and there is a clear sense that people have lost faith in some of Britain's most important institutions. This certainly applies to politicians and the political process.' Austerity has been introduced amid 'a growing disjunction between the stage-managed political theatres that the elites are engaged in and are projected on television screens and social media, and the reality of people's everyday political struggles to be heard and represented' (Davoudi and Steele, 2020: 113). Public confidence in government's ability to strive for a fairer and better society has been gradually diminishing. While in 1986, 38 per cent of the respondents trusted 'governments to put the nation's needs above those of a political party', in 2011, only 18 per cent did so (BSAS, 2013: 13, 16). In the future, a positive change depends largely on how the government handles the COVID-19 crisis. Judged by its initial laissez-faire approach and the lack of preparedness, especially in relation to testing and the provision of protective clothing for front-line workers, optimism may be premature.

Of the four conditions identified by Kynaston (2010), 'equity of sacrifice' is perhaps the most vivid manifestation of two ideologically driven approaches to austerity. Post-war austerity was seen as being shared by the majority of both working- and middle-class people; there was a sense of parity of sacrifice. This could not be more different from neoliberal austerity. Although the Coalition government tried to sell austerity measures through the use of rhetoric such as 'We're all in this together', it soon became evident that the poor were getting poorer during austerity, and the rich were getting richer because of it (Davoudi and Ormerod, 2021). Indeed, neoliberal austerity has hit the most vulnerable people (women, children, the disabled and the sick) and left-behind places (for example, post-industrial regions in the north of England) the hardest.

Although real GDP (which takes into account changes in prices such as inflation) in the UK grew by 5 per cent between 2012 and 2018, public expenditure on low-income families and children dropped by 44 per cent: from £403 in 2010 to £222 per person in 2018 (HRW, 2019: 50). The government's own statistics show a rise of 200,000 in the number of children in 'absolute poverty' compared with the previous year, reaching approximately 3.7 million children in 2018 (DWP, 2018: 8). Similarly, homelessness is estimated to have risen by 165 per cent since 2010, reaching 280,000 in England by 2019 (Shelter, 2019). As Garry Lemon, Director of Policy at the Trussell Trust (the UK's largest national food-bank charity), puts it, the 2010 date is important because it marked a change of government from centre-left to centre-right and the introduction of 'policies that radically cut state spending … the message was clear … we need to cut back to balance the books' (cited in McGee, 2020).

Through a number of policies, notably, the reduction in the size of welfare benefits, the increase in the conditions attached to it and the changes in the procedure by which it can be accessed, austerity has been used to radically restructure the welfare system, with devastating effects on the lives of the most vulnerable groups, as well as on their ability to cope with the consequences of the COVID-19 crisis. For example, homeless people are struggling to self-isolate despite the fact that they are 'three times more likely to have severe respiratory problems' (McGee, 2020). The inequitable impacts of austerity policies are not simply the result of economic miscalculation; they are deliberately designed to achieve the neoliberal goal of reducing the social role of the state. Indeed, austerity is a key tenet of neoliberalism. As Peck (2012: 626) argues, 'according to neoliberal script, public austerity is a necessary response to market conditions, and the state has responded by inaugurating new rounds of fiscal retrenchment'.

As Clarke and Newman (2012) suggest, austerity has evoked both the prospect of hardship and the memories of post-war solidarities. However, despite successive governments' rhetorical appeals to the latter in order to legitimise austerity, it is the former that is prevalent in the contemporary political and cultural landscape. While hardship has been felt deeply, especially among the most vulnerable, solidarity remained a distant memory, at least until the COVID-19 crisis, when it was foregrounded partly by reference to the post-war era. As a result, people's participation in austerity has been characterised by Clarke and Newman (2012: 309) as a 'passive consent' rather than a 'popular mobilization'. However, we argue that if the outcome of the referendum on UK membership of the European Union (EU) is anything to go by, the initial 'passive consent' turned into an 'active discontent' with neoliberal austerity, which was 'hijacked by far-right populist parties and turned into instruments of their regressive and divisive political agendas' (Davoudi and Steele, 2020: 115). The far-right's hijacking of the narrative has been facilitated because successive political leaders failed to condemn the market's intensification and its pernicious, harmful effects (Shenker, 2019: 40), which were apparent even before austerity's onslaughts. As shown in the 2019 election, the rising level of discontent with austerity could no longer be ignored by electioneers seeking to win the public's vote. At the time of writing and in the face of the COVID-19 crisis, public spending has reached a scale never seen during peacetime.

The inequitable effects of austerity have had a spatial dimension too, with some of the poorest cities and regions of England being hit hardest, including the North East region. Severe cuts to local governments' public spending (Bailey et al, 2015; Hastings et al, 2015) has compounded the inequitable social effects of austerity because, in these areas, disadvantage is concentrated and there is a heavy reliance on the public sector for jobs and services (Peck, 2012). The scale and severity of budget cuts, especially in the North East, has reduced local governments' ability to deliver services and to manage the recurring crises of capitalism. Proclamations from Boris Johnson's Conservative government to 'level up' the regional economic, employment and budget disparities remain exactly that, while actual actions for levelling up have become more imperative than ever as the COVID-19 crisis is widely predicted to exacerbate existing spatial and socio-economic inequalities (Partington, 2020). So far, central government activities regarding its response to the pandemic are foreboding. Critical responses – such as testing and tracing – have been centralised and privatised, against expert advice, while the role of the public sector and local public health networks has been overlooked. Furthermore, Public Health England has been effectively dismantled and the expertise and resources within local authorities and community organisations have hardly been utilised (Chakrabortty, 2020). However, amid the darkness of austerity Britain and the global pandemic, there have also been glimmers of hope in the form of a rising level of activities by civil societies.

## Proactive civil societies as the 'best of times'

> The idea of civil society failed because it became too popular. (Wolfe, 1997: 9)

This provocation refers to the faith in many concepts that travel far and fast and pick up different meanings at every stop along the way. 'Civil society' is not an exception; its history goes back to ancient Greece and its development as a concept began with the Enlightenment thinkers (notably, Alexis de Tocqueville) and continued through the works of many scholars, notably, Gramsci, who 'may be single-handedly responsible for the revival of the term civil society in the post-World War Two period' (Foley and Hodgkinson, 2002: xix). Today, its widespread popularity is due to the rising presence of non-governmental organisations (NGOs) on the global stage since the 1980s. The long history of civil society is coupled with its various theorisations. According to Edwards (2014: 10), there are at least three distinct schools of thoughts about what civil society is, each of which has its own historical root, normative claims and socio-political implications.

The first one considers civil society as a *part* of society that is distinct from states and markets; it is a form of associational life. Its origin goes back to de Tocqueville's view of the 19th-century US and the defence of individual freedom from the intrusion of the state. This view of civil society is particularly strong in the US and shares similar distrust of the state and desire for self-governance as that advocated by communitarians (Edwards, 2014: 7). It is, therefore, not surprising that one of its most influential contemporary advocates, Robert Putnam, has come from the US. The everyday references to, for example, the 'third' or 'non-profit' sector, which includes associations (notably, NGOs) whose membership and activities are voluntary, are often a reflection of this theory of civil society.

The second view considers civil society as 'good society' – as a *kind* of society characterised by positive norms and values, as well as success in meeting particular social goals. The third school of thought defines civil society as the 'public sphere'. This view was first developed by scholars such as John Dewey and Hannah Arendt in their theorisations of the 'public sphere' as a central component of political life and democracy (Edwards, 2014: 8). It then became influential through Jürgen Habermas's theory of 'communicative action' and 'discursive democracy'. For him and other critical theorists, civil society is that which 'is steered by its members through shared meanings that are constructed democratically in the public sphere' (Chambers, 2002: 94). Despite the diversity of views, it is the theory of civil society as a form of associational life that has become dominant in policy discourse and popular imaginaries. As Edwards (2014: 10) puts it, 'it is Alexis Tocqueville's ghost that wanders through the corridors of the World Bank, not that of Habermas or Hegel'.

The understanding of civil society as associational life (that is, distinct from states and markets) resonates with the 'third way' politics of the New Labour government in the 1990s, which claimed to be the middle ground between the state-oriented (welfarist) and the market-oriented (neoliberalist) solution to collective problems. While, in reality, the so-called 'third sector' has been made financially dependent on the state and the private sector, and the boundaries between them have become blurred, it is this third sector view that is often visualised in myriad so-called 'triple helix' diagrams.

It is interesting to note that civil society as *part of* society is often conflated with civil society as *a kind of* society, assuming that 'a healthy associational life contributes to, or even produces, the "good society" in ways that are predictable – while the public sphere is usually ignored' (Edwards, 2014: 10). Such a perspective overlooks the various forms of what Chambers and Kopstein (2001) call 'bad civil society': although they resonate with many of the principles of what a civil society is (coherence, trust and so on), they are exclusionary of and sometimes hostile to outsiders and 'Others'. Examples include the voluntary organisations that nurture hatred and fear.

There is another frequent conflation between civil society as an *end* and civil society as a *means*. According to Edwards (2014: 11), this is due to a number of political changes, epitomised by the fall of the Berlin Wall in 1989, when civil society 'became both ... a new type of society characterised by liberal democratic norms and a vehicle for achieving it'. An example of such a conflation can be found in the range of civil society roles that have been identified by the World Economic Forum (2013: 9), which suggests that civil societies act as: watchdog (holding institutions to account); advocate/campaigner (raising awareness and lobbying governments for change); service provider (related to education, health, food and security, and contributing to disaster risk management and emergency response); expert (bringing in local, experiential knowledge); capacity builder (providing education and training); incubator (developing solutions that may materialise in the long term); representative (empowering the marginalised or under-represented); champion of active citizenship (motivating civic engagement and supporting citizen rights); solidarity supporter (promoting fundamental values); and definer of standards (creating norms that shape market and state activity).

Many of these roles assume more organised forms of civil society, known as 'civil society organisations', 'non-governmental organisations' or, in England and Wales, the 'voluntary, community and charitable sector'. Perhaps arising from the conflations that Edwards (2014) identifies, the UK National Council of Voluntary Organisations (NCVO, 2019) highlights the disputed nature of the term 'civil society', suggesting that it encompasses a breadth of organisations extending beyond legally registered charities to include, for example, trade unions, universities and housing associations. The contention about the scope and definition of civil society makes it hard to quantify the total number of organisations. For example, the NCVO's scope is narrower than the Charities Commission as their count of 'general charities' excludes independent schools, housing associations and sacramental religious bodies, and instead bases its definition of general charities on the fulfilment of criteria such as independence from government, being non-profit and working for public benefit. According to this definition, in 2016/17, there were 166,854 general charities in the UK, of which 4,450 were in the North East of England, amounting to 1.7 organisations per 1,000 population – the lowest rate in England (NCVO, 2019).

Focusing on what they do rather than who they are does not reduce the diversity either; yet, in broad terms, much of their activities are directed at improving the well-being of citizens (Clifford, 2017). Despite some serious controversies around the aggressive marketing tactics of some charities and their accountability with regard to salaries, staff conduct and disciplinary policies, charities generally attract higher public regard than many other organisations, even though confidence in them may have fallen in recent years (Charity Commission for England and Wales, 2018). Keen and Audickas (2017) suggest that the sector is predominantly focused on the delivery of social services (18.2 per cent), followed by culture and recreation (8.7 per cent), which are activities that focus on well-being.

### The impact of austerity on civil society organisations

The long-term contraction of the state's social role and its capacity to deliver social services, compounded by neoliberal austerity, has significantly reduced civil society organisations' capacity to respond to rising demands (Jones et al, 2016). This has generated feelings of disempowerment and ineffectiveness, as shown in the following statement by a welfare adviser in Hull with 15 years' experience: 'A few years ago, we used to be able to help people with an answer, direct them somewhere for help, but increasingly there's not much we can do. The safety nets to which we used to direct them, which they may not have known about, aren't there anymore' (HRW, 2019: 15). In the North East, nearly half (46 per cent) of the organisations completing the Voluntary Organisations' Network North East's survey reported an 85 per cent increase in demand for their services, a decrease in their grant income from local authorities (Meegan et al, 2014; VONNE, 2016; Clifford, 2017) and staff redundancies. The effects are variable depending on their size, activity and location, with those more reliant on state funding and operating in disadvantaged areas experiencing a larger fall in their income (Jones et al, 2016), as is the case in the North East (Chapman and Hunter, 2017). Here, smaller charities in poorer areas also lack confidence, resources and skills to apply for grants from national bodies (Pharoah et al, 2014). While the COVID-19 lockdown has further increased demand and reduced their resources, the majority of the sector have continued their support. Some of the increased pressures have been driven from the government's attempts to redirect demand away from the public sector towards them, as is the case in the referral of patients to an already-stretched voluntary sector (NCVO, 2019).

The problem of the government offloading its responsibility onto civil society organisations' shoulders and overburdening them with what ought to be the responsibility of the public sector came to the surface during the outbreak of COVID-19, as reported by a volunteer in an independent food bank:

> The majority of our volunteers are retired. Some are not in good health because it's hard to be when you're over 70 ... We've given them the option of dropping out and obeying the government guidelines. But it does leave a hole. Now, if a family member coughs, people are gone at the drop of a hat. (Quoted in McGee, 2020)

Added to the reduced supply of volunteers was the limited amount of donated food as for the 'people who use the food bank, it's quite a hand-to-mouth existence. And now that food just isn't there' (quoted in McGee, 2020).

In response to neoliberal austerity measures, civil society organisations have stepped in to compensate for the loss of a safety net, creating a juxtaposition between the expression of solidarity ('the best of times') and the state's abdication of responsibility ('the worst of times'). Nowhere is this more apparent than in the growth of food banks in response to growing food poverty (HRW, 2019), as articulated by the Chief Executive of the Trussell Trust:

> Food banks have tried to stem the tide, but no charity can replace the dignity of people having enough money to afford a decent standard of living. The failure to tackle the structural problems at both a national and local level has left people with nowhere else to turn. We have the power to tackle these structural problems as a nation. (Quoted in HRW, 2019: 9)

These accounts highlight the limit to the perceived adaptability of civil society – compared with the state and the market – and its ability to align its core activities and values to maintain integrity and mission (Corner, 2014).

Transferring what were previously government services and assets to the charitable sector undermines democratic accountability. Instead of these organisations complementing state provision, they are increasingly operating 'as *substitute* for the provision of services by public sector professionals' (Lyall and Bua, 2015: 33, original emphasis). This risks undermining the relationship between citizens and the state, and between citizens and voluntary sector organisations, increasing the stigma and shame that many people feel. The sector is also changing through undertaking target-driven, performance-managed services where the government has set the agenda. The encroachment of 'new public management' approaches in the voluntary sector may bring with it the neoliberal discourses of responsibilisation (Powell et al, 2017), through which benefit recipients are denigrated. Such a discourse became commonplace through popular media and television programmes such as 'Benefits Street' in England and 'The Scheme' in Scotland (Mooney and Hancock, 2010; Marriott, 2017). As Clarke and Elgenuis (2014) argue, the Coalition government's 'skivers v strivers message is inflaming resentments between those affected by the economic slump', while 'benefit crackdown leads to divide and rule within poor communities', essentially breaking down civil society. Furthermore, the new public management approaches are changing the nature of volunteering, with negative effects on attracting and retaining volunteers, who become subject to the culture of performance indicators and an emphasis on competing with other civil society organisations to win contracts. The concept of 'joyless volunteering' (Dunn, 2017) has emerged, whereby volunteers are often expected to participate in strategic decisions concerning service provision and staff redundancies, and to be on the front line of hard-pressed services for citizens, bearing the brunt of expressed frustration.

Finally, we return to the idea of civil society as the 'public sphere', which goes beyond service delivery and focuses on the role of civil society in critiquing and shaping public policy (Williams and Goodman, 2011). This is where tensions arise in civil society organisations, whereby their role as the voice of the disempowered may contradict with their dependence on state funding and the delivery of services that are commissioned by the government. Both of these may hamper their willingness to confront and question government policy (Alcock, 2010), and compromise their autonomy and advocacy role, especially for disadvantaged communities. As a study by Hemmings (2017: 59) shows, austerity, the shift to the 'contract culture' (Bode, 2006), competition, professionalisation and 'self-muzzling' has restricted the ability of the voluntary sector to advocate for disadvantaged groups, and to challenge government policy – a role that was further curtailed by recent legislation.[2]

In many ways, the aforementioned empirical cases reflect the theoretical critiques of the public sphere as a static, essentialised and neutral space. Instead, scholars (notably, Chantal Mouffe) consider the public sphere as a contested space. Here, 'passive observance of moralist comprehensive doctrines' that underpin the liberal views of the public sphere is replaced with 'proactive engagement and sifting of ideas and actions' by political actors, who have 'their own visions and versions of the common good' (Baker, 2018: 258). This dynamic and relational perspective combines political values of agonistic pluralism with ethical values of shared civil imaginaries, which are 'mediated through rules and norms of conduct that help create a common bond and public concern' (Baker, 2018: 259). For us, it is this understanding of civil society as a *contested* 'public sphere' that presents hope in the dark (see also Davoudi and Ormerod, 2021).

## Concluding reflections

This chapter comes to a conclusion at a time of a global health crisis – the COVID-19 pandemic. We, the authors, are self-isolated in our homes. Businesses are shut down. Shops and schools are closed. Cities are eerily empty, quiet and locked down, and ambulance sirens are constant reminders that hospital beds are filling up and many lives are being tragically lost. While everyone is exposed to the virus, it is becoming evident that some are more vulnerable than others, not just due to their age, but also because of persisting social inequalities. Those who have borne the brunt of austerity measures are also the most vulnerable to the effects of the pandemic. The COVID-19 crisis has shone a light (if we can call it that) on the plight of those in poverty, without a job, without a home, without food and with poor health. The virus has exposed the cracks in our societies – cracks that have been widened by decades of austerity measures and disinvestment in public services and social safety nets. All this makes it hard not to think that it is 'the worst of times'.

In the midst of such despair, we look out of the window and see civil societies in action: neighbours are helping neighbours; volunteers are delivering food to families; charities have ramped up their work despite dwindling donations; and hundreds of thousands of people are volunteering to reduce the burden on essential public services, notably, the National Health Service (NHS) – the only legacy of the post-war welfare state that has not yet been fully privatised and neoliberalised. To further blur the boundaries of the so-called three sectors, businesses are providing free services to communities: laundries are washing key workers' uniforms; restaurants are delivering hot meals to hospital staff; hotels are opening their doors to homeless people; and supermarkets are donating to food banks. Similarly, public sector key workers – notably, nurses, doctors and carers – are working around the clock to save lives, and the government is promising to 'do what it takes'[3] to protect businesses and families. All this makes it easy to think that it is 'the best of times'.

Thus, there is no escape from the entanglement of hope and despair. And nor should there be because lying in their intersection is a political force that enables us to imagine how we might be otherwise, and engenders the condition of the possibility for alternatives to neoliberal social orders. The COVID-19 pandemic will abate sooner or later but its wider socio-economic impacts will last for many years to come. There will be a 'new normal' but what it will look like depends largely on the mobilisation of civil society, understood not simply as the provider of voluntary services, but crucially as a *contested* 'public sphere' infused with power and politics in which tensions and contradictions are played out, with uncertain outcomes. It is in this sense that civil society can be seen as the embodiment of *hope* in the midst of multiple and related crises, and the mobiliser of what Block (1986 [1954–59]: 43) famously called an 'ontology of the Not Yet', enabling citizens to step *out* of the undesirable present, rather than staying hopeful *in* it.

## Notes

[1] The value of goods and services produced over a specific period of time.

[2] The Transparency of Lobbying, Non-party Campaigning and Trade Union Administration Act 2014 (the Lobbying Act 2014).

[3] The phrase first used by the UK Chancellor of Exchequer when he presented the government budget in February 2020.

## References

Alcock, P. (2010) 'Better get used to bitten fingers', *The House Magazine*, University of Birmingham, 19 April.

Bailey, N., Bramley, G. and Hastings, A. (2015) 'Symposium introduction: local responses to "austerity"', *Local Government Studies*, 41(4): 571–81.

Baker, C. (2018) 'Aiming for reconnection: responsible citizenship', in S. Cohen, C. Fuhr and J. Bock (eds) *Austerity, Community Action, and the Future of Citizenship in Europe*, Bristol: Policy Press.

Barry, B. (2005) *Why Social Justice Matters*, Cambridge: Polity Press.

Block, E. (1986 [1954–59]) *The Principle of Hope, Volume 1*, Boston, MA: MIT Press.

Bode, I. (2006) 'Disorganized welfare mixes: voluntary agencies and new governance regimes in Western Europe', *Journal of European Social Policy*, 16(4): 346–59.

Bohland, J., Davoudi, S. and Lawrence, J. (eds) (2018) *The Resilience Machine*, London: Routledge.

BSAS (British Social Attitudes Survey) (2013) 'British Social Attitudes Survey 30, key findings'. Available at: www.bsa.natcen.ac.uk/media/1144/bsa30_key_findings_final.pdf

Chakrabortty, A. (2020) 'England's test and trace is a fiasco because public sector has been utterly sidelined', *The Guardian*, 17 September. Available at: www.theguardian.com/commentisfree/2020/sep/17/england-test-and-trace-public-sector-boris-johnson-covid

Chambers, S. (2002) 'A critical theory of civil society', in S. Chambers and W. Kymlicka (eds) *Alternative Conceptions of Civil Society*, Princeton, NJ: Princeton University Press, pp 90–113.

Chambers, S. and Kopstein, J. (2001) 'Bad civil society', *Political Theory*, 29(6): 837–65.

Chapman, T. and Hunter, J. (2017) *Third Sector Trends in the North of England: A Summary of Key Findings*, Manchester: IPPR North. Available at: www.ippr.org/files/publications/pdf/third-sector-trends-in-the-north-of-England_Mar2017.pdf

Charity Commission for England and Wales (2018) *Trust in Charities in 2018*, London: Charity Commission.

Clarke, T. and Elgenuis, G. (2014) 'Benefits crackdown leads to divide and rule within poor communities', *The Guardian*, 30 April. Available at: www.theguardian.com/society/2014/apr/30/benefits-crackdown-divide-and-rule-poor-communities-coalition

Clarke, J. and Newman, J. (2012) 'The alchemy of austerity', *Critical Social Policy*, 32(3): 299–319.

Clifford, D. (2017) 'Charitable organisations, the Great Recession and the age of austerity: longitudinal evidence for England and Wales', *Journal of Social Policy*, 46(1): 1–30.

Corner, J. (2014) *Backing Those Who Show Most Courage: Voluntary-Sector Leadership in a Time of Austerity*, Manchester: IPPR North. Available at: www.ippr.org/juncture/backing-those-who-show-most-courage-voluntary-sector-leadership-in-a-time-of-austerity

Davoudi, S. and Madanipour, A. (eds) (2015) *Reconsidering Localism*, London: Routledge.

Davoudi, S. and Ormerod, E. (2021) 'Hope and despair at the time of pandemic', *Town Planning Review*. https://doi.org/10.3828/tpr.2020.77

Davoudi, S. and Steele, J. (2020) 'Unaccountable city', in J. Dobson and R. Atkinson (eds) *Urban Crisis, Urban Hope: A Policy Agenda for UK Cities*, London: Anthem Press, pp 113–25.

Dickens, C. (1859) *A Tale of Two Cities*, London: Chapman and Hall.

Dunn, A. (2017) 'Austerity, Citizens Advice and living in poverty', presentation at the Great North Museum, Newcastle, 22 November.

DWP (Department for Work and Pensions) (2018) 'Households below average income: an analysis of the UK income distribution: 1994/95–2017/18', 28 March. Available at: https://assets.publishing.service.gov.uk/government/uploads/system/uploads/attachment_data/file/789997/households-below-average-income-1994-1995-2017-2018.pdf

Edwards, M. (2014) *Civil Society* (3rd edn), Cambridge: Polity Press.

Foley, M. and Hodgkinson, V. (eds) (2002) *The Civil Society Reader*, Hanover, NH: University Press of New England.

Hastings, A., Bailey, N., Gannon, M., Besemer, K. and Barnley, G. (2015) 'Coping with the cuts? The management of the worst financial settlement in living memory', *Local Government Studies*, 41(4): 601–21.

Hemmings, M. (2017) 'The constraints on voluntary sector voice in a period of continued austerity', *Voluntary Sector Review*, 8(1): 41–66.

HRW (Human Rights Watch) (2019) 'Nothing left in the cupboards: austerity, welfare cuts, and the right to food in the UK', 20 May. Available at: www.hrw.org/report/2019/05/20/nothing-left-cupboards/austerity-welfare-cuts-and-right-food-uk

John, P. (2014) 'The great survivor: the persistence and resilience of English local government', *Local Government Studies*, 40(5): 687–704.

Jones, G., Meegan, R., Kennett, P. and Croft, J. (2016) 'The uneven impact of austerity on the voluntary and community sector: a tale of two cities', *Urban Studies*, 53(10): 2064–80.

Keen, R. and Audickas, L. (2017) *Charities and the Voluntary Sector: Statistics, Briefing Paper Number SN0528, 16 August*, London: House of Commons Library. Available at: https://researchbriefings.files.parliament.uk/documents/SN05428/SN05428.pdf

Kynaston, D. (2010) 'Austerity was a hard sell in the 40s. Today it's harder still', *The Guardian*, 21 June. Available at: www.theguardian.com/commentisfree/2010/jun/21/austerity-hard-sell-budget-2010

Lyall, S. and Bua, A. (2015) *Responses to Austerity: How Groups across the UK are Adapting, Challenging and Imagining Alternatives*, London: New Economics Foundation. Available at: https://neweconomics.org/uploads/files/1ac29da8caad2f83c0_llm6b3u3v.pdf

Marriott, L. (2017) 'The construction of crime: the presumption of blue-collar guilt and white-collar innocence', *Social Policy and Society*, 16(2): 237–51.

Mattie, C. and Salour, S. (2019) 'Austerity is political choice, not an economic necessity', *The Guardian*, 2 September. Available at: www.theguardian.com/commentisfree/2019/sep/02/austerity-is-a-political-choice-not-an-economic-necessity

McGee, L. (2020) 'Coronavirus is revealing how badly the UK has failed its most vulnerable', *CNN*, 23 March. Available at: https://edition.cnn.com/2020/03/22/uk/coronavirus-homeless-intl-gbr/index.html

Meegan, R., Kennett, P., Jones, G. and Croft, J. (2014) 'Global economic crisis, austerity and neoliberal urban governance in England', *Cambridge Journal of Regions, Economy and Society*, 7(1): 137–53.

Mooney, G. and Hancock, L. (2010) 'Poverty porn and the broken society', *Variant Magazine*, issue 39/40. Available at: www.variant.org.uk/39_40texts/povertp39_40.html

NCVO (National Council for Voluntary Organisations) (2019) 'UK civil society almanac 2019. Data. Trends. Insights'. Available at: https://data.ncvo.org.uk/

*Oxford English Dictionary*. Available at: www.lexico.com/definition/austerity

Partington, R. (2020) 'UK must prioritise levelling up if economy is to get back on its feet', *The Guardian*, 26 July. Available at: www.theguardian.com/business/2020/jul/26/forget-levelling-up-the-uk-economy-must-first-drag-itself-back-up-on-to-its-feet

Peck, J. (2012) 'Austerity urbanism', *City*, 16(6): 626–55.

Pharoah, C., Chapman, T. and Choudhury, R. (2014) *An Insight into the Future of Charity Funding in the North East*, London: Garfield Weston Foundation.

Powell, K., Thurston, M. and Bloyce, D. (2017) 'Theorising lifestyle drift in health promotion: explaining community and voluntary sector engagement practices in disadvantaged areas', *Critical Public Health*, 27(5): 554–65.

Shelter (2019) 'This is England: a picture of homelessness in 2019', Shelter Report, 18 December. Available at: https://england.shelter.org.uk/media/press_releases/articles/280,000_people_in_england_are_homeless,_with_thousands_more_at_risk

Shenker, J. (2019) *Now We Have Your Attention: The New Politics of the People*, London: Vintage.

Solnit, R. (2004) *Hope in the Dark, Untold Histories, Wild Possibilities*, New York: Nation Book.

VONNE (Voluntary Organisations' Network North East) (2016) 'Surviving or thriving 2016: the state of the VCSE sector in the North East of England', VONNE. Available at: www.vonne.org.uk/sites/default/files/files/SnT-2016.pdf

Williams, B. and Goodman, H. (2011) 'The role of the voluntary sector', in S. Walklate (ed) *Handbook of Victims and Victimology*, Oxon: Routledge.

Wolfe, A. (1997) 'Is civil society obsolete? Revisiting predictions of the decline of civil society in "Whose keeper?"', *Brookings Review*, 15(4): 9–12.

World Economic Forum (2013) *The Future Role of Civil Society*, World Scenario Series, Geneva: World Economic Forum. Available at: www3.weforum.org/docs/WEF_FutureRoleCivilSociety_Report_2013.pdf

# 2

# The North East of England: place, economy and people

*Elizabeth Brooks and Mel Steer*

## Introduction: a portrait of the North East

This chapter introduces the North East of England: its people, industries, how it is governed, how it compares to other regions and its future outlook. Before this account, the origin of the idea of the North East is considered, bearing in mind that, at least in England, regions are both historically recent and fragile entities, their integrity challenged by a raft of devolution initiatives at sub- and supra-regional level. This sets the scene for the next section, a thumbnail portrait of the North East's geography, industry, heritage and culture. The section further explores the challenges of deindustrialisation and of governance and economic restructuring. A final section explores how the North East compares with similar regions in England and Europe. The chapter concludes with a brief consideration of what the future may hold for the region.

### The idea of a North East region

Although it may seem to have always been with us, the idea of a North East region is a relatively new one. Soon after its emergence as a nation, England was split up into counties for the purpose of governance, a division that is reflected in today's local government structure. Although regional terms such as 'The North' were in common usage, they were generally ill defined and subject to interpretation. The North East only began to be viewed separately from the North West during the mid-18th to early 19th century (Green and Pollard, 2007: 12–20), at which point academic interpretation, industrial specialisation and, mainly as a consequence of this, political interests clustered around the distinctive characteristics of the area, in particular, the varied commerce and industry based on the ready supply of energy from the Great

Northern Coalfield. The recognition of a North East region in England has subsequently waxed and waned, along with periodic attempts to address regional economic problems and create regional governance that have met with only temporary or partial success (Elcock, 2014). For this reason, studies and detailed analysis at the North East region level, though relating to a wide historical period, date mainly to the recent period of regional governance (1994–2010/12), with a number of notable exceptions outside of this period (for example, McCord, 1979; Jackson, 2019).

While the region continues to exist culturally and in official statistics, various decentralisation drives since 2009 have resulted in many supra- and subregional governance bodies, differently defined by economic, health and combined authorities, explored later in the section on governance; this has resulted in fragmented and overlapping governance structures, with consequences for transparency and accountability. Nevertheless, consideration of the historical path and current challenges of the constituent parts of the region suggests continued value in considering the region as a whole, as will emerge from the following sections.

## A thumbnail portrait of the North East

The North East region of England covers a varied urban, rural and coastal landscape, with diverse communities and 12 local authorities (municipalities) situated in the region (see Figure 2.1).

### Population

The North East is the smallest English region outside of London, extending over an area of approximately 850,000 hectares. In the 2012 mid-year estimates, the region also accounted for only 4 per cent of the UK population (2.6 million), giving it the lowest population of any of the English regions, and one smaller than Scotland and Wales, though still larger than Northern Ireland. Over much of the 20th century, the North East suffered from population decrease, mainly due to net outmigration. Even as early as the years between 1927 and 1938, a national scheme to relocate people living in poor mining areas moved around 100,000 people out of the North East. In the 1950s, the population of the region fell by around 70,000, largely due to people relocating to other regions in pursuit of work (Renton, 2008). By the end of the 20th century, the Government Office for the North East (GONE, 2008: 7) was reporting a decades-long trend of outmigration.

**Figure 2.1:** North East England and its constituent local authorities

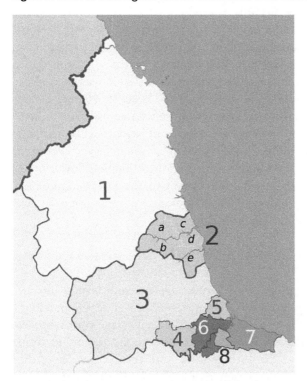

| | |
|---|---|
| 1 – Northumberland | 3 – County Durham |
| 2 – Tyne and Wear | 4 – Darlington |
| 2a – Newcastle upon Tyne | 5 – Hartlepool |
| 2b – Gateshead | 6 – Stockton on Tees |
| 2c – North Tyneside | 7 – Redcar and Cleveland |
| 2d – South Tyneside | 8 – Middlesbrough |
| 2e – Sunderland | |

Source: Wikimedia Commons (available under the Creative Commons CC0 License and the Creative Commons Attribution-ShareAlike License)

However, the trend began to reverse around 2008, as shown by the 2011 Census, which found that the population had risen by around 3.2 per cent since 2001.

Historically, the North East was always the site of population flows and exchanges, and archaeological artefacts bear witness to the diverse origins of troops sent to defend the Roman wall from across the Roman Empire, including Belgians, Dutch and even Syrian cohorts. The growing number of Christian foundations across Dark Age and medieval Northumbria embedded the importance of the region within wider European scholarship and exchanges, while invaders from what is now Scandinavia changed the population and influenced place names from the 8th century onwards.

The region has been a major centre for migration in two modern periods: the first was from 1820 to 1920, when it saw mass migration from Scotland and Ireland, mainly attracted by the high wages and abundance of work in the region; the second period has taken place since 1987 as a result of the government's dispersal scheme, which has sought to distribute refugee communities across the country to moderate the impact of international migration on London and the South East (Renton, 2008). Academic studies have connected recent arrivals with the history of the region's migration flows, while illustrating that their experience has varied with the type of community they have joined and the prevailing economic conditions (for example, Olsover, 1981; Lawless, 1995; Buckler, 2011).

## Industry

The national image of the North East has undoubtedly been shaped by its past economic and industrial strengths in coal, steel, shipbuilding, heavy engineering and armaments, and indeed as one of the cradles of the Industrial Revolution. It was economically important from around the middle of the 19th century until the last quarter of the 20th century. With the emergence of a global industrial system, the North East fell behind newly industrialising countries with abundant primary resources and a cheaper labour force. By the last quarter of the 20th century, the region's economic role in the UK had significantly declined, a decline accelerated by the withdrawal of government subsidies to heavy industry in the 1980s.

In general terms, the region has been riven with internal inequalities throughout its history and its industry also participated in generating inequalities elsewhere, having been imposed on other nations through the political power of the British Empire (Hudson, 2005). This history of severe and visible inequalities (McCord, 1979) had its counterpart in influential thinkers challenging the status quo, including the historical North Eastern reformers and activists Thomas Spence, Josephine Butler, W.T. Stead, Emily Wilding Davison and Ellen Wilkinson ('Red Ellen'). Spence was an early champion of rights for all, Butler and, fatally, Davison fought for women's rights, while Butler and W.T. Stead also worked to combat child prostitution. Wilkinson was a politician and journalist who became the first female Education Secretary in 1945, introducing free milk and school meals. Notably, the region has a prominent link with the civil rights movement that stretches from

Earl Grey (Foreign Secretary in 1806), who introduced the Act that abolished the slave trade, to Newcastle University awarding Martin Luther King an honorary doctorate in 1967. Between these periods, the important visitor Frederick Douglass (an abolitionist and former slave) lived for a time in Newcastle, where sisters-in-law Anna and Ellen Richardson raised the £150 to secure his freedom (Hodgson, 2016). The Richardsons also campaigned to refuse goods from slavery, to educate the poor and for teetotalism (Hodgson, 2016).

Deindustrialisation has resulted in improvements in air quality, healthier cities and a rural area that is increasingly attractive to ex-urban migrants, particularly in County Durham. The growing public sector and services economy that replaced industry created jobs that were accessible to, or even targeted, women workers (Hudson, 2005: 587). The range and quality of the region's educational institutions has led to its growth as a 'knowledge economy'. The low cost of property and land relative to the England average can provide a draw for in-migration and business relocation, and has allowed the development of a more outward-looking, multicultural region. The region's long and often strife-riven industrial history has left a legacy of successful workplace organisation and campaigning; today, the North East region is notable for having the highest number of workplaces with a trades union presence in England, with over a quarter of the workforce belonging to a union (DBEIS, 2017).

## Environment

In spite of its industrial reputation, around two thirds of the North East region is rural, with half of the rural area either designated as a national park (Northumberland and North York Moors) or as an area of outstanding natural beauty (AONB) (GONE, 2009). Although the imaginary of the North East in national policy continued to be centred around work and productivity, some awareness of its cultural and environmental assets emerged in the latter part of the century, when radio and television disseminated its traditions more widely (see later section on cultural regeneration) and tourism rose in prominence as part of its economy. In terms of environmental assets, the North East has been described as having 'some of the UK's finest high-quality and diverse countryside, and natural and built heritage, including a varied coastline ranging from extensive sandy beaches, dunes and inter-tidal flats, to spectacular cliffs, islands and rocky outcrops' (GONE, 2008: 6). The region was awarded two world heritage sites in the mid-1980s: Durham Castle and Cathedral from 1986; and Hadrian's Wall from 1987 – shared with the North West of England and part of the Frontiers of the Roman Empire international sites (GONE, 2008: 6).

Regarding its rural areas, the agriculturally productive land is mainly found along the coastal plain (particularly in Northumberland), while higher ground to the west provides large acreages of pasture (Faulkner and Gregory, 2010: 10). Along the line dividing the pasturage from arable land are located the region's main historic market towns – due to their origins as places for exchange between the different products of each type of farming. While the rising role of coal in the region's economy came to reduce their relative prominence, many of these towns retain regional significance as rural 'hub' towns and visitor destinations (Roberts, cited in Green and Pollard, 2007: 10).

There is a trend for the rural areas to increase in population at a higher rate than the urban ones, influenced by those from the urbanised parts of the region moving out to the rural west, as well as through in-migration from other regions by those in mid- to later life, who are particularly attracted to Northumberland and County Durham (Midgley et al, 2005: 6). At the 2001 Census, 16.9 per cent of the North East's population lived in a rural ward (Midgley et al, 2005: 4). By the 2011 Census, this proportion had increased to 18.4 per cent of the population, while 81.4 per cent were classed as urban dwellers (ONS, 2013).

### Governance restructuring

The North East's distance from central government in London, and its proximity to the Scottish Borders, is a thread that runs through the governance of the region. The dominant neoliberal emphasis on regional productivity and employment continues to shape a negative image of the North East nationally, and in England, central government exerts a high degree of control over investment and spending (Raikes et al, 2019). Attempts to increase regional autonomy were made in 2004, when the North East was the first English region to have a referendum on an elected regional assembly. Based on a turnout of nearly 50 per cent, the proposal was rejected and, as a consequence, similar referendums that were planned elsewhere were abandoned (Rallings and Thrasher, 2006). Nevertheless, regional structures, including its regional development agency (ONE North East) and GONE, endured until the regional tier was abolished by the Coalition government (2010–15).

While regional devolution failed, various other forms of devolved governance have been introduced that have produced a confusing and fragmented institutional array. There are now four layers of regional devolution, added to disparate catchment areas used by the health, emergency and police services. This creates a disjointed picture of governance, with impacts for public participation and accountability (Shaw and Robinson, 2018), and many of the new bodies 'fail to offer equity for rural communities and places' (Davoudi et al, 2017: 20).

Of the four layers of devolution, the first consisted of supra regional growth deals, including the Northern Powerhouse, which unites North East, North West and parts of North Wales. At the subregional level, the first was city-region devolution ('combined authorities'), introduced through the Local Democracy, Economic Development and Construction Act 2009. By April 2018, 12 devolution deals had been announced for England (at the time of writing, 11 remain). Eight of these, including the Tees Valley Combined Authority and the North of Tyne Combined Authority, have elected 'metro mayors' (Wilson and Paun, 2019). Of the eight combined authorities with metro mayors, the North of Tyne and Tees Valley have the fewest devolved powers (Wilson and Paun, 2019).

The second layer of devolution ('city deals') was brought about through the Localism Act 2011. In December 2011, the first wave of city deals was launched, offering new powers over finance and planning to more than 30 major UK cities to date. Newcastle was in the first wave of the eight largest British cities, while Sunderland and the North East were in the second wave (Ward, 2018). A separate round of local growth deals was launched in 2014, applying to local enterprise partnership areas: the North East, Tees Valley and York, North Yorkshire, and East Riding growth deals were all announced in 2015.

A further trend that may raise concern for regional cohesion and spatial justice is the breaking away of more from less prosperous subregions. Real growth in gross value added (a measure of the worth of goods and services generated) between 2009 and 2017 in (what has become since 2018) the North of Tyne Combined Authority set of local authorities was 13.8 per cent, while growth for the same period in the Tees Valley Combined Authority was only 2.8 per cent (ONS, 2018).

## Economic restructuring

The turn of the millennium saw a period of restructuring and improvement of economic performance for the North East. Regional gross value added for the North East grew by almost a third between 1995 and 2002 (Midgley et al, 2005: 4). The declining traditional industries (mining, steel, shipbuilding, chemicals and heavy engineering) gave way to a services economy, entrepreneurship, innovation and new forms of industry, including pharmaceutical, digital and biotech (GONE, 2008; CLES, 2014; Charles and Liddle, 2018). This transformation has been encapsulated in the phrase 'from coal to call centres, from ships to microchips'.

The strong growth trend, which coincided with a period of high levels of investment from EU structural funds prior to the accession of East European countries to the EU, peaked in 2004 and has never been attained again since (Charles and Liddle, 2018). Besides a reduction in EU funds, the economy was hit by the 2008 financial crisis and subsequent austerity; public sector jobs were particularly hard hit. Summary statistics from March 2008 to June 2017 show a decline in public sector jobs in the North East from 25.7 per cent of all jobs to 20.3 per cent of all jobs – effectively around 60,000 jobs, more than one in five, were lost to the public sector over this period (ONS, 2017). This was a greater proportion than any other English region and only comparable to Wales. This level of loss also generates local multiplier effects within the economy (CLES, 2014). By 2019, the North East had the lowest employment rate (72.2 per cent) of all nine English regions and UK administrations, even lower than that of Northern Ireland (ONS, 2019). Reciprocally, it had the highest unemployment rate nationally (at 5.8 per cent in 2019) (ONS, 2019), a labour market characterised by lower than average wages and high rates of poverty and poor health, demonstrating substantial challenges for social renewal.

### Cultural renaissance

The modern cultural image of the region was to a great degree shaped by post-war arts policy. At the end of the Second World War, developments in broadcasting and cultural policy fostered the development of 'cultural regions' in the UK. Radio programme makers in the North East gave an outlet for the kinds of pipe music, popular songs, stories and dialect associated with the area – 'The Blaydon Races' ballad being the best-known example – which may have supported the consolidation of a regional culture (Vall, 2011: 7). The North East has some well-established world heritage sites, as mentioned earlier, and several established museums of national importance, including the Bowes Museum in Barnard Castle and the Great Museum of the North (formerly The Hancock). Other formal expressions of culture, such as orchestras and art galleries, have historically been sparse in the region, but beginning in the 1980s, the provision of formal arts venues began to improve. Since the late 1980s, culture featured as a pioneering way to spearhead regeneration. The Gateshead Garden Festival in 1989 was one of the foundational initiatives in the region, using a cultural event as a way of attracting investment for regeneration, and attracted both national and international attention. Following on from its success, Northern Arts published a document entitled 'The case for capital' in 1995, which helped to bring in funding for culture-led regeneration, including the creation of what have since become iconic buildings and heritage attractions, and the improvement of existing features. Outstanding examples include the National Glass Centre in Sunderland and the Sage (international music centre) and Baltic (centre for contemporary art) in the Quayside area of Newcastle and Gateshead, with more projects, such as the Middlesbrough Institute of Modern Art (MIMA), following after the millennium. A recent addition is the Auckland Project, a museums complex in the Durham market town of Bishop Auckland that includes a restoration of the historic castle, a new Faith Museum, a viewing tower and a Mining Art Gallery. The original flagship regeneration projects, often with an arts focus, not only made the region a beacon for the economic benefits of a public and private sector mix in urban regeneration, but also raised its national and international profile (Vall, 2011: 11–12). The best-known example from this period may be the monumental steel 'Angel of the North' by sculptor Anthony Gormley, erected in 1998 on the site of a disused colliery overlooking both Newcastle's major road and rail arteries.

## Comparison with other regions

The North East can be compared with other European regions on a number of dimensions, including regions transitioning from an economy dominated by coal mining, deindustrialising regions and regions near internal borders (a source of current and future uncertainty that may become more significant should Scotland secede from the UK [see Cowie et al, 2018: 74]). While studies of deindustrialisation tend to focus on cities and city regions, comparisons with coal-producing regions include rural areas where extraction took place and so are more truly regional in the sense of this account.

The extensive decline of coal mining resulted in the loss of around 250,000 jobs in the UK in the 1980s and 1990s, and has been called 'the most dramatic contemporary example of social transformation in Britain since the Second World War' (Bennett et al, 2000: 1). While Bennett et al's (2000) report focuses on the former coal-mining areas of South Wales and North Nottinghamshire, many of its findings can be applied to the North East. Due to the density of habitation left over from the extraction industry, these former pit villages 'resemble many of the housing estates that ring the major urban centres' (Bennett et al, 2000: 2). There was now no clear reason for such dense rural settlements and the cost of their upkeep became politicised. Many jobs that replaced mining were lower-paid, service sector jobs, often taken up by women, leaving many men with no alternative but long-term unemployment or low-paid, part-time work, exacerbated by regeneration strategies that attracted enterprises to former coalfield regions based on the promise of cheap land and labour (Bennett et al, 2000).

Probably due to the difficulties for small and medium enterprises to locate to disadvantaged and remote places, a large part of regeneration policy depended on attracting external or foreign investment. While this was effective in the city areas, it was less so in rural and former coal-mining regions of the UK, and investment proved unstable and vulnerable to rapid closures and relocations when economic conditions changed. The vulnerability of the North East to what became known as 'branch plant syndrome' came to national attention in 1998 (Pike, 1999) and continues to feature as an issue, as demonstrated by the shockwaves following the closure in 2015 of the Thai-owned SSI steel makers in Redcar (Blackburn, 2016) – a closure as symbolically important as that of the Consett steelworks in the 1980s.

The mapping of regions in relation to economic indicators such as GDP, jobs and employment figures often grapples with the issue of where areas of low population appear advantaged by comparison with more densely populated regions. Put simply, mapping a sparsely inhabited region with high average economic performance might give a misleading image of that region's contribution to national prosperity and comparability with other regions. Ballas et al (2017) attempted to overcome this and compare European regions on a number of economic measures by expanding the size of the region to represent the number of people living there, so that a small but densely populated poor region shows up more strongly on the map than a large but sparsely populated wealthy one. Applying this, the rural two thirds of the North East all but disappear, swallowed up by the densely populated east-coast areas, which, on most economic measures, resemble Wales and Northern Ireland in terms of deprivation, as well as European areas such as Southern Italy, Southern Spain and Eastern Europe.

The UK's growing regional inequality and population concentration in the South East has been challenged (GOS, 2010; McCann, 2016;

UK2070 Commission, 2019). The UK's spatial economic strategy functioned effectively from the late 1940s up to the late 1970s to reduce inequalities between regional productivity and bring city sizes in line with other countries. However, the pattern stalled and then reversed due to focusing the new industries of vehicle manufacture, aviation and electronic and electrical goods into Southern England, along with a range of new service industries (UK2070 Commission, 2019: 34). Policies since the 1990s attempted to ameliorate the immediate impacts of decline rather than unlocking opportunities, and developed an approach of managed decline of 'left-behind' places. The UK2070 Commission's report draws a comparison between East and West Germany, which were much more spatially unequal than Britain in the 1990s; however, through a deliberate and unificationist policy, the situation was reversed, so that the UK is now regionally more unequal than Germany. Since the strong Conservative victory in the 2019 elections, including new gains of many traditionally Labour constituencies in the North East, various announcements have been made about 'levelling up' the English regions (Scott, 2019; Giles, 2020). The evolving COVID-19 crisis is likely to exacerbate existing spatial inequalities in the labour market. Although London has the highest percentage of self-employed workers (15 per cent), the self-employed in the cities of the North and Midlands have increased precarity, and more people in London and the South East are employed in occupations that can switch to home and remote working (Magrini, 2020). Within-region labour market inequalities between cities and towns in the North will become starker during COVID-19 as some Northern cities (such as Newcastle, Manchester, Warrington and Leeds) have been identified as having different economies that will better adapt to homeworking (Magrini, 2020). Pre-crisis proclamations of levelling up between the regions will need to account for these different regional and local economies and experiences once the COVID-19 crisis is over, as well as any implications of Brexit. However, based on the preference for a project-based as opposed to programmatic policy style, this may work to mitigate the uneven regional impacts of Brexit and COVID-19, rather than achieving a reduction in regional disparities.

## Conclusion

Various challenges, which are either rooted in history or arise from increased global connectedness, confront today's North East. Disadvantageous trading agreements following Brexit would have a major impact on the North East industrial sector. Some, however, hope that a weaker pound might create advantageous conditions for new trading agreements, though this has not been borne out by the actual figures since the Brexit vote (Edwards et al, 2018), at least until the COVID-19 crisis caused the pound's value to tumble in early 2020. At the same time, EU subsidies have been important to the North East region. Between 2007 and 2020, the North East received over £800 million of EU structural funds, utilised in programmes investing in businesses, innovation, reducing firms' emissions and upskilling workers (South Tyneside Council, 2017). Post-Brexit forecasts for the region anticipate the loss of the relatively politically neutral redistribution of EU regional funding streams, leading to further economic stress and sharpening the North–South divide, both economically and politically.

While EU structural funds are to be replaced by a UK Shared Prosperity Fund after the EU funding ends in 2020, concerns surround how it will operate, including: whether it will match or exceed EU investment; whether it will be devolved to regional decision-making or tightly controlled from the centre; whether there will be a smooth transition between EU and UK funds (Cowie et al, 2018); and whether the funds will become more politicised (Bell, 2017). Furthermore, the probable choice of the urban-located Local Enterprise Partnerships to manage the new fund has raised concerns over the future equity of distribution between urban and rural areas (Dwyer, 2018), which is of significance for the growing population of the North East that lives outside of its cities.

As this chapter has indicated, the North East region has an influential and varied cultural heritage, outstanding and diverse landscapes, with many distinctive cities, towns and villages, offering the potential for an excellent quality of life. Regional inequalities in wealth, prosperity and health, the effects of austerity, and the implications of Brexit present challenges for the foreseeable future. The outlook is uncertain for the economy and bleak for the vulnerable; however, the strength of the region rests in its people, and the case studies in the following chapters describe some of the initiatives that are offering hope.

## References

Ballas, D., Dorling, D. and Hennig, B. (2017) 'Analysing the regional geography of poverty, austerity and inequality in Europe, a cartographic perspective', *Regional Studies*, 51(1): 174–85.

Bell, D. (2017) 'Regional aid policies after Brexit', *Oxford Review of Economic Policy*, 33(1): 91–104.

Bennett, K., Beynon, H. and Hudson, R. (2000) *Coalfields Regeneration: Dealing with the Consequences of Industrial Decline*. Bristol: Policy Press. Available at: www.jrf.org.uk/report/coalfields-regeneration-dealing-consequences-industrial-decline

Blackburn, M. (2016) 'Judge awards £700,000 payout to SSI contract steelworkers', *Gazette Live*, 30 September. Available at: www.gazettelive.co.uk/news/teesside-news/judge-awards-700000-payout-former-11964467

Buckler, S. (2011) *Fire in the Dark: Telling Gypsiness in North East England*, Oxford: Berghahn Books.

Charles, D. and Liddle, J. (2018) *North East Future Finance Commission: Report on Funding for the Regional North East*, Newcastle upon Tyne: Northumbria University Business School.

CLES (Centre for Local Economic Strategies) (2014) 'A summary of austerity in the North East and a case study of Redcar and Cleveland Borough Council'. Available at: www.tuc.org.uk/sites/default/files/North%20East%20Final%20Report_0.pdf

Cowie, P., Mulvey, G., Peck, F. and Shaw, K. (2018) 'Brexit: implications for the rural North of England', report for Northumberland County Council and the Institute of Local Governance. Available at: www.ncl.ac.uk/media/wwwnclacuk/centreforruraleconomy/files/researchreports/brexitruralnorth-report.pdf

Davoudi, S., Turner, R. and Garrod, G. (2017) *A New Deal for the North: A Briefing Paper for the British Academy*, Newcastle upon Tyne: Newcastle University.

DBEIS (Department for Business, Energy and Industrial Strategy) (2017) *Trade Union Membership 2016: Statistical Bulletin*, London: DBEIS. Available at: www.gov.uk/government/uploads/system/uploads/attachment_data/file/616966/trade-union-membership-statistical-bulletin-2016-rev.pdf

Dwyer, J. (2018) 'Where is rural development and LEADER? Director's response to the Draft Agriculture Bill', 20 September. Available at: www.ccri.ac.uk/response-draft-agriculture-bill/

Edwards, T.H., Soegaard, C. and Douch, M. (2018) 'Brexit has already hurt EU and non EU exports by up to 13 per cent', World Economic Forum, 6 December. Available at: www.weforum.org/agenda/2018/12/brexit-has-already-hurt-eu-and-non-eu-exports-by-up-to-13-new-research

Elcock, H. (2014) 'Multi-level governance and peripheral places: the North East of England', *Local Economy*, 29(4/5): 323–33.

Faulkner, I. and Gregory, J. (2010) 'Introduction: landscape and north-eastern-ness', in I. Faulkner, H. Berry and J. Gregory (eds) *Northern Landscapes: Representations and Realities of North East England*, Woodbridge: The Boydell Press, pp 1–24.

Giles, C. (2020) 'Sajid Javid sets March 2011 date for Budget to "level up" UK regions', *Financial Times*, 7 January. Available at: www.ft.com/content/27daa4ee-3099-11ea-a329-0bcf87a328f2

GONE (Government Office for the North East) (2008) *North East of England Plan: Regional Spatial Strategy to 2021*, Newcastle upon Tyne: GONE.

GONE (Government Office for the North East) (2009) *The North East*, Newcastle upon Tyne: GONE. Available at: http://webarchive. nationalarchives.gov.uk/20100528154547/; www.gos.gov.uk/ nestore/docs/ourregion/99keyfactsandfigures

GOS (Government Office for Science) (2010) 'Land use futures: making the most of land in the twenty-first century'. Available at: https:// assets.publishing.service.gov.uk/government/uploads/system/ uploads/attachment_data/file/288845/10-634-land-use-futures-summary.pdf

Green, A. and Pollard, A.J. (2007) 'Introduction: identifying regions', in A. Green and A.J. Pollard (eds) *Regional Identities in North East England 1300–2000*, Woodbridge, Suffolk: The Boydell Press, pp 1–25.

Hodgson, B. (2016) 'Former slave "freed" by Newcastle couple is set to be honoured in Martin Luther King anniversary year', *Chronicle Live*, 5 November. Available at: www.chroniclelive.co.uk/news/ north-east-news/former-slave-freed-newcastle-couple-12126390

Hudson, R. (2005) 'Rethinking change in old industrial regions: reflecting on the experiences of North East England', *Environment and Planning A*, 37: 581–96.

Jackson, D. (2019) *The Northumbrians: North East England and its People – A New History*, London: Hurst and Company.

Lawless, R. (1995) *From Ta'izz to Tyneside: Arab Community in the North East of England in the Early Twentieth Century*, Exeter, Devon: Exeter University Press.

Magrini, E. (2020) 'How will coronavirus affect jobs in different parts of the country?', blog, 17 March. Available at: www.centreforcities.org/blog/ how-will-coronavirus-affect-jobs-in-different-parts-of-the-country/

McCann, P. (2016) *The UK Regional-National Economic Problem*, London: Routledge.

McCord, N. (1979) *North East England: The Region's Development 1760–1960*, London: Batsford.

Midgley, J., Ward, N. and Atterton, J. (2005) 'City regions and rural areas in the North East of England', Centre for Rural Economy research report, University of Newcastle upon Tyne. Available at: www.ncl.ac.uk/media/wwwnclacuk/centreforruraleconomy/files/city-regions-full.pdf

Olsover, L. (1981) *The Jewish Communities of North East England, 1755–1980*, Gateshead: Ashley Mark Publishing Company.

ONS (Office for National Statistics) (2013) '2011 Census analysis: comparing rural and urban areas of England and Wales'. Available at: http://webarchive.nationalarchives.gov.uk/20160105224826/http://www.ons.gov.uk/ons/rel/census/2011-census-analysis/rural-urban-analysis/comparing-rural-and-urban-areas-of-england-and-wales.html

ONS (Office for National Statistics) (2017) 'RPUB1 regional labour market: regional public and private employment dataset'. Available at: www.ons.gov.uk/employmentandlabourmarket/peopleinwork/employmentandemployeetypes/datasets/regionalpublicandprivateemployment

ONS (Office for National Statistics) (2018) 'Regional economic activity by gross value added 1998–2017', *Statistical Bulletin*. Available at: www.ons.gov.uk/economy/grossvalueaddedgva/bulletins/regionalgrossvalueaddedbalanceduk/1998to2017

ONS (Office for National Statistics) (2019) 'Regional labour market statistics in the UK: January 2020'. Available at: www.nomisweb.co.uk/

Pike, A. (1999) 'The politics of factory closures and task forces in the north east region of England', *Regional Studies*, 33(6): 567–75.

Raikes, L., Giovannini, A. and Getzel, B. (2019) 'Divided and connected: regional inequalities in the North, the UK and the developed world, state of the North 2019', IPPR. Available at: www.ippr.org/files/2019-11/sotn-2019.pdf

Rallings, C. and Thrasher, M. (2006) ' "Just another expensive talking shop": public attitudes and the 2004 regional assembly referendum in the North East of England', *Regional Studies*, 40(8): 927–36.

Renton, D. (2008) *Colour Blind? Race and Migration in North East England since 1945*, Sunderland: University of Sunderland Press.

Scott, G. (2019) 'Leading centre for technology modelled on MIT could be coming to Leeds', *Yorkshire Post*, 22 December.

Shaw, K. and Robinson, F. (2018) 'Whatever happened to the North East? Reflections on the end of regionalism in England', *Local Economy*, 33(8): 842–61.

South Tyneside Council (2017) 'Brexploration: charting a course for our post-Brexit future by engaging public and private sector community stakeholders in collaborative discussion'. Available at: https://northeastca.gov.uk/wp-content/uploads/2018/03/BREXploration-Commission-Report-circulated-at-the-meeting.pdf

UK2070 Commission (2019) 'Fairer and stronger: rebalancing the UK economy'. Available at: https://drive.google.com/file/d/1DaPlON pLXwxS1lE2kLu3aQVkOQEmFLwB/view

Vall, N. (2011) *North-East England Cultural Region: 1945–2000*, Manchester: Manchester University Press.

Ward, M. (2018) 'City deals', House of Commons Briefing Paper 7158. Available at: https://commonslibrary.parliament.uk/research-briefings/sn07158/

Wilson, J. and Paun, A. (2019) 'English devolution: combined authorities and metro mayors', Institute for Government, 15 July. Available at: www.instituteforgovernment.org.uk/explainers/english-devolution-combined-authorities-and-metro-mayors

# PART I

# The public sector and civil society

# 3

# The public sector and civil society: introduction

*Mel Steer, Simin Davoudi, Liz Todd and Mark Shucksmith*

There is no definitive, universally agreed definition of what social welfare is (Lowe, 1993), and in the UK, 'social welfare', 'social security' and the 'welfare state' are terms that are often used interchangeably to refer to the provision of a lifeline, a safety net, to help people cope during periods of disruption or crisis. While welfare provision is often associated with the post-war social-democratic states and, in Britain, the introduction of the NHS in 1945, Alcock's (2016) historical account demonstrates that charitable forms of welfare provision existed before, for example, the Poor Law of 1601 in England, where parishes administered relief to the destitute, and measures introduced in the 19th century that applied to large sections of the population regarding access to education, hospitals and sanitation. However, social infrastructures such as schools and hospitals were typically owned by churches and voluntary organisations, or funded by private individuals, rather than the state (Alcock, 2016). This tradition of charitable and voluntary welfare provision has continued to date, leading to the involvement of multiple actors and creating diversity in terms of the manner of service delivery, staff ethos and the purpose and accountability of the organisations.

Across the public, voluntary, community and private sectors, increased prominence is given to collectively produced welfare services through co-production and collaboration. The Organisation for Economic Co-operation and Development (OECD, 2011) simply defines co-production in terms of a model incorporating diverse organisations operating in distinct ways and with differing levels of engagement from and involvement of civil society organisations, service users and citizens. The case studies included in Part I of this book draw on co-production in its various forms and incorporate a number of different providers, addressing issues that affect different aspects of people's lives in interlocking ways that impact life chances and outcomes. All case-study chapters are co-written by university researchers and those working for organisations outside the university. Some of the case studies are well established and others represent relatively new initiatives or ways of working. A common thread running through the case-study practices is their aim to provide more than a lifeline through a crisis. Instead, they aim to deliver sustainable, transformative change that reshapes people's social and community connections and lives for the better in a way that encourages social renewal and promotes social justice, recognising that 'A more equal, cohesive society is simply a better, healthier place to live' (Marmot et al, 2020: 149).

The first case study in Part I of the book is the chapter 'Innovation outside the state', which outlines how the Glendale Gateway Trust started as a locally driven initiative in Wooler, North Northumberland, in 1996. The authors describe the trust's journey, how they navigated the challenges and tensions, and how a more favourable funding landscape at the start of the initiative enabled them to establish the trust and to ultimately acquire income-generating assets to ensure sustainability. The trust provides an example of how the community responded to perceived local needs and developed an innovative approach to capitalise on opportunities for social renewal. Although the initiative started in 1996 and benefited from successful community grant applications to create a community centre, the austerity cuts from 2010 presented a challenge to continued operation and later, ironically, opportunities. The library, tourist information centre and local police presence moved into the community centre, providing a stable income, and the trust acquired the old library building through local authority transfer and converted the building into affordable housing units.

The chapter 'The Byker Community Trust and the "Byker Approach"' argues that housing has been particularly badly affected by 'roll-back neoliberalism' (Peck and Tickell, 2002: 388) and austerity, and yet good-quality housing was central to the development of the post-war welfare state. The authors describe how Byker Community Trust (BCT) undertook the co-creation of the physical, social and environmental refurbishment of the historical and architecturally significant grade II★ listed Byker Estate in Newcastle, which is situated in an area of high socio-economic deprivation. The authors describe how BCT developed the holistic 'Byker Approach' to give tenants a strong voice and role in decision-making in the estate's renewal. BCT embraced a wide remit of responsibilities and worked with partners to alleviate some of the effects of health and social inequality, financial exclusion, and educational and employment disadvantage. Aiming to make Byker an 'estate of choice', active tenant engagement through 'value co-creation' (Grönroos, 2011) to enhance citizen well-being and to develop BCT to market its housing was supported by Newcastle University through a knowledge transfer partnership.

The chapter 'Cafe society' discusses how food sharing in a 'pay as you feel' community cafe in Chester-le-Street used donations of 'safe for consumption' surplus food to prevent waste, improve access to food and reduce social isolation. The chapter engages with social justice from the perspective of promoting an inclusive space that encourages people to value their own self-worth and contribution regardless of ability to pay as cafe customers are invited to pay with time, skills or money. Drawing on a co-produced research project between the cafe and Newcastle University that used photovoice and participatory action research methods, cafe visitors' experiences of the cafe and their views about the cafe's impact on visitors and community were gathered. They argue that the associations and interactions taking place in the cafe are based on reciprocity, which represents a 'quiet activism' inherent in cafe users' exchanges, providing a challenge to the critique that surplus food depoliticises food waste and food poverty, as well as to capitalist modes of production and consumption.

The chapter ' "Computer Says No" ' explores the components of fairness and justice in the design and implementation of the welfare system through online, digital services (as the UK government implemented the 'digital by default' initiative to access services). Based on data from a participatory action research project that was funded by UK Research and Innovation and led by a researcher from Newcastle University, the authors consider how, using a collaborative approach, people can be supported to use technology to achieve fairer outcomes. The authors demonstrate how the Parker Trust and the Pallion Action Group from Sunderland support those experiencing low income to navigate government welfare benefit services online and share their learning with other similar third sector organisations. Drawing on claimants' experiences, they acknowledge that lack of online access creates exclusion, though access alone is not a panacea for social justice. Rather, other issues, such as the absence of a human interface during stressful life events accelerates disconnection, that the online claim system is imposed and that people may inadvertently select the wrong tick box, create the potential for adverse consequences and severe outcomes for people accessing services.

The chapter 'Drive to thrive' describes how Gateshead Local Authority has been affected by austerity. The chapter outlines Gateshead's approach to partnership working during austerity and its work to improve outcomes on food and fuel poverty as part of the implementation of its 'Thrive' place-based initiative. It considers how the council advanced collaborative working to combine resources in order to meet community needs through working with the voluntary, community and social enterprise, and private sectors. It charts the development of a food distribution network that was established to distribute food to vulnerable households and considers how Gateshead facilitated the provision of free energy advice, home insulation and boiler replacement schemes for people experiencing fuel poverty. The authors situate place-based working in the context of central government cuts that affected the local authority and its partner organisations, and within the context of a large, powerful, bureaucratic organisation involved in multiple inter-organisational collaborations during times of severe and sustained financial pressure.

The chapter 'City of Dreams' illustrates that local authority cuts to arts and culture acted as catalyst for a new and exciting approach to enable children and young people in Newcastle and Gateshead to engage with culture and creativity. The authors suggest that City of Dreams – a collaboration between ten cultural and heritage organisations on a ten-year mission – actively involves young people in the design and delivery of the cultural offer, and has the potential to be transformative through the creation of new ways of working. It involved action research with representatives from NewcastleGateshead Cultural Venues, leading to the creation of a steering group of 16–25 year olds and a representative body of children and young people, which culminated in the development of the annual Big Culture Conversations. Newcastle University functioned as the key research facilitator for City of Dreams and established the City of Dreams seminar series, which brought academics and the wider arts, charity and other sectors working with young people together to discuss topics such as 'youth citizenship and culture'. It involved increasing engagements with arts and culture by young people, some of whom were from disadvantaged backgrounds, developing their confidence and life skills. In its role, Newcastle University sought to draw on its own research strengths, as well as those of other regional universities, to support and be a critical friend to the project.

Part I of the book concludes with the chapter 'Are we "all in this together"?', which critically reflects on austerity and the COVID-19 crisis. The author argues that there are clear connections between the unequal impacts of austerity and COVID-19 on disadvantaged groups in society, and highlights the risks of applying the same austerity ideology to the COVID-19 crisis and its aftermath. Consistencies between the state's expectations of the voluntary sector and the responsibilisation agenda are discussed in relation to austerity and COVID-19, while providing a focus on the implications of austerity and the COVID-19 crisis on young people, women and front-line workers.

## References

Alcock, P. (2016) *Why We Need Welfare: Collective Action for the Common Good*, Bristol: Policy Press.

Grönroos, C. (2011) 'Value co-creation in service logic: a critical analysis', *Marketing Theory*, 11(3): 279–301.

Lowe, R. (1993) *The Welfare State in Britain since 1945*, Basingstoke: Macmillan.

Marmot, M., Allen, J., Boyce, T., Goldblatt, P. and Morrison, J. (2020) *Health Equity in England: The Marmot Review 10 Years On*, London: Institute of Health Equity.

OECD (Organisation for Economic Co-operation and Development) (2011) *Together for Better Public Services: Partnering with Citizens and Civil Society*, Paris: OECD Public Governance Reviews, OECD Publishing. Available at: https://read.oecd-ilibrary.org/governance/together-for-better-public-services-partnering-with-citizens-and-civil-society_9789264118843-en#page2

Peck, J. and Tickell, A. (2002) 'Neoliberalising space', *Antipode*, 34(3): 380–404.

# 4

# Innovation outside the state: the Glendale Gateway Trust

*Patsy Healey, Tom Johnston and Frank Mansfield*

## Introduction

Our story is about a civil society initiative activated by local concern over the steady decline of economic and social opportunity in a 'remote' rural area in Northumberland. As with many other parts of the Western world, such areas are on the margins of political attention these days, experiencing youth out-migration, ageing populations and difficulties in sustaining needed services (Shucksmith and Brown, 2016). Social renewal in such areas means searching for pathways towards a sustainable future.

The Glendale Gateway Trust (GGT) has grown from the efforts of committed locals, experimenting with how to do things, into an established part of the governance ecosystem in the county of Northumberland. It started in the mid-1990s, centred on creating a community centre and facilities for young people in Wooler, the main centre in Glendale, North Northumberland. It then grew into providing a platform for a range of activities, which have established a community and business hub, generated improvements to the high street, built a locally significant amount of affordable housing, ensured the survival of the local youth hostel, and created a base for a range of other initiatives and programmes. Infused by a sense of the changing wider context, the GGT has developed an entrepreneurial culture, looking out for opportunities and innovating with new ways of doing things. Over time, the GGT has become a significant actor in local development in Northumberland. As a result, it has increasingly been in a position to grasp available opportunities, both economic and political, drawing down investment from the private, public and charitable sectors.

The initiative was motivated not by a particular driving ideology or a specific local crisis, but by locally widespread perceptions of the ebbing away of an old life and the search for practical ways to both renew community vitality and find a sustainable future for the area. On the one hand, the focus has been on remedying what has disappeared or been neglected; on the other, the GGT has tried to open up new opportunities, such as affordable offices for microbusinesses. It can be seen as helping the Glendale area move beyond the sense of a place 'left behind' by agricultural change towards alternatives based on what the area can offer in terms of local amenities and assets, notably, the attraction of the landscape, heritage and sense of community for visitors and in-migrants. The GGT has brought new knowledge, ideas and practices into play in local development work, and contributed to changing how the much-stressed public sector undertakes its various activities and responsibilities. Its contribution is not uncontested locally, with tensions between expectations rooted in the past and the arrival of new opportunities, as well as between different groups in the community as each seeks recognition for its various contributions. However, such tensions reflect the challenge for any community forced to find new ways to sustain itself into the future.

## Rural life on the margins[1]

Glendale lies just south of the Scottish border in Northumberland. In 2011, nearly 6,000 people lived here, in scattered hamlets, villages and the small 'town' centre of Wooler, where around 2,000 people live.[2] The nearest larger towns (Berwick and Alnwick) are around 17 miles (27 km) away, though these are small for English market towns. The large urban centres of the Tyneside conurbation are over 50 miles (80 km) away and Edinburgh is 65 miles (105 km) away. In economic terms, until recent decades, the main employment was in agriculture. According to Murdoch et al (2003), the area had the political economy of a 'paternalist countryside' and a 'welfarist' government regime. One facet of the GGT's activities has been to challenge this culture.

Tourism has been important for many years and the visitor economy is now as significant in terms of employment as farming. Meanwhile, many former farm workers' cottages have been converted into holiday homes, or sold to more affluent incomers and second-homers. There is a steady inflow of people starting microbusinesses in a range of sectors, as well as professionals working from home. Young people are still leaving the area, driven by the search for wider horizons and especially the pull of urban lifestyles, along with limited work and leisure opportunities at home. In contrast, in recent years, there has been an inflow of those in middle age seeking a different lifestyle. This has resulted in an increasingly skewed demography. Nearly 26 per cent of people in Glendale in 2011 were aged 65 and over. The inflow of people from especially Southern England has put pressure on house prices in an area where, for many, incomes remain low and precarious.

The result is a transforming local economy, an increasingly skewed demographic and an accelerating crisis of housing availability and affordability. Despite a widespread appreciation of a strong feeling of 'community' in the area, there are also potential social tensions – between locals and incomers, the professionally skilled and those with less formal education, and those in Wooler town and in the outlying small villages and hamlets. Therefore, as in many rural areas across Europe, Glendale is experiencing not just significant economic and social change, but an existential challenge to find a sustainable future.

The scale of this challenge has been exacerbated by a decade of austerity. With a combination of low incomes and an ageing population, there is an increasing need for affordable and appropriate housing. Budget cuts have amplified the difficulties of sustaining services, from health and social care to adequate local shops, in an area where people are geographically scattered. In this situation, the GGT's implicit development strategy has focused on limiting the continuing outflow of younger people and the decline of the services that support them, while accepting the energy and investment of retiring incomers and providing for the needs of increasing numbers of older people. This demands continual recognition of the complex interrelations that make for place quality – work, housing, transport, health, education, training, social care, leisure and sport, and community vitality. It also requires an appreciation of a geography in which physical distance still really matters.

Meanwhile, formal government has become increasingly distant. Up to the mid-20th century, many services were provided in the different farming communities or through the churches, often on a parish basis. Until 1973, the lower-tier local authority was the Glendale Rural District Council (GRDC), based in Wooler, which covered the area to which the GGT now relates. The GRDC was merged into Berwick Borough Council, which, in turn, was merged into the higher-tier authority, Northumberland County Council, in 2008. This became a unitary authority covering a large and varied area. Grasping and responding to this changing context, while managing the merger of several districts into a single organisation and, at the same time, dealing with continual severe funding cuts, has been a fraught challenge for county politicians and staff. Yet, the county has been keen to promote community initiatives and social enterprises, and, in the past decade, has become much more interested in working with civil society actors such as the GGT.

Northumberland County Council's capacity is severely limited by its dependence on national government for funding. During the 1997–2010 government, there was a rich and varied flow of 'targeted' resources, with investment programmes in regional development through the regional development agency (One North East) and coordinated through the Northumberland Strategic Partnership, as well as regeneration funds for rural areas, market town improvements, playgrounds, community enterprises and national park initiatives. Many of these programmes provided resources for which civil society initiatives could bid and from which the GGT benefitted. However, this flow came to an end with the financial collapse of 2007/08 and the change of government in 2010. It has been replaced by the North East Local Enterprise Partnership, which focuses primarily on the industrial parts of the region and has a much smaller budget than One North East. At the national level, the Department of Environment, Farming and Rural Affairs had a small rural development programme, the Rural Growth Network, from which the GGT benefitted during 2012–14. Community enterprises could also bid for funding for social housing for rent from the national Homes and Communities Agency, so long as they were set up as registered social providers.[3] Even this opportunity was much reduced after 2015 as national policy swung against building more social housing for rent. The GGT has also had access to the EU LEADER programme over the years, a source that will presumably disappear after Brexit.

Along with many other small trusts and charities in Northumberland that had grown up in the 2000s providing local services, the GGT was catapulted into a much harsher funding environment. Yet, during the 2010s, the challenges for a rural area such as Glendale increased: the farming economy has contracted and is even more mechanised, along with forestry, and farming activity may contract further as a result of Brexit; the retail sector has been transformed by Internet trading, with shops closing in Wooler High Street, along with banks; public services have been further cut and centralised, being subject to funding regimes that have little recognition of the challenges of dispersed populations in rural areas; and the uncertain economic climate generated by Brexit has held back investment in potential projects. This has increased people's sense of being abandoned, both economically and politically, which, in turn, increases the potential for angry hostilities to break out, threatening the sense of a cohesive community.

Yet, there are opportunities to be grasped too: the Internet enables people to live in Wooler but work across the world; firms can similarly develop trading links in a wide geography; the beautiful landscape and the feeling of community attracts not only older people from further afield, but also those seeking to raise families in such an environment; and tourism continues to expand, offering attractive options for those interested in encountering the natural environment through walking and cycling. It is in this shifting context of the past 20 years or so that the GGT has evolved into a significant local development organisation.

## Case study: creating a community hub[4]

The GGT was formed in 1996, following discussions about how to improve Wooler's future facilitated by the then Rural Community Council. These had identified the need for a better community centre, which could combine meeting places for community groups, business spaces for start-ups and a base for key local services, as well as improved services for young people. It is run by a small employed staff and trustees from the locality. A drop-in facility for young people was created in a vacant building on the high street, while the neglected former offices of the Glendale Rural District Council, formerly a workhouse, provided an opportunity to create a community centre, now the Cheviot Centre. The building was transferred to the GGT by the then owner, Berwick Borough Council. The case study focuses on how the Cheviot Centre was transformed into a joint community–small business hub that not only helped save and enhance local services, but also, in time, came to be financially sustainable, largely by clustering services together. In parallel, while created to manage the development and operation of the community centre, the GGT grew into a multifaceted community development organisation with an entrepreneurial and proactive culture. In its early days, the GGT's activities were backed by funding from the Rural Community Council (now Community Action Northumberland) and the Northumberland Strategic Partnership.

For the first few years of its existence (1996–2000), the primary focus of the GGT's work was on converting the building. The challenge involved taking on ownership of the building, raising funds and organising the conversion process. To guide this work, as well as the creation of the drop-in centre, the GGT was created as a charitable trust, with a board combining local people and representatives of local government. This time is remembered as a risky, nail-biting experience as trustees embarked on ambitious projects, taking on grants and loans

**Figure 4.1:** The Cheviot Centre from outside

Source: Rachel Sinton

against uncertain achievement. However, this was the era of relatively accessible grants from government and other institutions.

By 2001, the job was done (see Figure 4.1) – a couple of community rooms were available for hire and there was a kitchen, office space for GGT staff and a few rooms left over that were rented to local businesses. The local Tourist Information Centre took one of the upstairs rooms, and there was initial talk of Wooler Library moving in, though Northumberland County Council procrastinated for many years over this idea. A key tenant of the community rooms was the local University of the Third Age (U3A),[5] which helped generate income. The Cheviot Centre slowly evolved as a base for delivering services, such as the Citizens Advice Service, the local credit union, a day centre run by the Royal Voluntary Service (RVS) and the Wooler Work Web. It also provided local offices for several voluntary sector services, which provided useful rental income.

The building was old, so it was not cheap to run; in addition, a full-time manager was needed. Fortunately, this early period coincided with generous national government funding for local initiatives of various kinds. This meant that, after the first couple of years, the Cheviot Centre operated at a reasonable surplus, based on a number of tenants who were themselves the recipients of public or charitable funding. Meanwhile, the GGT expanded its activities by investing in high-street improvements, funded by the national Market Towns Initiative, creating affordable housing for rent and taking over the local youth hostel. These initiatives helped to expand the revenue-earning asset base of the GGT, though public funding was still an important contribution. The financial basis of the GGT was therefore significantly affected by public sector budget cuts and the reduction of charitable funding opportunities in the 2010s. The revenues for the Cheviot Centre itself no longer covered running costs.

So, what to do about this? The GGT was aware of potential demand for more office space from the increasing numbers of microbusinesses in the area. The national charity RVS also located its regional office in the building, where they had begun to run a day event for older people. In 2012, the GGT saw an opportunity to do three positive things in an interrelated way. First, the trust applied for, and got, £212,000 in grants from the Rural Growth Network and the National Lottery for a major refurbishment of the building. It was pretty much gutted inside, providing extra office space without losing community facilities (the GGT made sure that local groups, especially Wooler U3A, the biggest customer of the Cheviot Centre, were kept onside during what was potentially a worrying time for them). Three 'pods' were also put in the garden – attractive one- or two-person units designed for start-up businesses. These have proved very popular (see Figure 4.2). Some small businesses have indeed moved on to larger premises and the GGT has never had any problems letting them. One early tenant who had been commuting to a job in Newcastle started their own business in the one-person pod, switched to a two-person pod within a year and then moved into one of the larger offices in the main building when they took on another employee.

Therefore, the first positive achievement was a significant improvement in the small business offer in Glendale – particularly

**Figure 4.2:** The pods

Source: Meg Vickers

for start-ups. Currently, more than 20 people are employed, either full-time or part-time, in the various businesses and activities based in the Cheviot Centre. In parallel with this refurbishment, the facilities of a community room were improved, raising the roof to provide for a Wi-Fi-connected sound system, which has not only allowed for film shows, but also provided a useful seminar space for business and community use.

At the same time, and after more than a decade of trying, the county agreed to move Wooler Library into the Cheviot Centre. By 2012, Northumberland County Council was beginning to suffer the cuts that have since further eroded their capacity for service delivery. This forced officers to seek new ways to deliver services. Meanwhile, by this time, the GGT had established a reputation as a capable local agency. The second achievement in this period was to bring Wooler Library and the Tourist Information Centre together with a single front desk. Sharing Northumberland County Council and GGT staff makes both services much cheaper to run and therefore more viable. The former library building just off the high street was transferred to GGT for £1 and was converted into two attractive affordable homes for the over 55s. The old library had been open for just two half days a week; the new library is now open six days a week, with a very evident uptake in usage. The Tourist Information Centre moved from their upstairs office to the reception area, thus creating a far more visible presence in the town. There is now a single reception desk for all activities in the Cheviot Centre, staffed by one person. As far as Northumberland County Council is concerned, these two services are now being operated efficiently as a much improved service is being provided at a very much reduced cost – so much so that the county have used the Glendale model as a template elsewhere.

A couple of years after this major redevelopment, another opportunity arose. The Police Authority for Northumbria decided to close a number of stand-alone police offices, including Wooler. The authority looked around the town for suitable, smaller premises to move into, and also considered moving out of Wooler altogether. At that stage, the GGT was very concerned to retain a police presence in the town. The individual police officers themselves were none too keen to lose their historic 'police station', but moving into the Cheviot Centre meant much reduced running costs – and it was preferable to a move out of town. The GGT did not want the whole character of the Cheviot Centre to change, with uniformed officers walking in and out of the front door all day, so the building was rapidly adapted to provide a degree of self-containment. This provided another 'anchor tenant', paying a significant rent on a long-term basis.

This brings us to the third achievement: the trust now runs a popular and successful community centre that actually makes a surplus. In other words, it is sustainable, as is the GGT as a whole. The small staff team (two full-time and two part-time, including the accountant) works collaboratively and flexibly, and the GGT continues to take new initiatives. When Active Northumberland pulled out of the marketing operation for tourist information centres across the county in 2018, the GGT decided to take it over and do it itself. The reception staff probably know better than outsiders what will sell to the visitors and locally, and it can be done without upsetting local traders on the high street too much (see Figure 4.3) – and staff enjoy trying out new lines.

The Cheviot Centre now exists as a thriving operation, realising the ambition to combine community and business activities, encouraging the cross-fertilisation of ideas. The Cheviot Centre is also the office base of the GGT, which has come to manage a varied portfolio of assets: 18 affordable housing units; commercial properties on the high street; and the Youth Hostel, now leased to a locally based operator. In 2019, the GGT has taken on another major conversion project. In addition, it has come to act as a platform for generating initiatives that, in time, become self-supporting, from the Wooler Youth Drop-In,

**Figure 4.3:** The reception area

Source: Rachel Sinton

to the Wooler Wheel cycle events that now run twice a year, and a small grant fund, created in partnership with Northumberland County Council's promotion of health and well-being. All those who interact with the GGT, from tenants to representatives of national and local government, experience it as a friendly face in the midst of the flow of multiple activities.

To achieve all this, the GGT has had to act in an innovative and imaginative way, trying out new ways of doing things and demonstrating what a community-sensitive service delivery culture can look like. It has always been infused by the idea of 'partnership', both among proactive people in Glendale and in relations with external agencies. In this way, the GGT has become valued by formal government agencies forced into finding ways to 'co-produce' public goods and services with market and civil society agencies. Throughout, it has been important to maintain a strong vision, along with a commitment to finding new, more entrepreneurial and more approachable ways of providing community services, challenging traditional public agency practices but also helping them to change. But what has been its role in relation to agendas of 'social renewal' and 'social justice'?

## Social renewal and social justice in a 'remote rural' context

It would be difficult to deny that the activities of the GGT have made a difference to the quality of life and opportunities available in Wooler and Glendale. It has: created a multifaceted community hub; provided 18 affordable housing units for rent through conversions, targeted at young people starting out and the needs of older residents; helped to enhance the vitality of the local high street and sustain the visitor economy; become a 'go-to' place with a face for many looking for information and advice; and acted as a platform from which to draw down resources from elsewhere and present a voice in larger arenas relevant to the area. In this way, it has created significant value for the 'public' of Glendale. This value has been material, in terms of drawing down resources for investment and producing both capital assets and services. However, it has also been institutional, both in creating a presence locally and more widely, and in demonstrating a proactive and entrepreneurial way of working. Along with other initiatives locally – by landowners, farmers, a few firms and the lively array of community groups in Glendale – it is working to help create a sustainable future to replace that based on the traditional labour-intensive agricultural economy.

The GGT can thus be understood as a vigorous agent for social renewal in the area. In this situation, social renewal must be understood in terms of structural adjustment from one economic geography to another. The experience has been of continual existential threats and opportunities. How far will it be possible to retain some of the old sense of a lively working and living community, centred around connections with the land and landscape, while adjusting to the changes in possibilities available to those who live and create a living in Glendale? Is the future, as some fear, to become a 'retirement' locale or a haven for those seeking to escape from the stress of an urban world? Does an Internet-based economy offer real potential for attracting a wider range of economic activities into Glendale, or will its impact be to reinforce the closure of shops and services, and the replacement of face-to-face interaction with live-chat, YouTube and email? Will there be enough variety of economic opportunity to support young people entering the workforce, or will they continue to leave? If so, where will the workforce to support existing local businesses and services, let alone staff new enterprises, come from?

The GGT is feeling its way through innovation and experimentation into an unknown future. In this sense, the challenge involves socio-economic reinvention rather than just renewal. It is also about political reinvention, showing a different way of acting for the public benefit to that long associated with increasingly stretched and distant public agencies. Creating a forward-looking and innovative culture of action, prepared to try out new things, means being open-minded and outward-looking, rather than introvertedly focusing on what has always been done. It means encouraging a proactive attitude towards doing things, rather than waiting for some public authority to 'authorise' or 'lead' a new activity. It means working with others, locally and more widely, to drive initiatives forward.

Not surprisingly, the GGT and its activities are not uncontested locally. Some feel that the Cheviot Centre is not a relevant locus for 'their' part of the community. For others, the way the GGT articulates a community voice is a challenge to other possible representations. Elsewhere, agencies such as the GGT have been created from within a local parish council. In this case, though one of the Glendale parish councils was, until recently, represented on the board of trustees, there is always the potential for conflict over who should be the community voice. Many people say the GGT places too much emphasis on Wooler, rather than the wider area of Glendale. Sometimes, the GGT's legitimacy is questioned, or its priorities. Part of this critique is about competition over 'who is in charge'. However, it is also fuelled by feelings of nostalgia for a disappearing past and fears for the future, driven by all kinds of misapprehension, which is not easily dispersed.

The trust is aware that its legitimacy, within Glendale and beyond, depends not on who it represents, but on what it does and how it does it. Here, the GGT also has to counteract some local critique that implicitly casts it into a new generation of 'paternalists': professionally educated people acting for, rather than with, the fellow citizens of Glendale. Social renewal is no easy process and is inherently conflict-ridden. In this context, the GGT is always taking a bet on how the future may work out. It is committed to finding ways into the future that look as if they can be sustained while that future unfolds uncertainly in front of us. However, one issue that rumbles away under the surface of the GGT's work is who in the community most benefits from what is done. How do the GGT's activities stand up to the criterion of social justice, and is that a relevant criterion for activities such as this?

'Social justice' is an abstract term. Some definitions centre on the fairness with which life opportunities and resources are distributed. Others link the term specifically to the notion of a hierarchy of classes and income groups, arguing that a socially just policy or outcome is one where the differences between classes or groups are minimised (see Bell and Davoudi, 2016). In the political economy of a country such as ours, the levers for promoting such fairness and redistribution are far beyond the reach of micro-local agencies such as the GGT. Moreover, recent national policies have contributed to the sense that many people locally have of experiencing unfair treatment in the way national resources are distributed. Those on low and often precarious incomes have been badly impacted by welfare reforms. Education and health services in rural areas are not just stretched, but also experience the spatial difficulties of the concentration of services in larger centres, supported by outreach that ignores the time costs of rural geography. As services get ever-more Internet-based, little attention is given to those who find it difficult to engage with the fast-changing practices of technological innovation.

In such a context, what contribution to social justice can a micro-organisation such as the GGT make to promoting greater fairness and supporting those at most risk in rural areas? The GGT has seen its responsibility in this respect, in part, as promoting community vitality and economic opportunity, both materially and through advocacy. The creation of the Cheviot Centre, the provision of offices for small-scale businesses and investing in Wooler High Street all make a contribution here. The Cheviot Centre provides several opportunities for social interaction and activity for older people. An early initiative of the

GGT was to create a drop-in facility for young people. The GGT's housing contribution is specifically targeted at groups whose needs are neglected by the market. The first investments in conversions to flats above high-street shops were targeted at young people. When a local sheltered housing facility for older people was closed, the GGT refocused its efforts in housing provision on the needs of older people. The GGT continues to promote local economic opportunity through providing training courses of various kinds at the Cheviot Centre. Overall, though, the emphasis is less on the needs of particular groups in the locality than on asserting the needs and potential viability of the area as a place with the possibility of a positive future, thereby challenging the urban-centred (and Southern-centred) politics that infuse our national and regional political economy.

## In conclusion

The mission that inspires both the staff who have worked for the GGT over the years and the many people who have acted as trustees has been to 'benefit the people of Glendale'. Our locality is understood as a place full of actual and potential vitality, though at the margin of attention nationally and regionally. We have a strong sense that we are 'on our own' and that it is 'up to us' as a community to work to realise the potential that will sustain that vitality. The role of the GGT in this context is to act as a micro-local community development agency, aware that economic, social and cultural life are interrelated in how people live their lives in a place such as ours. We give value to direct face-to-face interaction between the providers and users of services. We continually balance the creation of community benefit now with the need to sustain our operation over the long term. We regularly make links with external agencies that could bring benefit to our area, while being aware of the ongoing dangers of being 'co-opted' into acting as agents for their policies. Understood more widely, we are one of the many civil society initiatives across the country, and to be found elsewhere in Europe and North America more generally, experimenting with new ways of promoting local futures. Our experience shows the value of building up a revenue-generating asset base and we were fortunate that we could begin this asset-building process in the years before the financial crash and subsequent austerity policies. However, there are no simple models for building initiatives like ours as each is specific to its particular time and place. Those seeking to encourage experiences like ours should focus instead on creating the conditions of possibility for such innovation and experimentation to occur.

## Acknowledgements

Our thanks to Rachel Sinton, Mark Shucksmith, Mel Steer and other chapter authors for helpful comments on this chapter.

## Notes

[1]   This section has been partly adapted from Healey (2015: 12–14), with permission of the copyright holder.
[2]   The population of Glendale fell from over 12,000 in 1871 to around 8,000 in 1951. The population of Wooler itself has remained constant and is now slowly increasing.
[3]   GGT became a registered social provider in 2013.
[4]   For an account of the overall history of the GGT up to around 2014, see Healey (2015).
[5]   The U3A is a national organisation with local chapters led by and for local participants.

## References

Bell, D. and Davoudi, S. (2016) 'Understanding justice and fairness in and of the city', in S. Davoudi and D. Bell (eds) *Justice and Fairness in the City: A Multi-Disciplinary Approach to 'Ordinary Cities'*, Bristol: Policy Press, pp 1–20.

Healey, P. (2015) 'Civil society enterprise and local development', *Planning Theory and Practice*, 16(1): 11–27.

Murdoch, J., Lowe, P., Ward, N. and Marsden, T. (2003) *The Differentiated Countryside*, London: Routledge.

Shucksmith, M. and Brown, D.L. (2016) 'Framing rural studies in the Global North', in M. Shucksmith and D.L. Brown (eds) *Routledge International Handbook of Rural Studies*, London: Routledge, pp 1–26.

# 5

# The Byker Community Trust and the 'Byker Approach'

*John Pendlebury and Jill Haley*

## Introduction

Newcastle's Byker Estate is one of the last heroic post-war attempts in Britain to provide better housing for a working-class community. Its aspiration of providing decent homes for all now seems a distant memory, with the demonisation and residualisation of social housing and successive turns of the screw in recent years, such as 'the bedroom tax' and Universal Credit.

The Byker Community Trust (BCT) housing association was created in 2012, acquiring both the council's housing stock and land, and its management responsibilities, in what is one of the poorest wards in the country. This unique approach to ownership and management followed from the decision in 2007 to heritage 'list' the Byker Estate for its architectural and historic qualities.

This chapter describes the work of the BCT to bring much-needed investment to the estate. This has been accompanied by the 'Byker Approach', developing a leadership and empowerment culture aimed to be inclusive of all and give tenants a key voice and role in decision-making, with a focus now upon a thriving Byker where people *want* to live – 'an estate of choice'.

## Social housing in an era of neoliberalism and austerity

The term 'multiple deprivation' was coined in the 1970s in recognition that people are often living with material and structural disadvantage, combined at the level of both the individual and the neighbourhood, including poor housing. Such deprivation can contribute to poor educational achievement, poor health, high crime rates and poor employment prospects, and cumulatively lead to poor life chances for those affected. Ever since, government policy has been, ostensibly, to combat such multiple deprivation. Yet, in a perfect storm of ideologically and austerity-driven policy since 2010, successive governments seem to have been intent on concentrating and increasing levels of multiple deprivation in England, through changes to a raft of legislation and social policy. Most obviously, this includes the housing and welfare systems, though it ranges far more widely and extends to, for example, the criminal justice system.

When the post-war welfare state was developed, improved housing was understood as one of the essential social goods across the political spectrum. Yet, within this apparent post-war consensus, there were some significant political differences. The aspiration of the post-war Labour government was for council housing to be a tenure of choice for a broad range of social groups, but for the Conservatives, council housing was always considered as provision for the poor. Large-scale programmes of building were sustained through the 1950s, 1960s and into the 1970s, including the Byker Estate.

A critique of such building grew in parallel, which was entrenched by the late 1960s. The social consequences of comprehensive redevelopment had been documented in Young and Willmott's (1957) pioneering work, and a shift to high-rise, system building and other non-traditional forms was increasingly linked with failed technologies, poor-quality construction (sometimes as a consequence of corruption) and perceived problems in the intrinsic design principles used in many estates. Alice Coleman's (1985) work on this latter point was enthusiastically personally picked up by Margaret Thatcher as it fitted her narrative that far from being a remedy for social problems, the welfare state was one of their causes (Jacobs and Lees, 2013).

While construction and management failings of the sort described were common, most council housing stood as good-quality housing. Nevertheless, all council housing was tarnished by the negative images attributed to some estates, typically portrayed as 'concrete jungles', however inaccurate these stereotypes and however unrepresentative of the bulk of council housing these were. The political Left and Right broadly accepted these critiques of particular forms of council estate and the post-1997 Labour governments did little to change the direction put in train under Conservative administrations. Integral to this was a hostility to the local state, with the end of large-scale house building, the removal of stock from the public domain under 'Right to Buy'[1] as part of the chimera of a property-owning democracy and the removal of the management of housing to arm's-length organisations. Within this process, there has been a fundamental repositioning of social housing (no longer *council housing*) through a process of residualisation. In the long decline in the political position of social housing, its presentation has been shifted steadily from homes for all to a small sector geared only to the poorest citizens or those with social vulnerability. While the focus of this chapter is upon a deprived community, all social housing has been affected to a greater or lesser extent by the attendant stigmatisation that has occurred with these trends, and an attendant image of crime, decay and being the housing of those with no choice.

Focusing specifically on the period since 2010, the government's approach to housing, and specifically its assault on social housing, was characterised early on as 'class war conservatism' (Hodkinson and Robbins, 2012). We have seen attempts to remove the lifetime security of tenure for those living in social housing, the targeting of 'high earners' to pay market-level rents, caps on Housing Benefit and, broadly, an ideological view that social housing should be used 'efficiently' and purely as a 'safety net'. This carries an implicit message that social housing is a generous gift from the state that can be withdrawn. One manifestation of this is the retrospectively applied 'bedroom tax', introduced as part of the Welfare Reform Act 2012, which has forced residents out of their long-term homes. Punitive definitions of what constitutes surplus rooms (for example, children under 16 of the same gender are expected to share a room) lead, through benefit reduction, to effective rent rises of 14 per cent for one 'extra' bedroom and 25 per cent for two. Furthermore, those under 35 years old are paid Housing Benefit for only a single room and therefore cannot afford to rent a one-bedroom flat. Ironically, as a result of the bedroom tax, Byker has seen an increased demand for its previously unpopular one-bedroom flats, of which it has an unusually high proportion.

These changes to housing, combined with other changes in benefit, such as the disastrous and pernicious implementation of Universal Credit,[2] have resulted in making a difficult situation worse for, first, and most importantly, those caught in this poverty trap, as well as those agencies that interact with tenants experiencing new levels of extreme deprivation. In the words of John Boughton (2018: 268, emphasis original): 'we now have a state which, while it once promised its citizens security, seems to be offering – and valuing – *insecurity*'. Rather than a view of the welfare state as having a broad application in various forms to many citizens, it is a grudging view whereby a minimal state provides a minimal provision for citizens who are deemed to have failed. However, it also actively creates conditions that, having fallen into the poverty trap, there is little prospect of escaping. Furthermore, austerity-driven politics has extended throughout the welfare state, with, for example, food banks becoming a depressing part of everyday life for many. Poor housing, poor nutrition and so on place inevitable extra burdens on the NHS, among other public agencies. The unravelling of the welfare state has many consequences, presumably unintended. To give one example, a recent report has shown how the loss of Sure Start centres has had particularly negative effects in disadvantaged areas, including the increased hospitalisation of primary school-aged children (Cattan et al, 2019). Social housing landlords have often been left trying to pick up the pieces caused by these policy changes, within a political environment that has sought to encourage the private rented sector, through various deregulatory initiatives.

There are small signs of a more positive outlook for council housing developing. Many local authorities have re-engaged in small-scale house building and a government Housing Green Paper has acknowledged the important role of social housing, and the need to reverse the stigma attached to it. It remains to be seen whether this is a significant turning point.

## The Byker Estate

The Byker Estate, designed by Ralph Erskine and colleagues for Newcastle City Council, is one of the last large-scale post-war attempts to provide better housing for a working-class community before such council housing programmes were stopped by the Conservative governments of Margaret Thatcher. It is one of the greatest achievements of its age in public housing anywhere in the world, celebrated nationally and internationally for its architectural design and its novel processes of engaging with working-class residents. The designers encouraged a co-creation approach in Byker and sought to create something of enduring social worth.

Erskine was appointed in 1968 to redevelop the high-density 19th-century neighbourhood of terraced houses and 'Tyneside flats'. Erskine had the view that the physical fabric of the place could be transformed without disrupting relational resources. This was a step change from clearance elsewhere, where the focus had been upon housing as defective bricks and mortar rather than housing as homes and places of attachment. The most well-known architectural feature of the estate is the perimeter block – 'the Byker Wall' – defining the northern part of the site. Designed to reduce the noise from a planned urban motorway to the north, and to create the feeling of a village within the city, it is also a strong visual signal of a separate place, with few pedestrian and vehicular access points. Beyond the 'Wall', low-rise dwellings of various sizes were constructed. Extensive use was made of light materials, including brightly coloured timber cladding and metal roofs. Materials had to be cheap, were often not durable and were non-standard. The integration of a strong landscaping framework into the estate was a key integral feature and cars were mostly kept at the periphery of the estate. New social facilities introduced included a large number of 'hobby rooms' for social enterprises, clubs and individuals to use. Space heating was provided through a district heating system. Erskine envisaged Byker as an estate that would change and develop to meet community needs but each of these latter points – in terms of materials, car parking, changing social practice and an expensive heating system – has been a source of subsequent problems, exacerbated by lower-than-anticipated management budgets and, arguably, the subsequent restrictions of heritage status.

Erskine's practice set up an office in a former undertaker's premises in the heart of the area, where their open-door policy allowed a demystifying of the architectural process (Drage, 2008). Acknowledgement was made of the mistakes that had been made in post-war housing policy, both in terms of a lack of sensitivity to the value and importance of social relationships in existing communities, and in terms of the material form of estates. A rolling programme of clearance and rebuilding attempted to reduce the displacement of residents. The emancipatory goals of Byker were underpinned by the work of Newcastle City Council, which, as landlord, pre-allocated dwellings with a strong concern for facilitating the retention of neighbourly contacts that were seen to be supportive. However, ultimately, less than half of the old Byker residents returned, in part, because of industrial action that left residents in limbo for longer than anticipated. A subsequent moratorium on large-scale local authority house building meant two large sites were not developed according to the original plan. The Byker redevelopment ultimately comprised 2,010 dwellings. There is a rich mix of dwelling types, ranging from small apartments and maisonettes to family homes, and including sheltered housing and care homes, with the different housing types widely spread, with few easily plotable patterns.

From the 1980s, Byker was hard hit by industrial decline through the loss of shipbuilding, mining and allied industries, with consequent rising unemployment, and the residualisation of social housing in the UK. A cash-strapped local authority struggled to maintain a built environment that had used cheap and relatively short-lived materials extensively, and service charges rose as problems with the district heating system escalated costs. Increasing worklessness was accompanied by problems of vandalism and anti-social behaviour, and people who could leave often did so. As a very different physical environment that outsiders could find intimidating and hard to navigate, Byker quickly began to develop a poor reputation in the local media that it has struggled to shake off ever since. The demographics of Byker also began to change, with the original white working-class community gradually developing into a multi-ethnic and multilingual one. Problems in the southern part of the estate led to the abandonment of some property, and by the late 1990s, the city council had concluded that it needed to undertake some demolition.

The possible demolition of a part of such a lauded estate triggered controversy in the Byker Estate, as well as in the city and beyond, and led to a local and national campaign for the estate to be listed as of 'special architectural or historic significance'. In 2000, English Heritage recommended that the government list the Byker Estate and after a long hiatus the entirety of the Erskine-designed estate was listed at grade II* in January 2007.[3] The long delay over the listing decision was a source of local frustration for both residents and the various agencies involved; however, at the same time, it has been argued that significant numbers of residents in Byker hold to a sense that Byker is special. There is a consciousness of the estate's very particular physical characteristics. There is also a consciousness of the history of a community and how, in part, it was involved in a process of redevelopment that led to continuity in space while the nature of the physical environment was utterly transformed. This history is embedded within the institutions of neighbourhood governance and civil life, as well as in the networks of kinship and friendship from that early period that, in part, still survive (Pendlebury et al, 2009).

Listing raised consciousness that the long-term management of Byker required a non-standard solution to those usual in the management of social housing, not least as physical interventions might be more expensive in recognition of the heritage status. It was within this context that the then Labour government convened a commission to look at the long-term future of the estate. The commission examined various governance models, with the eventual proposition put to residents of a new housing association with a transfer promise that 'tenants would have more influence on how the estate is managed and have more opportunities to be involved'. The significant 'sweetener' offered alongside this was a government commitment to write off the estate's debt. After a hiatus around the 2010 general election, the Coalition government decided to honour this offer, and following a unanimous vote in favour of the proposals by Byker residents in 2011, the stock transferred to the BCT in July 2012.

## The BCT and the 'Byker Approach'

Since its creation, BCT has embarked on an ambitious and transformative programme of physical renewal of the housing stock, other buildings under its influence and the wider landscape, significantly exceeding the promises made at stock transfer in the process. However, the physical challenges that Byker faces are the tip of the iceberg. Much harder to resolve are issues of deep and systemic poverty, disempowered residents, and a negative place image, with decades-old stories endlessly recycled by the local media. One of the 'golden threads' running through all that the BCT does, now explicit in its *Thriving Byker Strategy* (Byker Community Trust, no date), is 'making Byker an estate of choice': if Byker is to be successful, it needs to be somewhere people want to live, rather than being forced to live through a lack of alternative. Linked to this has been the key goal of empowering residents in the governance and management of Byker.

The BCT has progressed through two phases since its creation and is now in its third strategic period. Initially, the BCT had to find its feet quickly and start delivering on stock-transfer promises. In practice, at the beginning, the BCT was unable to act as independently as it would have liked, operating within a rather tangled context of legacy agreements. For example, it was tied into four-year service contracts with Newcastle City Council and Your Homes Newcastle, its arm's-length management organisation. Furthermore, as other social landlords, it was hit by Coalition government policy that forced rents down year on year. This was made worse by Byker-specific problems such as an expensive service charge (linked to the district heating system), the difficulties and cost of works due to the listed status, and, above all, deep-seated poverty and disempowered tenants, exacerbated by austerity and a negative place image quite different from its celebrated architectural value. Cumulatively, these issues also left the BCT walking a financial tightrope.

While not all these problems have in any way been overcome, the BCT was able to stabilise and move forward with its vision in a second phase. Since 2012, the BCT has committed £47.5 million of investment up to 2025 in the physical fabric of the estate through major programmes addressed at the Byker Wall, the lower-rise housing, substantial upgrades to sheltered housing blocks (see Figure 5.1), the district heating system and, to come, the landscape. This considerably exceeds the £39 million pledged over 20 years in the stock-transfer document. Improved management practice has seen rent-collection rates rise from 93.9 per cent to 99.97 per cent,

**Figure 5.1:** Tom Collins House, at 12 storeys, is BCT's tallest building and one of two sheltered housing accommodation facilities for older people. Sir Keir Starmer relaunched both sheltered housing schemes following a £2 million regeneration project, in November 2018. Pictured are (left to right) Jim Coulter (BCT Chair), Charlie Hardwick (local actor), Councillor Nick Kemp, Sir Keir Starmer, Nick Brown MP and Jill Haley (BCT Chief Executive)

Source: BCT

despite the implementation of Universal Credit. Staff surveys show an empowered staff. Most importantly, a robust participatory governance framework has been developed.

The achievements made have often been against the odds. Capital projects are frequently made more complicated, and are delayed and made more expensive, by listed status. For example, reroofing costs have been twice what might otherwise have been the case and the 20 different types of non-standard bricks used in constructing Byker cost up to five times the cost of a standard brick. These dramatically higher costs are a problem and a frustration; however, at the same time, there is a recognition by the BCT that the distinctive architecture of the estate is one of the things (along with its people) that make Byker special. Other investments have included buying back 'Right to Buy' properties when the opportunity arises and converting disused 'hobby rooms' into additional housing as part of growing both the BCT's housing stock and the diversity of its offer. The BCT has worked with other partners as part of this physical transformation. One example is the reuse of the disused Avondale House, a historically unpopular and underpopulated sheltered housing scheme. This has been brought back into use in partnership with the charity Armed Forces' and Veterans' Launchpad. It now forms 35 flats and houses for members of the armed forces struggling with the transition back into civilian life who have experienced homelessness and/or a range of other problems, and is combined with a programme of activities and events to integrate the residents into the community. The whole of the Byker Estate is serviced by a district heating system. Since taking over ownership of the estate, the BCT has frozen the heating and hot water costs to tenants, and in December 2012, it commissioned a new biomass boiler and combined heat and power plant, resulting in a greener and more economical system for all. One of the difficulties that the BCT faces in seeking to manage place is that tenants' experience of Byker may be negative due to factors over which the BCT has little or no control. As an example of this, waste management and issues of fly-tipping can have a significantly detrimental impact on the experience of place but are principally the responsibilities of the local authority. The BCT works in close partnership with Newcastle City Council to try to overcome these issues.

While investment in the physical fabric of Byker and good stewardship are vital, it is clear that the biggest challenge Byker faces is ultimately the impact of deep-seated poverty and deprivation, exacerbated by austerity and welfare reform. Byker is one of the poorest wards in the country, for example: life expectancy is a decade or more less in Byker than in more affluent wards in the city; four food banks operate in the area; educational achievement is low; only 13 per cent of tenants have Internet access other than through a mobile phone; and, to complicate matters further, 19 languages are spoken on the estate. A particular challenge for the BCT has been welfare reform and the introduction of Universal Credit and the brutal hardship this has created for many of the BCT's residents; 68 per cent of residents claim benefits of some sort and two thirds of these have been migrated to Universal Credit, and the BCT has had an important role in helping tenants with debt management. The BCT runs pre-tenancy workshops to better prepare future tenants for the responsibilities they will assume, and has sought to maximise access for local people to employment, training, health and educational opportunities. This includes, for example, working with contractors to provide training and educational opportunities for Byker residents and children. Vulnerable people tend to attract those that prey on those vulnerabilities. Therefore, an important part of the BCT's approach has been a zero-tolerance approach to those tenants who, through various forms of criminality, such as drug dealing, seek to exploit these weaknesses. Working closely with the police and the council, the BCT has sought closure orders and to evict such tenants.

The BCT's *Thriving Byker Strategy* (Byker Community Trust, no date) includes 27 different community partners and has further emphasised the importance of measures extending far beyond those of a traditional landlord (see Figure 5.2). Aimed at meeting the corporate objective of engaging, empowering and supporting residents, and contributing to the economic health of the neighbourhood, the strategy has five key themes:

- Health and well-being and the links between housing and both physical and mental health, including issues of food poverty.
- Financial inclusion in terms of providing opportunities for tenants to access training and employment, as well as increasing the range of financial services tenants can access.
- A safer Byker through tackling crime and the fear of crime.
- Children and young people in terms of young people in Byker having the best opportunities to raise educational attainment and raise aspirations.
- Community investment and the use of a fund (the Byker Community Chest) to enable tenants to initiate community projects.

At the heart of the BCT's work is the 'Byker Approach', which gives tenants a key voice and role in decision-making, and influence in service provision and standards. Beyond this, it is a strategy to build

**Figure 5.2:** Community fun days and get-togethers are a regular occurrence in Byker. The picture shows a community barbeque in Felton Walk, Byker organised by the neighbourhood tenants and residents association

Source: BCT

leadership capacity among residents and staff alike. Central to this process is building trust, empowering and training both staff and residents, and building closer working relationships. The BCT aims to extend this philosophy through all its actions. In its framework for engaging with tenants, it has a series of mechanisms for customer care and ten different residents' groups of different kinds through which it has a more formal engagement. At the apex of these is the formal governance structures of the BCT, with a Customer Scrutiny Committee, comprising nine tenants plus a number more as observers, of whom between three and five sit on the 12-member board of the BCT. Demand from tenants for these empowered roles is highly competitive. Tenants are guided, supported and trained when engaging in these processes, and tenant board members of the Customer Scrutiny Committee are remunerated.

Nevertheless, as indicated, substantial challenges remain and further work is needed to 'make Byker an estate of choice'. While housing supply and shortages are major problems at the national level, in the east end of Newcastle, the BCT finds itself in competition with six other registered social landlords, as well as the private sector. Its own exit surveys have shown that the most common reason for tenants to leave is that they feel they have a better offer from somewhere else locally, albeit that turnover rates on the estate have steadily fallen year on year since the BCT's creation. The goal is to create a more balanced social and economic mix of residents as part of building a more resilient community. Building its relationship with its tenants, or customers, has been a central activity for the BCT over its life so far. To help drive this further, the BCT has made a concentrated effort to understand its data better and to work with its community partners to develop and grow its co-creation approach. Community engagement remains challenging in the context of the range of languages spoken in Byker, low rates of digital inclusion and the marginalised nature of many tenants. An extensive tenant engagement and communication framework was established in 2018 to encourage more residents from hard-to-reach groups to work more closely with the BCT.

All this reinforces the importance of the third phase mentioned previously, with the BCT seeking to jump from the stabilisation of the estate achieved over the last few years into a deeper transformation. At the heart of this is a programme of major investment. Partly, this is about addressing an environmental transformation to improve street and play facilities and the overall appearance of the estate, as well as further investment in property. Improving the wider environment is the one promise from the original stock transfer that has not been fully addressed. Consultants have been employed to produce a strategy that encompasses objectives such as addressing the lack of management of trees, the replacement of some by fruit trees, play facilities for different ages, waste collection arrangements and, importantly, safety and security. Further work is needed to houses and flats to bring them in line with contemporary expectations. For example, properties were provided with baths but no showers, and modernisation, where it has occurred, has been on a component basis, leaving a hotchpotch of kitchen and bathroom fittings and fixtures, with many 1970s' fixtures remaining. The potential to build more new houses exists within the estate, and this will be important in terms of providing property types that Byker has a relative lack of, such as level-access homes. However, the BCT does not have the wherewithal at the moment to fully implement all these measures. The next section returns to the implications of this.

The BCT is rightly proud of its achievements and is active in entering these into various award schemes, with much success. Notable awards, all in 2017, include being awarded 'Great Neighbourhood' by the Academy of Urbanism, 'Outstanding Innovation' by the Chartered Institute of Housing in the North East for the 'Byker Approach' and 'Best External Publication' by the Chartered Institute of Public

Relations for its tenants' newsletter. These are important as part of developing pride in Byker. Furthermore, the BCT was named a 'Top 50' landlord in the UK in 2018 and 2019, and was awarded 'Customer Service Excellence' accreditation in 2020. The external assessors awarded the BCT the highest possible marks for 'leadership', 'using customer insight' and 'working in partnership'.

## Discussion and conclusion

Decent housing, along with education and health provision, was one of the pillars of the welfare state in providing a decent and just society for all. While education and health face severe pressure, it is with housing that the welfare state has been most comprehensively unravelled over the last four decades and this has, in turn, further undermined education and health. Government policy since 2010 has exacerbated the long residualisation of council housing and drastically eroded support for the poorest and most vulnerable people in society as part of an ideological programme of austerity. This has left social landlords having to manage increasingly marginalised communities. The need to manage places better in a holistic way is not new, but it has acquired a new urgency in this context.

The ideals that underpinned the construction of Byker seem to belong to a very different era. Indeed, the recognition of the architectural importance of the estate through its listing bestowing it heritage status formally places it into the historical record. However, this happenstance of listing has also led to a very different strategy for managing the estate – one rooted in place, which has helped enable a responsiveness to the particular needs of Byker. As well as seeking to be a good, responsive landlord, the BCT has had to become a surrogate arm of the welfare state, working for Byker and endeavouring to make it a good place to live and a place of choice, despite indifference and hostility from the national government. The BCT contributes to the local economy by investing in its people and communities, supports local schools and a wide range of community organisations, and reinvests any surplus or additional income back into the area.

Against the odds, a transformative programme of material quality and social relationships has been developed and implemented. Above all, the BCT has sought to empower its residents and develop their capacity for leadership through carefully supporting, developing and extending their integration into the management and governance of the estate. Trust has been built with a community that had become disengaged, disempowered and distrustful of all external authority. In doing so, as this chapter has outlined, major achievements have been made, which have been demonstrated in performance and customer service measures that have steadily improved. This is the Erskine vision of developing the estate in line with community needs and the BCT stands as a model of good practice of what can be achieved.

Equally, the BCT is acutely conscious that it has not solved all of Byker's problems. Specifically, the BCT's vision of 'making Byker an estate of choice' requires a degree of transformation that is beyond its current means. Achieving these goals may involve contemplating a new future for the BCT and closer working or amalgamation with other, larger, organisations with more resources. However, critically, residents have been empowered to lead that decision-making process, rather than having it imposed upon them. This is truly in the emancipatory tradition envisaged by Erskine and his team.

## Notes

[1] The Right to Buy scheme is a policy in England (originally in all the UK) that gives local authority tenants the legal right to buy, at a discount, the house they are living in.

[2] Universal Credit is a UK social security payment designed to simplify the benefits system with a single monthly payment if someone is out of work or on a low income.

[3] Buildings can be listed as grades I (the highest grade), II★ or II. The higher grades are used sparingly, with over 90 per cent of buildings being grade II.

## References

Boughton, J. (2018) *Municipal Dreams: The Rise and Fall of Council Housing*, London: Verso.

Byker Community Trust (no date) *Thriving Byker Strategy 2019–2022*, Newcastle upon Tyne: BCT.

Cattan, S., Conti, G., Farquharson, C. and Ginja, R. (2019) *The Health Effects of Sure Start*, London: The Institute of Fiscal Studies.

Coleman, A. (1985) *Utopia on Trial: Vision and Reality in Planned Housing*, London: Hilary Shipman.

Drage, M. (2008) 'Byker: surprising the colleagues for 35 years, a social history of Ralph Erskine's Arkitektkontor AB in Newcastle', *Twentieth Century Architecture: The Journal of the Twentieth Century Society*, 9: 147–62.

Hodkinson, S. and Robbins, G. (2012) 'The return of class war conservatism? Housing under the UK Coalition government', *Critical Social Policy*, 33(1): 57–77.

Jacobs, J.M. and Lees, L. (2013) 'Defensible space on the move: revisiting the urban geography of Alice Coleman', *International Journal of Urban and Regional Research*, 37(5): 1559–83.

Pendlebury, J., Townshend, T. and Gilroy, R. (2009) 'Social housing as heritage: the case of Byker, Newcastle upon Tyne', in L. Gibson and J. Pendlebury (eds) *Valuing Historic Environments*, Farnham: Ashgate, pp 179–200.

Young, M. and Willmott, P. (1957) *Family and Kinship in East London*, London: Routledge and Kegan Paul.

# 6

# Cafe society: transforming community through quiet activism and reciprocity

*Jane Midgley and Sam Slatcher*

## Introduction

This chapter is about food sharing in a community cafe in North East England. The chapter draws from an original co-production research project between Newcastle University and a local social enterprise RE<sup>E</sup>USE Community Interest Company (CIC). RE<sup>E</sup>USE collects 'safe for consumption' surplus food from local food retailers and manufacturers, and by intercepting food in this way, prevents it from going to waste. The food is then transformed into meals and snacks that are available in its 'pay as you feel' (PAYF) cafe in the town of Chester-le-Street. This environmentally motivated activism also aims to bring beneficial impacts to the local community, such as greater access to food and reducing social isolation. RE<sup>E</sup>USE is a member of The Real Junk Food Project, a collective network and effort involving 120 projects in seven countries that intercept, distribute and share food within their communities (TRJFP, 2019). In this chapter, the social and community impacts of the cafe are documented, which are specifically explored through the ideas of reciprocity and 'quiet' activism in social renewal actions that aim to improve social justice outcomes.

## Context

This research and the cafe project is, in part, located amid the growth in UK food industry donations of 'safe for human consumption' surplus foods to charitable and social redistributors, as well as commercial food redistribution organisations (such as social supermarkets) that work to make this surplus food available to individuals and communities either free or at reduced cost. For example, recent UK figures identified that the estimated extent of surplus food used for charitable and social redistribution amounted to 43,034 tonnes in 2017, which was consequently diverted from entering the waste stream (WRAP, 2018). This reflected an increase of 80 per cent in the amount of available food offered between 2015 and 2017, and of the 2017 total amount, UK charitable and social redistributors (such as RE^FUSE) handled 20,935 tonnes, which was mainly sourced from food retailers (WRAP, 2018).

While the focus of redistribution actions is often associated with preventing safe, edible food from going to waste *and* improving the provision of food to those experiencing food poverty and insecurity, here, the opportunities that are offered by community cafes and other food sharing offers (which may or may not utilise surplus food) to address the increasing harsh realities of life for many in austerity Britain amid the continued retrenchment of collective welfare provision are highlighted. In the UK, there has been a well-documented growth in the numbers of households that are turning to charitable sources to gain emergency access to food in order to avoid hunger. The UK's leading food-bank network estimated that during 2017–18, it experienced a 13 per cent increase in demand for its three-day emergency food parcels, distributing 1,332,952 meals to people in crisis, of which 484,026 went to children (The Trussell Trust, 2018). Food redistribution and sharing activities seek to explicitly challenge the model of conditional charitable food aid that is typically denoted by eligibility requirements for emergency support in the form of food parcels offered by food banks. Indeed, community cafes and other organisations that offer opportunities for social eating and food sharing have been shown to proffer alternative and often unconditional support to individuals experiencing chronic (long-term) food insecurity and social isolation in contemporary society (Midgley, 2018). Thus, this chapter challenges the critique often levelled at surplus food actors of depoliticising issues by taking care of the symptoms of food waste and food poverty (Poppendieck, 1998), and highlights the possibilities of political and participatory actions that look to more 'progressive possibilities' (Cloke et al, 2017) based on the encounters and connections found within the cafe and stimulated by its activities. The focus here is on the use of the concepts of quiet politics and activism (Askins, 2015; Kneafsey et al, 2017) to help frame and explore the work of the cafe and its social impacts, both for individuals and for the wider community, which have become centred around reciprocity.

It has been suggested that people often become involved in food-based initiatives such as growing projects and community cafes, which are transformational for themselves and also for their wider community, but may not perceive themselves as political actors or their behaviour as being radical (Kneafsey et al, 2017). Kneafsey et al's (2017) study of community gardens in Coventry identified unintentional transformations in people's lives, such as improving access to fresh own-grown vegetables and/or an ability to express greater control in their own lives, which led to commitments to change wider practices in the food system, as well as community-focused activities. The practices generated by these spaces were termed 'quietly radical' (Kneafsey et al, 2017: 624) and created the possibility that through 'sharing, repairing, gifting and bartering', beneficial social and environmental impacts could occur (Smith and Jehlicka, 2013: 155). In contrast, rather than activism being achieved as an outcome of either accidental or incidental practice in shared everyday spaces, Askins (2015: 476) has argued that these spaces can produce 'more than implicit actions', which she refers to as 'quiet politics'. Exploring encounters between refugees and asylum seekers and their befrienders in spaces such as cafes, Askins (2015: 476) notes how these mundane spaces 'allow for, and demand, shifts in perceptions of Self and Other, nudging established discourses of alterity, and anticipating new social relations'. As such, this quiet politics is explicit and purposeful, and expresses a political will to (re)make communities. On a different note, Cloke et al (2017: 720) have suggested that encounters between food-bank volunteers and recipients enable changes in perceptions and relations that can encourage subtle subversions of the prevailing system of conditional support, and contribute to creating 'political and ethical ruptures in the art of the possible within capitalist realism'.

A crucial means by which such quiet politics and activism can be facilitated is through thinking about reciprocity and the relations that can shape this practice in everyday life. Informed by Young (1997: 343) and her promotion of 'asymmetrical reciprocity', the authors suggest that it is through dialogue, encounters and interactions with others that we learn to respect difference, that is, their particular histories and situations, which 'acknowledges and takes account of the other'. This asymmetrical position contrasts with other ethical positions that start by assuming that we can put ourselves in the place of another, and understand others by substituting our socially structured differences (such as gender, class or religion), and our experiences, emotions, morals and expectations, for theirs. Young gives an example of how following an initial gift of a jar of marmalade, weeks later, the recipient offers a loaf of bread and this exchange creates and reaffirms reciprocity – there is no attempt to equate each item, but there is an opening to recognition, equality and continuing relations. Nor is the relationship based on ideas of obligation or compensation. This movement away from the usual immediacy of commodity exchanges is suggestive of more plural practices of sharing and exchange that can be seen as being 'a constitutive practice of sociality, community, and being together' (Barnett and Land, 2007: 1073). Recognising social as well as economic diversity and difference, and how these may be collectively performed and shared, leads us to think about how these are articulated: as quiet or loud political actions that can challenge systems from outside; or from within by enabling alternative forms of practice to be recognised and valued (Gibson-Graham, 1996). The diversity of political and community activism(s) reflected by diverse food sharing economies, such as 'pay as you feel' cafes, cooperatives, discounted offers to people in need, food redistribution and the relational flows and social connections that result from these practices, become more visible as contributing to social change (Pottinger, 2018; Davies, 2019; Hall, 2020). Therefore, attention to reciprocity, particularly its asymmetrical form, may contribute towards recognition of the greater diversity of actions and arrangements that promote social justice and renewal as part of an everyday quiet activism.

## The RE$^E$USE cafe case study

RE$^E$USE began its life as a collective of individuals who were campaigning about the amount of food wasted in the city of Durham. In 2015, Nikki, now Co-director of RE$^E$USE, was working at a chain hotel in the city and volunteering at a local food distribution centre for homeless people. Alarmed by the stark contrast between the amount of food going to waste in the hotel and the need for food at the distribution centre, Nikki and her friend Mim began discovering the amount of food wasted elsewhere in the city, such as local supermarket bins, and discussed how they could address the problem of huge amounts of edible food being thrown away. After a launch event in June 2015, Nikki, Mim and a team of volunteers served a meal to 256 people, bringing together people from different backgrounds. They set up a CIC and became part of 'The Real Junk Food Project'. Relying on small start-up grants to employ Nikki part-time, by the end of 2016, RE$^E$USE had hosted 26 pop-up events, fed 3,000 people and saved 3,800 kg of food from being wasted. In the winter of 2016/17, they successfully crowdfunded £15,000 to subsidise the costs of a van and the rent for a cafe on the main high street of the nearby town of Chester-le-Street (as a CIC, RE$^E$USE pays usual business costs such as rent and utilities, its income is generated through PAYF, and it returns surplus to benefit the community). After a nine-month renovation project, the cafe opened in April 2018 in a former kitchen showroom and warehouse. The cafe initially opened to the public three days a week (Thursday, Friday and Saturday), and by October 2018, the cafe opened a further two days. By December 2018, it employed five people and intercepted roughly 1 tonne of surplus food per week. The cafe is decorated with upcycled materials, and a wooden board hangs on the wall with black paint and coloured words that read 'Food is *not* free. It is valuable and so are you, so Pay as You Feel: donate your time; pay with money; pledge your skills' (see Figure 6.1).

The original research informing this chapter came about through a comment made by Nikki when interviewed by the author in 2017, as Nikki explained the plans for the cafe's opening and the outcomes that RE$^F$USE hoped to achieve. Nikki was aware that the anticipated impacts would need to be identified and evidenced but was uncertain how this could be done. This conversation informed the development of the co-production research project reported in this chapter, which aimed to: (1) identify and evidence the social and community changes in the immediate months following the cafe's opening, and how these impacts were valued; and (2) develop a method that would be repeatable and useable by the cafe and other community cafes to identify and evidence their impacts.

**Figure 6.1:** The cafe

Source: Newcastle University

The research method chosen and adapted was 'photovoice' (Wang and Burris, 1997; Sutton-Brown, 2014; Sitter, 2017). In this participatory action research method, a pre-existing group of people who are known to each other agree to collect photographs that they have chosen to take, which prompts discussion. Together, these data identify what characteristics or things they may collectively wish to see change in future, and, in turn, work together with others to achieve. However, as there was no pre-existing group, other than visitors to the cafe, the authors worked with different individuals on a one-to-one basis to document and identify what the cafe and community meant to them, in essence, what they valued about the cafe and its impact on their lives and that of their community. Initially, we collected data from different individuals visiting the cafe on an anonymous basis, whereby we left 'open invitations' to participate in the research by writing and drawing on placemats in response to the ideas of the 'RE$^E$USE cafe' and 'community'. The placemats were left, collected and replaced on the cafe tables over a three-week period in May 2018. These provided the authors with greater contextual knowledge of how the cafe was beginning to impact on people and how people valued the cafe (see Figures 6.2 and 6.3). The invitation to provide comments or images also included the author's contact details if people were interested in taking part in the next stage of the research project. While we had a huge response to the placemats, few people came forward for the next stage of research without the researchers or cafe link researcher (Sam) having an informal chat with people who they either saw completing a placemat or recognised as people returning to the cafe. This approach allowed the authors to provide information sheets on what further participation entailed, explain the research in more detail and answer any questions. Five individuals participated in the final stage of the research during summer 2018. Each person was given an instant camera to take photographs, which they brought to discuss with a member of the research team on a fortnightly basis (or as convenient to the participant). Each participant selected the final images and associated comments that they were willing to put forward into the public domain. Integral to this method is that the curation of the image and comments are not controlled by the researcher; rather, the images that are initially discussed are then further reflected upon by the participant with an awareness of what was discussed in connection to them, with the decision for the potential inclusion of images and discussions denoted by participants handing over their selection to the researcher(s). This enabled the research relationships to progress on a more equal basis and allowed for potentially sensitive

**Figure 6.2:** Placemats in the cafe

Source: Newcastle University

issues to be voiced and acknowledged but controlled by the participant. The data were analysed by the research team and shared with the cafe and participants at a workshop where the narrative and content of the findings were decided, alongside the final image choices and the extent to which they wished their participation to remain anonymous (for wider discussion of the methodological design and findings in the final report, see Midgley et al, 2018). In writing this chapter, the authors have continued to respect the levels of anonymity chosen by participants (hence, we may use a pseudonym, a real name or no name), and for people to be referred to as cafe users and/or participants.

**Figure 6.3:** Completed placemat extracts

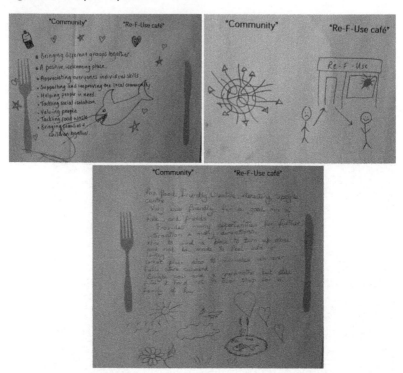

Source: Newcastle University

This approach has always been intended to complement the standard estimated measure of social benefit that is commonly used by the food industry, redistribution actors and funders, which converts amounts (weight) of surplus food into meals (420 g of foodstuff is typically equated to one meal serving, regardless of food type or nutritional balance). During its first year (2018/19), the cafe saved 39.9 tonnes from 20 food manufacturers and retailers, which was transformed into 12,248 meals (RE^FUSE, 2019). As such, the strength of the approach outlined earlier enables participants to identify, evidence and voice what they agreed were individual and shared impacts in their lives that reached beyond the transformation of food items into meals (Midgley et al, 2018).

## The cafe: a quietly transformative community space

This section is organised around three themes. The first theme explores reciprocity and how this was both performed and worked to challenge values and open up different relations and possibilities for change. Some of the changes in individual and family life are explored under the second theme, which is termed 'quiet transformations'. The third theme focuses on self-declared political actions and expressions of quiet activism by participants undertaken in the community in connection to the cafe.

### Reciprocity

Reciprocity was practised by participants in a number of ways. Participant 1 was an active practitioner of the opportunities for reciprocity offered by the cafe: with respect to the PAYF format, she was often seen clearing tables and valued the community fridge (discussed in the next section), recognising its value to herself, friends and acquaintances that she met in the cafe. In the following quote, Participant 1 explains how the cafe's PAYF format works to challenge both expectations of people's behaviour and ways in which value can be expressed: "When they go to cafes, that's what they expect, [crockery] to get cleared up. Here, it's a different kettle of fish. Yes. It's supposed to be for everybody to [muck] in and have a go with everything."

The ability to interpret PAYF by each cafe user enabled people to acknowledge the support and value of the food to themselves in their own way. For example, while Participant 1 liked to clear tables of used crockery and cutlery, others – despite having a limited budget – valued the opportunity to be able to make a monetary payment based on what they could afford and make a contribution to the cafe in this way. In doing so, this not only acknowledges the value and contribution of the cafe to their lives, but also works to disrupt capitalist forms of exchange and value as the anonymity of the payment (placed in an envelope without indication of its contents) enables everyone to participate in the social norms of consumption. The reciprocity expressed in the cafe through the PAYF basis brings to life the ethos expressed on a board hung in the cafe (illustrated in Figure 6.1).

The anonymity provided by the practice of PAYF opened up concepts of value – of the food, of people and of the cafe in the community – as well as how this exchange came to reflect collective efforts taken in 'being together' (Barnett and Land, 2007). This was illustrated by Oliver when he discussed his friend's behaviour as we looked at his photograph depicting his friend holding the envelope and considering what monetary contribution to make:

'[A friend] was wanting to make his "pay as you feel" sum amount appropriate and correct, something which would keep the place going, but he didn't know how much it should be. He was saying, "Should we check out other menus and base it on that, or is there some other criteria?" … I think he was working on the basis that he would rather and would even be happy to pay too much if it meant the place survived.'

This donation reflects an extension of asymmetric reciprocity suggested by Young (1997), in that while this was a monetary payment to recognise the food consumed by Oliver's friend, this transaction went beyond simple payment for the consumption of a good and acknowledged different economic and social values associated with the cafe's offer and its activities (Gibson–Graham, 1996). As intimated by Oliver's account, this included the perceived value of the cafe as an alternative food provider for individuals and families in the community experiencing uncertainty regarding their access to food (food insecurity), and the opportunity for social interactions in the space. The anonymity of the PAYF provided for this expression of openness to others and the continuation of the diverse relations centred in the cafe.

Mark discussed his decision to donate some allotment-grown scallions to the cafe, which he had chosen to take an image of. He initially discussed this as avoiding the scallions going to waste (his own political action that was attuned to the ethos of the cafe). The conversation highlighted the opportunities that the cafe offers for sharing and mutual reciprocity, and how this enables a more diverse and direct expression and participation in contributing to his community, as well as his support for and appreciation of the cafe in the local community:

'So I brought them in one day … and the chap told us that they were used on a garnish on a salad. Just liberally, because they're quite strong. I thought it was nice to know that some of the food that I have brought in has helped in the cafe … They were spare … And I thought, "Well, the cafe would appreciate them."'

## Quietly transforming lives

Participants reflected on the personal changes that the cafe had brought to their daily lives (for example, having somewhere friendly to visit on lunch breaks [Oliver] or its changing menu options and the variety brought to their diet [Mark]), as well as more explicit articulations of envisaged (better) futures. For example, Oliver discussed an evening meal at the cafe, its conviviality and the possibility of future changes to his social circle: "I was in the company of new friends, someone I'd never met before, someone that I know and his friend. So we were

**Figure 6.4:** Evening in the park

Source: Newcastle University

striking up the beginnings of conversations which will continue in the future, laying down the foundations of future ... that's a lasting benefit." Moreover, when discussing a photograph she had taken (see Figure 6.4) in connection with the meal she had eaten in the cafe one day, Participant 2 explained:

> 'After I'd been in here on a night-time, I was in a good mood, so I took the baby out for a walk and caught the skyline ... [it] was beautiful and ... I put it [the camera] onto the night mode and tried to take a decent picture. And that came out and I thought, "Well ..." I was just in a lovely mood because I'd obviously been fed, I don't know, I just thought, like, it gave me an olive branch, sort of thing, another chance.'

This participant also discussed the cafe and its openness and acceptance of diverse groups of people as providing a positive and hopeful experience, in part, as it gave her and her child the opportunity to meet and interact with people from elsewhere in the town and beyond. This was reflected in her commenting that "I'm proud to be part of this cafe, it's like an extended family, it's really nice" (Participant 2). Her comment affirms the importance of everyday or ordinary interactions in the space and how this can provide opportunities for collective action and connection – the feeling of belonging to a community centred on the cafe. Her accounts reflect how '[r]elationality becomes both a personal and political tool in austerity' and its survival (Hall, 2020: 250).

## Quiet activism

Underpinning many participants' engagement with the cafe was a quiet yet explicit advocacy for actions to reduce the amount of food going to waste. This was expressed in terms of both countering environmental impacts (such as landfill-generated greenhouse gas emissions) and reducing the lost opportunity that this represented for consumption by someone who may be going without a meal. For example, Mark noted how "everywhere [food businesses] should be aware now that there's no such thing as throwing food away", and particularly how the cafe's commitment to tackling food waste was important to him personally: "I love the idea of this one ... The idea of food that would otherwise have been thrown away ... It's all about recycling these days, not just the plastic, but the food."

The political actions in their own lives and behaviours extended to participants frequently mentioning how they recommended the cafe to friends and suggested that others try the cafe and the food, moving towards more vehement and impassioned advocacy, where participants directly challenged others' perceptions of the cafe and the food offered. This was discussed by Mark when he recollected how he 'stood up' for the cafe when making a purchase elsewhere in the town:

> 'I only went there to buy a ticket and then ended up having an argument [laughter]. But I was sticking up for this place, though and I've stuck up for this place a couple of times, when people were saying it was out-of-date food. So, I said, "Well, have you been in and tried it?" And the bloke says, "No." So, I said, "Well, why are you saying things that you don't know anything about?" I was getting a bit aerated.'

A further way in which the cafe's own advocacy and practice encouraged political action on food waste and food access was the presence of the community fridge on the premises. The community fridge (see Figure 6.5) was managed by REFUSE and, as such, provided an opportunity for food that they had collected and that others had donated to be taken and used by anyone without payment or

**Figure 6.5:** The community fridge

Source: Newcastle University

contribution. The decommodification of food in this context reflects the key imperative that the food is consumed and hence valued rather than being wasted. In turn, the presence of the community fridge and its free-to-use offer also worked to raise awareness of the accessibility and affordability of food for households in the town. By being publicly accessible and run on the ethos of the prevention of food waste, this attempted to alleviate concerns about the stigma of using the fridge to access food in this way. For example, Participant 1 had taken a photograph of the community fridge and people choosing food from it, and explained when discussing her picture that this had captured the importance of the opportunity for choice and dignity in people's food provisioning practices (a feature that contrasts with the lack of choice of preselected food items given in food-bank parcels): "Well, it was how much was donated ... which is good ... Because it's more for people to choose if they want to choose, come in and choose what they need or what they want."

Some participants expressed their actions as directly contributing to sharing in a collective political response. For some people, this was oriented to food waste actions; for others, this was joined with an awareness of members of the community experiencing food insecurity. As Oliver explained, when using the community fridge, his actions to prevent food waste were tempered with an awareness for others' immediate needs:

> 'If I think to myself, "I could go and buy that in the supermarket, maybe somebody else couldn't, so maybe I should leave it for them", but that's not the right attitude. I think what I should do is just reflect it in the donation and take it. That's what I'm going to do today ... there's more than one of a particular item so that makes it easier ... just in case someone else asks later in the day and would be in desperate need of it.'

## Conclusion

In concluding this chapter, the authors recognise that they have drawn from one particular case. However, this can be read as a contribution to the growing number of examples of food sharing initiatives that are contributing in different ways to transforming cities and communities globally (Davies, 2019). The chapter has suggested the incremental awareness raising and actions taken with attentiveness for others in the community and, in turn, the sense of community that has been demonstrably built among those choosing to support the cafe. The cafe has opened up opportunities for asymmetric reciprocity that recognises difference and diversity of experience, and does not profess to impose the self into the understanding, but is ready to bring people into new and different social, economic, material and political relations – though whether that is embraced is a further step in such processes of renewal (Young, 1997; Askins, 2015). The PAYF concept enables people to access the cafe and not to feel socially alienated or excluded from enjoying consumption experiences and the opportunity of being with and interacting with others due to price. Moreover, the cafe provides a choice and alternative food provisioning practice for those who may be food-insecure, whether temporarily or on a more persistent basis, and, as such, explicitly challenges pervading concepts of worth and value in society framed by dominant narratives of capitalism (Gibson-Graham, 1996), and how we choose to respond to structural inequalities that become reflected in differential access to food and the generation of food waste. While performing economic and exchange relations differently, the PAYF approach also generates opportunities for greater social interaction, as well as offering an opportunity for reciprocity and other expressions of respect and inclusiveness to be performed and practised in the cafe. The cafe's presence and its political intention and activities that work to reduce food waste have made a relatively 'loud' statement in the town. The chapter has shown how the cafe's opening has also led to quiet but, at times, considerable transformations in people's everyday lives.

## Acknowledgements

This work was supported by the Economic and Social Research Council Impact Accelerator Account (Grant ref ES/M500513/1, Newcastle University).

## References

Askins, K. (2015) 'Being together: everyday geographies and the quiet politics of belonging', *ACME: An International E-Journal for Critical Geographies*, 14(2): 470–8.

Barnett, C. and Land, D. (2007) 'Geographies of generosity: beyond the "moral turn"', *Geoforum*, 38(6): 1065–75.

Cloke, P., May, J. and Williams, A. (2017) 'The geographies of food banks in the meantime', *Progress in Human Geography*, 41(6): 703–26.

Davies, A. (2019) *Urban Food Sharing: Rules, Tools and Networks*, Bristol: Policy Press.

Gibson-Graham, J.K. (1996) *The End of Capitalism (as We Knew It): A Feminist Critique of Political Economy*, Oxford: Blackwell.

Hall, S.M. (2020) 'The personal is political: feminist geographies of/ in austerity', *Geoforum*, 110: 242–51.

Kneafsey, M., Owen, L., Bos, E., Broughton, K. and Lennartsson, M. (2017) 'Capacity building for food justice in England: the contribution of charity-led community food initiatives', *Local Environment*, 22(5): 621–34.

Midgley, J. (2018) '"You were a lifesaver": encountering the potential of vulnerability and self-care in a community café', *Ethics and Social Welfare*, 12(1): 49–64.

Midgley, J., Jeffries, J., Aitken, D., Dravers, N. and Skinner, M. (2018) *A Recipe for Success? Identifying Social and Community Impacts in the Work of Community Cafés: the case of Re-F-Use Pay as You Feel Café*, end-of-award project report, Newcastle upon Tyne: Newcastle University.

Poppendieck, J. (1998) *Sweet Charity: Emergency Food and the End of Entitlement*, New York: Penguin.

Pottinger, L. (2018) 'Growing, guarding and generous exchange in an analogue sharing economy', *Geoforum*, 96(1): 108–16.

REFUSE Café year 1 (2019) Blog. Available at: https://refusedurham. org.uk/2019/08/08/refuse-cafe-year-1/

Sitter, K.C. (2017) 'Taking a closer look at photovoice as a participatory action research method', *Journal of Progressive Human Services*, 28(1): 36–48.

Smith, J. and Jehlicka, P. (2013) 'Quiet sustainability: fertile lessons from Europe's productive gardeners', *Journal of Rural Studies*, 32(1): 148–57.

Sutton-Brown, C.A. (2014) 'Photovoice: a methodological guide', *Photography and Culture*, 7(2): 169–85.

TRJFP (The Real Junk Food Project) (2019) 'Homepage'. Available at: https://trjfp.com

Trussell Trust, The (2018) 'End of year stats (2017/18)'. Available at: www.trusselltrust.org/news-and-blog/latest-stats/end-year-stats/ #fy-2017–2018

Wang, C. and Burris, M.A. (1997) 'Photovoice: concept, methodology, and use for participatory needs assessment', *Health Education and Behaviour*, 24(3): 369–87.

WRAP (Waste and Resources Action Programme) (2018) 'Surplus food redistribution in the UK; 2015 to 2017', information sheet. Available at: www.wrap.org.uk/content/surplus-food-redistribution-wrap%E2%80%99s-work

Young, I.M. (1997) 'Asymmetrical reciprocity: on moral respect, wonder, and enlarged thought', *Constellations*, 3(3): 340–63.

# 7

# 'Computer Says No': exploring social justice in digital services

*Clara Crivellaro, Lizzie Coles-Kemp and Karen Wood*

## Introduction

Digitalisation of public services is an ongoing project in many developed countries around the globe. The rise of new and emergent technologies, such as machine learning and artificial intelligence, promises to further accelerate the transformation of public services. The integration of these complex data-driven technologies in public services is seen as an attractive proposition as they could potentially render services more efficient, tailored to the needs of specific communities and responsive to a range of significant societal issues. Yet, the use of computing, data science and machine learning to guide decisions in the design and delivery of public services has also raised significant concerns. These are associated with the embedding of potential social and technical biases, and thus their potential to further exacerbate existing socio-economic inequalities and social division (Eubanks, 2018). These concerns have raised broader questions globally as to the role of digital systems in social justice and in the safeguarding or formulation of new human rights (Abebe et al, 2020).

In the UK, the fast pace of public service digital transformation has been documented as having detrimental effects on the most vulnerable communities (Cheetham et al, 2019). Despite this, the implementation and use of new and emerging technologies to support public service delivery is still positioned as a necessary step in austerity Britain. In times of crisis, such as COVID-19, as new technologies facilitate everyday activities when physical distancing is in order, the importance of face-to-face community relations and existing digital inequalities comes more prominently to the fore. This chapter describes the initial stages of a collaboration with a charity based in Sunderland, the Parker Trust, which set out to explore what may constitute fairness and justice in the design and implementation of the welfare system and digital services. The chapter examines the impact of the digitalisation of services and considers the way collaborations between academia and third sector organisations can lead to the development of practical responses to the neoliberal crisis and in support of democracy.

## Digital inclusion, equity and social justice

Government discourse focuses on a positive story about digital innovation and the digitalisation of services. The 'digital by default' strategy (Cabinet Office, 2012), which created a single online portal for government digital services delivery, was seen as a way of promoting customer choice, convenience, efficiency and speed of response. While, in the era of austerity, 'digital by default' had largely been motivated by challenging financial socio-economic conditions, with continued budget cuts to reduce costs, online service delivery was framed as inevitably enhancing the lives of *all* in society. To this end, the digital inclusion strategy (Cabinet Office and Government Digital Service, 2014) aimed to provide the assisted digital support necessary to adjust to the project of ongoing transformation of government digital services for those unable to use or access the Internet. In the words of Francis Maude MP for the Cabinet Office 2010–16: 'to make sure the web is truly for everyone, we need to provide more than just access. We need to equip the whole country with the skills, motivation and trust to go online, be digitally capable and to make the most of the internet' (Cabinet Office and Government Digital Service, 2014). Yet, while the Internet and technologies have become an integrated part of everyday life, the government's 'digital by default' rendered Internet access and use not so much a matter of motivation, but a (rhetorical) question of whether there is *choice*. The experiences of citizens most in need regarding their ability to access and benefit from the Internet and now digitalised services tell a much more complex account.

Despite government efforts to promote an approach to digital skills training tailored to people's needs, and calls for concerted efforts through partnerships with third sector organisations to facilitate digital access (Government Digital Service, 2014), warning signs of serious long-term implications of the 'digital by default' strategy were already in sight in 2012. From spatial inequalities in terms of Internet provision, with patchy connections in rural areas, to existing socio-economic inequalities that significantly complicate digital engagement and access for those with physical and mental disabilities or experiencing financial hardship, digital inclusion does not solely concern the (un)equal distribution of resources to enable access and use, but necessitates a *recognition* that people live under different socio-economic conditions (Ogbonnaya-Ogburu et al, 2018; Coles-Kemp and Jensen, 2019; Heath et al, 2019). The number of people accessing the Internet as a way to measure (un)equal access is an inappropriate method as it fails to tell how people who experience hardship and deprivation are actually *benefiting* from the Internet. While the discourse on digital inclusion initially focused on digital resources distribution, attention has shifted to the way digital exclusion and disadvantage contributes to being unable to effectively use or capitalise on digital technologies, highlighting how digital exclusion can actually reinforce the multiple dimensions of existing social inequalities (Park and Humphry, 2019).

Today, inequality is still deeply rooted in Britain – where class, disability, ethnicity and gender play a critical role in the 'poverty trap' (Social Mobility Commission, 2019). People from working-class backgrounds still face higher levels of unemployment, and individuals from more disadvantaged areas are more likely to suffer lower levels of well-being. Many are without regular Internet access or, in some cases, have no access at all. Moreover, those with Internet access and the basic skills do not necessarily understand and know the implications of using the Internet (Miller et al, 2018). A 2018 survey highlighted a major understanding gap around technologies, revealing that: only a third of people were aware that data they have not actively chosen to share have been collected; a quarter had no idea how Internet companies make their money; and nearly half did not know how ads are targeting them and the origin of news on the Internet. Digital inequalities today take different forms and are entangled with understanding of how technologies operate in the background. This is all the more compelling as the collection and analysis of citizens' data are becoming an integral part of government. These inequalities are foregrounded in critiques of Universal Credit, the UK's flagship 'digital by default' programme and welfare reform. Universal Credit was developed to simplify the welfare benefits and tax credits system by combining six separate benefits payments into one singular payment, thus reducing system fraud and error. Cheetham et al (2019) show how a digitalised welfare system and a five-week wait for payments entails significant disadvantages for communities in the North East of England. Their research is echoed and amplified by the report from the UN's Special Rapporteur on Extreme Poverty (United Nations, 2019), in which the use of digitalisation to marginalise those in need of welfare is clearly described. More recently, increases in Universal Credit claims due to the COVID-19 crisis overwhelmed the online and telephone appointments system (Brignall, 2020), creating a situation that is particularly dire for claimants without Internet access and those needing claims assistance as physical distancing measures have resulted in the closure of libraries, community centres and places where face-to-face support and Internet access is provided.

New developments and advances in big data, machine learning and artificial intelligence are seen as having the potential to optimise services further, for example, helping identify families or children at risk so that resources can be geared towards where they are most needed (Cabinet Office, 2014; GOS, 2015). In the US, Eubanks (2018) outlined a rise of a 'regime of data analytics' in public services, detailing uses of, for example, automated welfare eligibility systems and the use of predictive risk models in child protective services. In the UK, Dencik et al (2018) issued a report demonstrating how citizens' data sets are increasingly used to provide insights for public service design and delivery. The COVID-19 public health emergency has justified the use of surveillance techniques, where the latest technologies are deployed to trace citizens' contacts (Clarke, 2020). This push to further accelerate innovation in digital public services raises significant concerns over the negative impact that these technologies can have on the most vulnerable and citizens' privacy, and over the assumptions and biases embedded in algorithmic systems.

Such developments have motivated academics, organisations and think tanks to advocate for a social justice dimension in digital innovation, calling for a political stance and a widening of our understandings of digital inclusion as inevitably entangled with questions of citizenship and democracy: 'Seeing high tech equity only as broadly shared access to existing technological products ignores other social values, neglects decision making processes, sees citizens only as consumers, and ignores the operation of institutions and social structures' (Eubanks, 2012: 26). Technologies actively shape social relations, affecting and producing our commonwealth, our society and the cities we live in. Many have argued for 'voice' and cooperation, that is, opportunities for people to provide accounts of what affects their lives, as well as the co-creation of forms of communal living, as critical values challenging neoliberal politics and the democratic crisis (Boyte, 2004; Couldry, 2010; Tronto, 2013). Here, opening participatory spaces to create the conditions that enable adapting, contesting and shaping the way technologies are entering and changing our lives is paramount.

As part of this growing movement, our case study is contextualised within 'Not-Equal', a three-year UK Research and Innovation-funded project that aims to develop understanding and explore fairness and social justice in everyday technology-supported civic and welfare service interactions, taking a place-based approach to social change that positions people as citizens rather than consumers or users of digital services (Olivier and Wright, 2015). 'Not-Equal' sets out to foster partnerships and productive collaborations between technologists and service innovators, local governments, service providers, and citizens in order to co-create responses to benefit the most vulnerable in our societies. To this end, the project delivers activities designed to open spaces of dialogue and inquiry, and to inform the commissioning of innovative research that responds to issues experienced by service providers and citizens in service interactions (Crivellaro et al, 2019a). The authors – Clara (Director of the 'Not-Equal' project), Lizzie (Co-director of the 'Not-Equal' project) and Karen (Sunderland City Councillor and Parker Trust Manager) – are university researchers.

## Understanding and exploring fairness and social justice in digital services in Sunderland

At the start of our 'Not-Equal' journey, we wanted to involve our partners' organisations to begin exploring the issues they saw as relevant to their day-to-day lives and what fairness in digital innovation might mean for them. Our engagement was grounded in work that had been undertaken between 2012 and 2013 (Coles-Kemp et al, 2014). This work comprised observations and a focus group, and examined how digitalised welfare services might in the future change the nature of the relationship between welfare claimants and welfare service providers, with a particular focus on notions and practices of safety and security for both parties. We returned to this initial study site and contacted Karen Wood, the manager of two charities, Parker Trust and Pallion Action Group (PAG), based in Sunderland. A small city in the North East of England, Sunderland is one of the 20 per cent most deprived districts/ unitary authorities in England, with high levels of health inequalities, employment deprivation and children living in low-income families (DCLG, 2015; PHE, 2018). Sunderland was also one of the first districts to assert its support for Brexit. Here, economic stagnation, the transformation of the job market reducing financial security and the experience of disenfranchisement and marginality appeared to lead to a mistrust that political elites and the political economic system was benefiting 'ordinary' working-class men (Bromley-Davenport et al, 2019).

Parker Trust and PAG are community-based charities providing a range of support services designed to enable people living in Pallion and West Sunderland to participate in society as 'independent, mature and responsible individuals'. Founded in 1993 by a group of local residents wishing to take action in response to issues experienced in their local community, today, both charities deliver programmes of activities aiming to develop skills, further education and relieve unemployment. Through their tailored programme of activities, Parker Trust and PAG provide support for those experiencing loneliness, health deprivation, financial hardship and unemployment. They also aim to be resources for other charities doing similar work and places for people to get together and help one another. Karen Wood has worked with communities in Sunderland researching, creating and delivering services and activities for over 20 years, and, more recently, has become an elected member of Sunderland City Council. She works closely with residents, community centres, schools and the local farm, and strives to find solutions to their problems and needs in an empathic way. The communities Karen works with are among the most vulnerable, excluded, isolated and affected by the impact of digital services and digital exclusion.

Following initial discussions, we worked with Karen to develop activities that would facilitate the exploration and articulation of issues in order to inform 'Not-Equal' future activities. We structured our initial engagement activities in three parts:

- Pre-study design: based on insights developed in prior work (Coles-Kemp et al, 2014), in collaboration with Karen, we developed an engagement activity titled 'Computer Says No'. The activity focused on issues and barriers to accessing digitally mediated services from essential service providers.
- Workshops: we conducted two 'Computer Says No' workshops with 14 participants in July 2018. Participants included Parker Trust service users, volunteers and front-line service providers. At the workshops, participants were invited to articulate an instance of difficulties in using technology and analyse it in detail, thinking through what was at stake, who was involved and how they felt. Participants were also invited to pinpoint 'one thing that could make a difference' in their situation, write it on a postcard and address it to the relevant person or institution.
- Follow-up interviews: two interviews were conducted with Karen to reflect on the value of the work to the community in question.

In line with a participatory action research approach (Kindon et al, 2007), our engagements were specifically designed to alter the traditional power relations between researchers and participants, according to four principles (Coles-Kemp, 2018): cede control; make visible all data to participants; use everyday spaces to carry out the research; and encourage participants to envision positive change to an aspect of their working environment.

These principles aim to create a space for participants' voices, enabling them to construct and refine the research questions, while encouraging critical reflection on accessible and (un)fair interactions in essential services, and on possible directions for the future. In line with participatory action research and co-design traditions, the approach is a means of transferring power away from researchers and towards the communities themselves, which often runs counter to expert conceptualisations of security (Vaughan-Williams and Stevens, 2016). Next, we provide an account of what emerged from our workshops and follow-up interviews with Karen and the people we engaged with at Parker Trust.

For many of our workshop participants, digital innovation, though perceived as something potentially beneficial, could turn into 'evil' if in the 'wrong' hands. Digital services, whether public or commercial, were experienced as something imposed and that they had no control over – as something that left them no choice, for example, on what to use and whether to use it, and about buying 'new upgrades'. This lack of control was associated with their ability to make choices on how to lead their lives. Our participants' concerns about the Internet, digital services and social media were expressed in terms of: the ways they affect their capacity to relate to the 'real' world; increasing loneliness; and, in some cases, how using digital technologies made them feel exploited by large digital companies – in the words of one of our participants, "it's as if we are working for them". While being digitally illiterate was identified as not fitting the status quo, they pointed out how having digital skills was often based upon assumptions that abilities to use social media necessarily translate to using 'anything digital', which is frequently not the case.

In our 'Computer Says No' workshop, participants mapped: instances of error or miscommunication in health services, where digital prescriptions were lost or not recorded; instances of personal details being automatically shared with other services when using social media applications; and instances where lack of transparency in the use of a digital service created confusion in terms of the failure of transactions and payments. Participants felt that digital services complicated situations and, at times, altogether prevented them from participating in daily activities (for example, from making payments using a bank card, to other, more complex operations). For some of our participants, getting through the week with the money available was a real struggle. In this context, Internet access was certainly not a priority, unless essential services relating to seeking work, applying for benefits or paying bills were only available online. In a workshop discussion, Karen reflected: "If the only existing social security system is an online one but free Wi-Fi in the city is not given, then what we are contending with is a system that is fundamentally unfair from the outset."

Furthermore, Karen explained that even if current statistics might indicate how many people have managed to access Universal Credit systems, they do not report *how* people do it, who helped them, how long it took and so on:

> 'The data … is based on what other people like professionals have inputted, [it is not about] the hidden families, not the hidden people who are not talking to professionals … If there is no data about you, you simply don't exist, so data is not a true reflection of society.'

The complexities involved in online activities mean that benefiting from the Internet is not simply related to possessing a technical artefact and having a connection, but linked to the ability to 'read the small print' and fully understanding the implications of using particular systems. For example, a wrong meter reading or ticking the wrong box in an online form or job-seeking application translates into sanctions. Parker Trust has seen a 60 per cent increase in people who are now in rent arrears and at risk of losing their homes because the system assumes that they are capable of looking after their own finances. In the new system, Housing Benefit is no longer paid directly to landlords and people are expected to manage their finances effectively. Karen told us in harrowing detail how, in practice, ticking the 'wrong box' means that her service users, whose lives are complex and very chaotic, have to wait for weeks or months to receive a payment, with sometimes devastating consequences. Karen told us how two Parker Trust service users lost their lives. In one case, a young man experiencing alcohol addiction issues lost his job and family, became homeless, and while waiting for Universal Credit support, struggling to manage his day-to-day life, took his own life. Over the same period, a single young mother of three children who suffered from diabetes struggled to use the online system, kept forgetting to order her prescriptions and eventually died. Karen reported these two recent instances to exemplify how chaotic the life of a person with complex care needs is or can quickly become.

The logic behind the Universal Credit system appears to assume equal capabilities (and equal access to goods and resources). Much like neoliberalism, there is an apparent 'freedom' bound up with the Universal Credit system – where the individual is given 'freedom' and is solely responsible for managing their income. Yet, a system like this quickly becomes an oppressive system if those capabilities are not in place. The reality is that the current system is putting them straight in debt due to delays in payments. For our participants, 'the new system is putting everyone into poverty', and this is invisible to the computer's mind's eye. While managing funds *for* people would not be the answer, Karen and people at Parker Trust know that information technology education is one of the key solutions. Yet, the level of stress that people are being subjected to does not create the right frame of mind for learning.

From Karen's perspective, poverty and the issues people are facing today have actually "always be[en] there" but they are now amplified by the introduction of digital technologies that are making it much harder. A critical aspect of the digital transformation is the lack of human presence. Many are struggling because they do not know how to express a problem or ask a question in writing. Parker Trust is often the first point of contact for people experiencing crisis. As Karen tells us: "In times of crisis, you want a human being. You want empathy. You want somebody to come along and just go, 'It's going to be all right. I'm going to help you.'" This is not simply about getting the Universal Credit application rectified, ordering the right medicines online or paying gas and electric for someone denied funds due to a miscalculation; it is also about making sure that the things that make us 'human' are in place. For example, on Christmas Eve, Parker Trust volunteers delivered presents to families affected by errors/miscalculations/delays in Universal Credit payments.

In some respects, this is what Parker Trust really encapsulates: people being there for each other, coming together and looking for solutions. One thing people have in common is thinking that the system is unfair as it assumes that everybody has digital skills and digital equipment. Therefore, rather than relying on learning information technology (IT) skills that are not fit for purpose, people help one another, teaching each other how to do digital tasks that are essential for their everyday life.

The previous 2012/13 study was referred to several times during the interview with Karen as an example of how participatory research with a community is an accurate indicator of likely changes in service provision. Insights from the initial study meant that Karen and her team were more prepared for and made provision for potential hardships and challenges:

> 'So, we started writing bids for private trusts and funders to have things like emergency money for gas and electric. We started networking with supermarkets. We started getting our staff up to speed on things and looking for solutions, we knew people wouldn't be able to afford gas and electric, food, and things like that.'

The collaboration legacy included tools like 'problem and solution sheets', which are still used for community collaboration to examine a problem and to seek collective solutions. This collaboration meant Parker Trust could use the tools to respond effectively to the crisis, compared to many other third sector organisations. Furthermore, this knowledge was used to scale out methods for responding to the crisis, sharing good practice and sharing resources:

> 'I just share everything I know ... I'm not territorial about any research I've done ... for helping people get on job sites easier or things like that. So, I'll share that with people so they can have it, so that's happening on a very local level here so people are able to get the right help and support, but that's only very local.'

Much of Parker Trust's work is responsive, flexible and run by the community, which is its strength. Yet, as Karen told us, it is responsive in a way that is not sustainable or that is difficult to scale because of the magnitude of the issues, amplified by the digitalisation of public services. Rather than a partnership between third sector organisations and the government, Karen voiced an expectation for the third sector in the UK to "clean out the mess and sort it all out" and a lack of recognition for the work done, as well as an ever-growing distance between the government and people, and between the government and the third sector.

## Towards collaborative responses to social (in)justice in digital services

Developing themes from earlier studies, our conversations with people at Parker Trust show that digital inclusion is facilitated not simply by access to a device, but also by understanding the implications of using a particular service, and by being able to make choices through a digital service and thus benefit from it. These are particularly important capabilities when dealing with complex systems such as Universal Credit, where the implications of incorrect choices result in financial, emotional and social harms. The conditions of digital access to a complex system such as welfare are shaped by the logic of the public policy and its encoding into the design of services and their technologies. The design of such systems determines not only how individuals are understood by the state, but also how individuals feel about themselves (their dignity and worth) and about the state. Within such a framing, citizenship is constructed upon an assumption of the individual as an autonomous being, which shapes how rights and capabilities are understood, and of the responsibility for anyone's welfare as pertaining to the individual alone. Citizens' current mistrust and disbelief that the state is there to support them is not surprising. This is further complicated by the way digital connectivity and access to welfare digital services is bound to the commercialisation and marketisation of the elements that are necessary to access these services (Duffield, 2016), crowding out all other values (Brown, 2015).

In contrast to the framing of the autonomous digital citizen, what we found at Parker Trust is an understanding of citizens and individuals as vulnerable beings who survive through their connections to others, as well as in terms of how they care for and about each other. Our engagement at Parker Trust calls for an understanding of social justice that is based not on pursuing individual liberty and the freedom to choose, but on social solidarity and the need to 'belong' (Brown, 2010). Our conversations with people at Parker Trust point to the need to recognise that the possibilities to benefit from access to digital services have to be understood within the contextual complexity of people's lives and the vulnerabilities people can experience at any given time of their lives. Such an understanding resonates with feminist democratic ethics of care (Tronto, 2013), where individuals can only be understood as existing within relationships and networks of solidarity and care, with varying degrees of autonomy and dependency. In this perspective, all humans are vulnerable and fragile. These positions of vulnerability and fragility are exemplified during crises such as the spread of COVID-19. Yet, the neoliberal management of the crisis meant that the UK government's response was slow due to a desire to protect the economy (Watts, 2020). Lives have been lost because of this, while the goal should be to enable everyone to live as well as possible and participate meaningfully in democratic life.

Yet, it is precisely the kind of vulnerabilities and stress experienced by the people we encountered at Parker Trust and front-line service providers that prevent them from participating. Fraser's (2008) perspective on social justice highlights how its different economic, cultural and political dimensions intertwine in complex ways, hindering or supporting the identification of social justice issues and the development of directions and strategies for redress. Fraser's notion of 'abnormal justice' refers to the ways that institutional social justice concerns rarely match those of the citizenry. This mismatch is significant in the context of the design and delivery of digital services – how these are imagined and then delivered. Lack of representation of those who are economically and culturally marginalised in the discursive spaces and processes at play in making and contesting digital services and their underlining policies needs critical attention. Such cultural and political inequalities and divides between those who can influence these processes and those who cannot, as Couldry (2010) suggested, might be just as important as the distributional inequalities that have characterised discourses on the digital divide. Our approach intended to open spaces for people to begin to define what might be (un)just in their experiences of digital services and to develop capacities to articulate and formulate what could be understood as 'new rights'. Creating spaces for personal issues and experiences to connect to public concerns is critical for collaborative responses to inequalities (Fraser, 1990), which also acknowledge care as vital in community relations. Creating such spaces is all the more important when digital means are the primary way to work and deliver services in times of global crises such as COVID-19. The oppressive impacts of online services on people's lives are likely to be exacerbated when the social infrastructure that supports and enables access to those services is taken away due to the closure of places such as Parker Trust in times of a pandemic. Furthermore, the community organising that characterises places like Parker Trust, and its ethos of belonging and trust, are fundamental to the welfare of communities and their social capacity but are not easy to achieve when engaging in physical distancing.

Our case study shows how the development of modest yet practical tools (such as problem sheets) can really make a difference in supporting the day-to-day collective planning of work in third sector organisations. It also shows how participatory research can be a powerful tool for community and third sector organisations to articulate issues and argue for changes to service provision. Participatory spaces to voice concerns enable civic organisations grappling with complex social issues to have a role in developing organisational responses that are sensitive to their practical experiences and related complexities (Crivellaro et al, 2019b). Yet, the case study presented here shows that while third sector organisations might have a willingness to open such spaces and to connect and create coalitions with other organisations, the lack of resources hinders their capacity for collective action. Here, partnerships and collaborations with academia could play an important role in catalysing and adding capacity to support and strengthen coalitions and solidarity between organisations, and thus build an evidence base for advocacy that can be connected with larger processes of change. However, these would require researchers to commit in the long term.

Previous place-based 'programmes' have been criticised for failing to address the structural causes of poverty – pointing to how change cannot be achieved simply at the neighbourhood level, but that local action needs to connect with regional and national policy (Taylor and Buckly, 2017). We acknowledge that change is also needed in academic cultures. Thus, on the one hand, the challenge is finding ways to develop spaces and opportunities for people to voice their concerns and for meaningful concerted efforts to connect people's claims, issues and lived experiences with the institutional procedures (policymaking) that shape the social worlds arising from the promises of technological progress. On the other hand, we must nurture a culture of care and reflexivity among technology designers and developers, and develop pedagogical approaches and tools to enable them to ensure social justice in society. The people at Parker Trust showed us that the present and the future need solidarity. The challenge is to spread this message among institutions and academics who believe that other social realities benefiting the many, rather than the few, are not just desirable, but altogether possible.

## References

Abebe, R., Barocas, S., Kleinberg, J., Levy, K., Raghavan, M. and Robinson, D.G. (2020) 'Roles for computing in social change', in *Proceedings of the 2020 Conference on Fairness, Accountability, and Transparency (FAT* '20)*. New York: Association for Computing Machinery, pp 252–60. https://doi.org/10.1145/3351095.3372871

Boyte, H.C. (2004) *Everyday Politics: Reconnecting Citizens and Public Life*, Philadelphia, PA: University of Pennsylvania Press.

Brignall, M. (2020) 'Universal Credit: "almost impossible" to complete claim as more than 500,000 apply', *The Guardian*, 26 March. Available at: www.theguardian.com/world/2020/mar/26/universal-credit-claims-almost-impossible-as-more-than-500000-apply

Bromley-Davenport, H., MacLeavy, J. and Manley, D. (2019) 'Brexit in Sunderland: the production of difference and division in the UK referendum on European Union membership', *Environment and Planning C: Politics and Space*, 37(5): 795–812.

Brown, C. (2010) 'On Amartya Sen and the idea of justice', *Ethics and International Affairs*, 24(3): 309–18.

Brown, W. (2015) *Undoing the Demos: Neoliberalism Stealth Revolution*, Cambridge, MA: MIT Press.

Cabinet Office (2012) 'Government digital strategy', November. Available at: https://assets.publishing.service.gov.uk/government/uploads/system/uploads/attachment_data/file/296336/Government_Digital_Strategy_-_November_2012.pdf

Cabinet Office (2014) 'HM government Horizon Scanning Programme. Emerging technologies: big data', 18 December. Available at: www.gov.uk/government/publications/emerging-technologies-big-data

Cabinet Office and Government Digital Service (2014) 'Government digital inclusion strategy', December. Available at: www.gov.uk/government/publications/government-digital-inclusion-strategy/government-digital-inclusion-strategy#executive-summary

Cheetham, M., Moffatt, S., Addison, M. and Wiseman, A. (2019) 'Impact of Universal Credit in North East England: a qualitative study of claimants and support staff', *BMJ Open*, 9(7). Available at: https://bmjopen.bmj.com/content/9/7/e029611

Clarke, L. (2020) 'How will the NHS Covid-19 contact-tracing app work and when will it go live?', *NS Tech*, 2 April. Available at: https://tech.newstatesman.com/security/nhs-covid-19-contact-tracing-app-rollout

Coles-Kemp, L. (2018) *Practising Creative Securities*, London: Royal Holloway University of London. Available at: https://bookleteer.com/collection.html?id=28

Coles-Kemp, L. and Jensen, R.B. (2019) 'Accessing a new land: designing for a social conceptualisation of access', in *Proceedings of the 2019 CHI Conference on Human Factors in Computing Systems*, New York: ACM, p 181.

Coles-Kemp, L., Zugenmaier, A. and Lewis, M. (2014) 'Watching you watching me: the art of playing the panopticon', in *Digital Enlightenment Yearbook 2014: Social Networks and Social Machines, Surveillance and Empowerment*, Amsterdam: IOS Press, p 147.

Couldry, N. (2010) *Why Voice Matters: Culture and Politics after Neoliberalism*, London: SAGE.

Crivellaro, C., Coles-Kemp, L., Dix, A. and Light, A. (2019a) 'Not-equal: democratizing research in digital innovation for social justice', *Interactions*, 26(2): 70–3.

Crivellaro, C., Anderson, R., Lambton-Howard, D., Nappey, T., Olivier, P., Vlachokyriakos, V., Wilson, A. and Wright, P. (2019b) 'Infrastructuring public service transformation: creating collaborative spaces between communities and institutions through HCI research', *ACM Transactions on Computer-Human Interaction (TOCHI)*, 26 March, pp 1–29. Available at: http://understanding.doteveryone.org.uk/files/Doteveryone_PeoplePowerTechDigitalUnderstanding2018.pdf.

DCLG (Department for Communities and Local Government) (2015) *The English Indices of Deprivation 2015*, London: DCLG. Available at: https://assets.publishing.service.gov.uk/government/uploads/system/uploads/attachment_data/file/465791/English_Indices_of_Deprivation_2015_-_Statistical_Release.pdf

Dencik, L., Hintz, A., Redden, J. and Warne, H. (2018) *Data Scores as Governance: Investigating Uses of Citizen Scoring in Public Services*, Cardiff: Data Justice Lab, Cardiff University.

Duffield, M. (2016) 'The resilience of the ruins: towards a critique of digital humanitarianism', *Resilience*, 4(3): 147–65.

Eubanks, V. (2012) *Digital Dead End: Fighting for Social Justice in the Information Age*, Cambridge, MA: MIT Press.

Eubanks, V. (2018) *Automating Inequality: How High-Tech Tools Profile, Police, and Punish the Poor*, New York: St Martin's Press.

Fraser, N. (1990) 'Rethinking the public sphere: a contribution to the critique of actually existing democracy', *Social Text*, 25/26: 56–80.

Fraser, N. (2008) 'Abnormal justice', *Critical Inquiry*, 34(3): 393–422.

GOS (Government Office for Science) (2015) 'Artificial intelligence: opportunities and implications for the future of decision making'. Available at: https://assets.publishing.service.gov.uk/government/uploads/system/uploads/attachment_data/file/566075/gs-16-19-artificial-intelligence-ai-report.pdf

Government Digital Service (2014) 'A checklist for digital inclusion – if we do these things, we're doing digital inclusion', blog, January. Available at: https://gds.blog.gov.uk/2014/01/13/a-checklist-for-digital-inclusion-if-we-do-these-things-were-doing-digital-inclusion/

Heath, C.P.R, Clara, C. and Coles-Kemp, L. (2019) 'Relations are more than bytes: re-thinking the benefits of smart services through people and things', in *Proceedings of the 2019 CHI Conference on Human Factors in Computing Systems (CHI '19)*, New York: ACM, paper 308.

Kindon, S., Pain, R. and Kesby, M. (eds) (2007) *Participatory Action Research Approaches and Methods: Connecting People, Participation and Place*, London: Routledge.

Miller, C., Coldicutt, R. and Kitcher, H. (2018) *People Power and Technology: The 2018 Digital Understanding Report*, London: Doteveryone. Available at: https://doteveryone.org.uk/report/digital-understanding/

Ogbonnaya-Ogburu, I.F., Toyama, K. and Dillahunt, T. (2018) 'Returning citizens' job search and technology use: preliminary findings', in Association for Computing Machinery (ed) *Companion of the 2018 ACM Conference on Computer Supported Cooperative Work and Social Computing (CSCW '18)*, New York: Association for Computing Machinery, pp 365–8.

Olivier, P. and Wright, P. (2015) 'Digital civics', *Interactions Magazine*, 22(4): 61.

Park, S. and Humphry, J. (2019) 'Exclusion by design: intersections of social, digital and data exclusion', *Information, Communication and Society*, 22(7): 934–53.

PHE (Public Health England) (2018) 'Local authority health profile 2018: Sunderland'. Available at: www.sunderlandccg.nhs.uk/wp-content/uploads/2019/04/Health-Profile-2018.pdf

Social Mobility Commission (2019) 'State of the nation 2018–2019: social mobility in Great Britain, summary'. Available at: https://assets.publishing.service.gov.uk/government/uploads/system/uploads/attachment_data/file/798687/SMC_State_of_Nation_2018-19_Summary.pdf

Taylor, M. and Buckly, E. (2017) *Historical Review of Place Based Approaches*, London: Lankelly Chase. Available at: https://lankellychase.org.uk/wp-content/uploads/2017/10/Historical-review-of-place-based-approaches.pdf

Tronto, J.C. (2013) *Caring Democracy: Markets, Equality and Justice*, New York: New York University Press.

United Nations (2019) *Visit to the United Kingdom of Great Britain and Northern Ireland: Report of the Special Rapporteur on Extreme Poverty and Human Rights*, Geneva: Office of the High Commissioner for Human Rights Commission, United Nations.

Vaughan-Williams, N. and Stevens, D. (2016) 'Vernacular theories of everyday (in)security: the disruptive potential of non-elite knowledge', *Security Dialogue*, 47(1): 40–58.

Watts, J. (2020) 'Delay is deadly: what Covid-19 tells us about tackling the climate crisis', *The Guardian*, 24 March. Available at: www.theguardian.com/commentisfree/2020/mar/24/covid-19-climate-crisis-governments-coronavirus

# 8

# Drive to thrive: a place-based approach to tackling poverty in Gateshead

*Mel Steer and Michael Walker*

## Introduction

In the UK, central government implemented public sector funding cuts following the global economic crash in 2008. These cuts were applied from 2010 and local authorities are at the forefront of central government's austerity measures. This chapter describes Gateshead Council's approach to place-based working during austerity and an initiative it developed. Austerity measures meant that existing levels of service provision were impossible to maintain, and within the council, there was increasing awareness that many residents were also feeling the effects of austerity and were in precarious financial and socio-economic circumstances. Gateshead's response endeavours to coordinate stretched resources, working in collaboration with colleagues from other organisations to influence partnership working in order to achieve better outcomes for residents.

The approach, 'Thriving for All – Tackling Poverty in Gateshead' (originating from Gateshead Council's 'Making Gateshead a place where everyone thrives' (Gateshead Council, no date) strategy and referred to as Thrive in this chapter), was launched at a conference in February 2018 and brought people together from diverse organisations to tackle key social justice issues around poverty and inequality. The chapter begins by outlining local authority austerity and its effects, and considering the development of partnership and place-based working and the role of the local authority. The development of the Thrive approach is described, reflecting how it might contribute to social renewal and social justice, and the challenges of implementing the approach.

## Local authority austerity

To reduce the public deficit caused by the global financial crash in 2008 and the additional debt that was incurred through the British government's rescue of UK banks, austerity measures were introduced that resulted in public sector spending cuts (Blyth, 2013). Between the financial years of 2010/11 to 2017/18, the amount of central government funding to local authorities almost halved (a 49.1 per cent reduction) (Comptroller and Auditor General, 2018: 7). Local government's response to the cuts has increasingly been to limit, begin charging for or reconfigure non-statutory services (Hastings et al, 2015a, 2015b), as well as cutting levels of staff (Lowndes and McCaughie, 2013). In Gateshead, from 2010 to the 2019/20 financial year, the core grant from central government fell by 52 per cent (higher than the national average), meaning a loss of £400 per person and £900 per property (Ramsey, 2018: 11). In addition to the loss of 2,400 local government posts during this period, Gateshead's estimates for the five-year period 2019–24 suggest a shortfall of £77 million in income from council tax, business rates and central government funding (Ramsey, 2018: 1), indicating that substantial financial challenges remain. Proposals to deal with budget cuts in 2019/20 range from stopping non-statutory pest control, bowling green and football ground maintenance, to reducing the number of management and family intervention worker posts, and cutting an unfilled public health consultant's post (Ramsey, 2018).

The large reductions associated with the spending cuts and the length of austerity implementation constitute a catastrophe for local government (Bailey et al, 2015; Hastings et al, 2015b). Disadvantaged former industrial areas, mainly those in the north of England, characterised by the legacy of deindustrialisation and higher levels of unemployment, lower wages, and poorer health outcomes (Beatty and Fothergill, 2013; Marmot et al, 2020), face particularly detrimental effects from central government cuts (Hastings et al, 2015a). Furthermore, UK public sector debt recovery action involved welfare reform that revised entitlement and reduced benefit payment rates, which increased hardship (Child Poverty Action Group Scotland, 2016), exacerbating poverty and inequality.

Despite the bleakness of austerity and some changes in function, local authorities remain an important provider and facilitator of services and are a key organisation within their communities. Their ability to adjust to changes in obligations such as assessing Council Tax Benefit claims, as well as to adapt to more fluid working conditions (John, 2014) and the return of public health responsibilities, has been highlighted. However, the improved autonomy coincided with local government's reduced financial resources and their having to make very difficult decisions regarding the provision of local services (Lowndes and McCaughie, 2013; Hastings et al, 2015a). Potentially, the demise of many regional bodies such as government offices (regional offices of decentralised civil servants that closed in 2011) and regional development agencies (closed in 2012) may offer an enhanced profile for local authorities and key civil sector organisations. However, research on regional governance in the North East region over the last two decades revealed that changes to local governance structures, including devolution deals and the election of mayors, have been detrimental for accountability, and that the governing bodies of many of these key organisations are 'not properly representative of those [communities] that they serve' (Shaw and Robinson, 2018: 855).

Furthermore, the developing COVID-19 crisis has demonstrated the pivotal role that local authorities play in our communities for services such as public health, education, social care, child protection, housing and homelessness. However, if the depth of local authority cuts has largely been hidden from the public's view, COVID-19 will bring them sharply into focus (Toynbee, 2020), perhaps with recognition that the local contextual knowledge within these areas represents an argument for more, not less, central government decentralisation to local bodies such as councils and combined authorities as they implement emergency actions (Longlands, 2020).

## Partnership and place-based approaches

Austerity measures may have forced local authorities to consider more resourceful ways of delivering services but partnership and area-based initiatives existed before austerity. Interest in place-based approaches developed under the New Labour government, which implemented the 13 'Total Place Pilots' in 2010 (HM Treasury and CLG, 2010). The proliferation of area-based initiatives (such as health action zones and education action zones) is particularly associated with the New Labour government (Sullivan et al, 2006) and the 'third way' (Rees et al, 2007: 261). The third way combined state and non-state provision of services (often through working with organisations from the voluntary, community and social enterprise sector) through partnership working (Rees et al, 2007). Area-based initiatives (focused on specific, relatively small localities) differ from person-based initiatives that are directed at people regardless of residency, though sometimes initiatives combined aspects of both these approaches (Lupton and Turok, 2004). More recently, there has been an emphasis on place-based working, which, as such, has no agreed definition or geography, but instead represents a whole-systems approach to combining resources in an area to deliver services (Taylor and Buckly, 2017). Place-based working emphasises partnership working (in common with area-based and people-based) initiatives. Typically, however, place-based approaches emphasise harnessing various (existing) local resources through coordination and streamlining, and involving communities and organisations to develop services that are responsive to communities' needs and generated by them, being 'bottom-up' and 'person-centred' (Munro, 2015: n.p.). Hence, the purpose of place-based working is to improve outcomes on social issues in a coordinated and cost-effective way (Public Health England, 2019). It differs from area-based initiatives because it is not developed for, or directed at, a specific area or accompanied by an additional budget for delivery. Instead, it is about organisations working together to achieve a common purpose using fewer public resources (HM Treasury and CLG, 2020), and according to Taylor and Buckly (2017), who draw on Anheier and Leat's and the Association for the Study and Development of Community's work, place-based:

> is currently used to describe a range of approaches, from grant-making in a specific geographic area to long-term, multifaceted collaborative partnerships ... In most cases, it is more than just a term to describe the target location of funding; it also describes a style and philosophy of approach which seeks to achieve 'joined-up' systems change.
>
> These approaches centre on a recognition of the need to reconfigure relationships between governments, philanthropy, civil society organisations, the private sector and citizens in order to achieve change by developing collaborative approaches to address the underlying causes of community problems. (Anheier and Leat, 2006; Association for the Study and Development of Community, 2007, cited in Taylor and Buckly, 2017: 9)

This model of place-based working situates local authorities as 'place leaders' (DCLG, 2016a: 4), representing an extension to the chief executive's role of leading local authorities (Hambleton et al, 2012) as they promote cohesive and strategic working in the local authority area across sectors and within their own organisations. It represents a change from earlier divisional and directorate-driven initiatives but does not entirely remove the danger that departments continue to work in isolation to each other (Hambleton et al, 2012). Given that local authorities are typically large, bureaucratic and politically driven organisations, there can be a risk that coordination is likely to be difficult to achieve internally without the added complication of working with external partners.

Various governments have promoted bottom-up, 'person-centred' initiatives through whole-place community budgets and 'total place' to improve outcomes and use public sector resources more effectively (DCLG, 2016b: 4). The extent that these initiatives successfully achieved integrated, joined-up working has, however, been questioned (Hambleton et al, 2012). Local authorities have a central role in place-based approaches, and austerity provided a strong incentive to review and coordinate services (and although an emergency response on the scale of the COVID-19 crisis could not be anticipated, relationships established or consolidated through place-based working could be beneficial in responding to public health emergencies). Gateshead adopted the strategy 'Making Gateshead a Place Where Everyone Thrives' ('Thrive') as a strategic, 'priority-led' place-based approach (Ramsey, 2018: 1).

## Gateshead

Gateshead Council is a unitary authority that serves a population of 202,500 (ONS, 2020: 1). A total of 94.08 per cent of Gateshead's population is white British, compared with 93.6 per cent of the population in the North East region, which has the highest percentage of white British residents in England and Wales, and some of the least diverse local authority areas: County Durham, Northumberland, and Redcar and Cleveland (ONS, 2018). It shares its name with the town of Gateshead, which is the largest town in the local authority area, and there are four other towns (Rowlands Gill, Whickham, Blaydon and Ryton). Two parliamentary constituencies (Gateshead and Blaydon, both with Labour MPs) are in Gateshead Council's boundary and there are 22 wards (defined administrative areas in local authorities for electoral purposes). Using government data and local housing data, Hirsch and Stone (2020: 8) indicate that in 2018/19, 30 per cent of children aged under 16 years in Britain lived in households with below 60 per cent of median household income after housing costs and in Gateshead local authority, the percentage was 33.5%, an increase of 8.8% since 2014/15 (and eight of the ten local authorities with the highest percentage increase were in North East England).

In 2018, levels of economic inactivity in Gateshead (21.0 per cent) were similar to the UK average (21.1 per cent) but lower than the average for the North East region (24.3 per cent), yet the percentage of those requiring work in Gateshead (22.0 per cent) was very slightly higher than the averages for the North East (21.8 per cent) and the UK (20.9 per cent) (ONS, 2020: 2). Gross full-time weekly pay was lower in Gateshead (£498.70) than the averages for the North East (£531.10) and the UK (£587.00) (ONS, 2020: 4). A higher percentage of people were employed in caring, services, sales, plant and machine operation, and elementary occupations (occupational groups 6–9) in Gateshead (42.3 per cent) than the North East (38.7 per cent) and the UK (32.7 per cent) (ONS, 2020: 3). Also, the numbers of people achieving NVQ level 4 qualifications and above were lower in Gateshead (30.4 per cent) than in the North East (31.1 per cent) and the UK (39.3 per cent) (ONS, 2020: 3).

### Early origins and the development of Thrive

Before austerity, Gateshead Council was aware that some households were on low incomes and experiencing financial hardship (Cheetham et al, 2018). A financial inclusion strategy was developed in 2008 and led to the development of a financial inclusion network of organisations from the voluntary, community and social enterprise sector. Between 2008 and 2012, when a new financial inclusion strategy and the Financial Inclusion Network was established, Gateshead (jointly with Sunderland and South Tyneside) was one of the 13 'Total Place Pilot' projects (HM Treasury and CLG, 2010). The 'Total Place Pilot' focused on developing a place-based approach to drug and alcohol services and included family intervention projects (HM Treasury and CLG, 2010). Insights from the pilot identified the importance of communication and the coordination of resources to create efficiencies by reducing the likelihood of duplication and improving the chances of better outcomes being achieved (HM Treasury and CLG, 2010). Perhaps informed by some of the organisational learning from this and the national 'Total Place Pilots', and as austerity impacted, Gateshead looked more closely, and holistically, at the emerging issues of poverty, engaging with partners from the voluntary, community and social enterprise sector.

Considerably later, in February 2018, the council hosted its inaugural 'Tackling Poverty in Gateshead' conference. It was attended by over 140 cross-sector partners, including a range of support organisations, food banks, charities, banks, credit unions and private businesses. The conference sought to identify what could be done collectively to improve the lives of residents. Recognising that the council had fewer resources and could not deliver the same services it used to, they positioned themselves as 'place leader' (DCLG, 2016a) and summarised their strategic vision in the Thrive series of pledges (see Box 8.1), which were launched at the conference by the Chief Executive of Gateshead, Sheena Ramsey. The council's Thrive agenda focused on 'Making

Gateshead a place where everyone thrives' (Gateshead Council, no date: 8). Gateshead outlined that over half of its residents were either 'managing or just coping', and more than 30 per cent were in need or in precarious circumstances (Gateshead Council, no date: 8). Thrive aimed to 'change those statistics' to make Gateshead a place with fewer people in need of council support and more people thriving (Gateshead Council, no date: 8).

---

**Box 8.1 Thrive pledges**

The council set five pledges to enable Thrive to succeed:

1. Put people and families at the heart of everything we do
2. Tackle inequality so people have a fair chance
3. Support our communities to support themselves and each other
4. Invest in our economy to provide sustainable opportunities for employment, innovation and growth across the borough
5. Work together and fight for a better future for Gateshead

Source: Quoted from Ramsey (2018: 12)

---

The intention was that the strategic approach would drive the major policy directions. A 'Tackling Poverty in Gateshead' board was established, comprising of influential, senior figures from across Gateshead, including the council's deputy leader as chair and the chief executive of Citizens Advice Gateshead as vice chair. The board directed the poverty agenda and attempted to embed the principles of Thrive.

Originating from feedback from the conference, seven key themes were agreed as areas of focus: food poverty, fuel poverty, child poverty, housing, financial inclusion, financial education, and employment skills and wages. The board created a series of themed network discussions in 2018 to allow the organisations operating across the area the opportunity to inform how each theme could be delivered, and food poverty and fuel poverty were identified as priorities (which unfortunately, as the pandemic later unfolded, many more people were to experience).

## Partnership and collaboration

The local authority was clear that austerity meant operational capability was reduced, yet they remained ambitious for their communities and their way forward was working with local partners to deliver on their pledges. Two examples are provided of how the council attempted to embed place-based working under the pledge 'Tackle inequality so people have a fair chance', with actions related to alleviating food and fuel poverty.

Food poverty occurs when people lack resources to access an adequate supply of nutritious food (Cambridge English Dictionary). Over 40 organisations within Gateshead established the Gateshead community food network. This led to the creation of a food sharing network, utilising relationships established during the council's successful bid to the Department for Education's 'holidays and food' fund. This secured funding of £204,000 in 2020 to deliver over 12,500 free places, providing free meals and social, recreational and development activities to Gateshead children, particularly targeting those on free school meals over the school holidays who may otherwise have gone hungry or suffered social isolation. The 'holidays and food' programme followed on from the 'fill the gap' holiday hunger provision that the council and its third sector partners have delivered since 2015.

Work on fuel poverty (said to occur when people pay more than the average (national median) amount on fuel, causing household income to fall below 60 per cent of median household income (DBEIS, 2019a: 3)) was complicated and protracted. The initial proposal included a potential partnership with uSwitch (a price comparison and switching service) to enable Gateshead to host their switching link on its website in order to encourage people to switch to more cost-effective tariffs (and to generate a fee for the council which would be reinvested into its tackling poverty work streams – an attempt to generate income given austerity cuts). This was complicated to progress given the complexities surrounding the energy sector in general, especially in relation to access to social tariffs and advice around fuel and other debt. Partial progress has been made as the council's energy services team has brought the Local Energy Assistance Programme (LEAP) to Gateshead through the third party provider AgilityEco (who provide support to vulnerable households on energy efficiency and utility bills). LEAP is a free service for fuel-poor and vulnerable households, offering energy advice, a tariff review and free energy-saving measures, as well as onward referrals to the Emergency Central Heating Offer (ECHO), which provides free insulation and/or boiler replacements to some of Gateshead's most vulnerable households (DBEIS, 2019b). LEAP also makes referrals to IncomeMax, a national charity that checks welfare benefit entitlement, energy grant eligibility and offers free independent debt advice.

## Social justice and social renewal

Place-based services incorporate the principles of Marmot's 'proportionate universalism' (Marmot et al, 2010: 41; Marmot et al, 2020: 142) because services are available to all in an area but are often targeted at those places and communities most in need. The food and fuel poverty initiatives arguably fulfil these criteria and may contribute to social renewal by providing adequate and sufficient food and warmth, and improving people's wellbeing. The spatial aspect of place-based working acknowledges that disadvantage is often concentrated in specific areas (Curtis and Rees Jones, 1989) because where people live is, by and large, a reflection of socio-economic status (Stafford et al, 2007). The creation of the Gateshead food poverty network provided outreach support in times of severe social and financial distress, and tapped into a web of wider support that was already established. However, although place-based targeting may be justifiable, tackling poverty and disadvantage requires national strategies as people living in poverty are dispersed across different areas (McLoone, 2001). Although thoughtful targeting may avoid stigmatising service users (Marmot et al, 2010), it does not guarantee it, and there may be people who would benefit from, but nevertheless do not access, the services that are available. Furthermore, place-based working works within the framework of existing structural inequalities. Although the local delivery and implementation of national social policies matter and can make a positive difference, fundamentally, there is no redistribution of resources from the rich to the poor, or any extra money available to councils to support place-based working, despite already operating in severely straitened circumstances.

Local authorities have a key role to play as their wide-ranging remit of responsibilities covers aspects of people's lives that affect the social determinants of health (Marmot et al, 2010). They engage with residents, the private sector and the voluntary, community and social enterprise sector, and they have a pivotal position in the places in which they are located (Marmot et al, 2010; Hambleton et al, 2012). This means that they are potentially well positioned to make cross-sectoral links with different stakeholders. According to Taylor and Buckly (2017), most explanations of place-based working appreciate that acquiring knowledge involves developing relationships over time, acknowledging how these might change. Moreover, a place-based working approach requires openness and transparency about its aims, and has to be embedded, not just be championed by a few people. The Thrive approach is an attempt to develop these relationships across and within the different sectors. However, Gateshead Council's fuel-switching initiative demonstrates that joint working is complex and does not necessarily deliver tangible outcomes within the time frames envisaged. Furthermore, austerity does not create the best conditions for joint working (Hastings et al, 2015a) as organisations are under intense pressure, and with staff reductions and organisational restructures, resources for partnership and collaborative working are unlikely to be available.

According to Sullivan et al (2006), in general, partnership working has formal entities created to facilitate working together, whereas collaboration refers to common values, purposes and activities. In practice, collaboration combines these attributes, and as a precursor to collaboration, it is necessary to scope local capacity and willingness (Sullivan et al, 2006). Gateshead's conference in 2018 and its follow-up conference in 2019 are arguably examples of scoping local capacity and an attempt to define a shared purpose (perhaps representing a symbol of hope). However, a strategy is necessary to garner capacity through to sustained collaborative action (Sullivan et al, 2006) but working in organisations that are reducing staff and restructuring is unlikely to be conducive to developing strategy and a smooth transition (Hastings et al, 2015a). Key themes from the conferences and a board were established but the development of a cohesive, dynamic strategy connecting the themes and overall direction of the initiative is necessary and needs adequate resourcing to enable officers to work with partners regarding delivery.

The examples of coordinated activity around food and fuel poverty demonstrate that partnership working is labour-intensive and prolonged, and that involving private and voluntary sector providers, even when there is common purpose, commitment and resources, is difficult and does not necessarily deliver as expected, as the fuel-switching initiative demonstrated. Some of the barriers related to structural issues that were difficult to resolve (such as consumer protection around debt and fuel poverty advice); however, others could relate to historic, organisational and relationship issues that are also difficult to overcome. As noted by Sullivan et al (2006), organisational capacity, current relationships and the relative power of organisations affect collaborative working. Some in the voluntary and private sector might perceive the local authority as adversarial or authoritarian due to its powerful position as place leader, as an organisation that allocates funding and determines priorities, and as a regulator. Operating during austerity is unlikely to strengthen relationships, and although austerity stems from central government's budget decisions, local authorities are at the front line of implementation – which inevitably, if often unfairly, means that they are at the front line for blame. Some decisions will be unpopular with partners, staff and communities, and this is likely to undermine credibility regarding the Thrive pledges. For example, in spite of its pledges, the council's budget consultation for 2019/20 proposed cuts of £100,000 to the Gateshead Fund, even though it acknowledged that it could affect Thrive, and proposed cutting three of its contracts with Mental Health Matters (a charity providing support to people experiencing mental health issues and homelessness) (Ramsey, 2018). This demonstrates how difficult it is for councils to meet austerity budgets, and although Gateshead's approach is 'priority-led', it will have no option but to prioritise statutory services. Good-quality relationships are key to the fulfilment of positive actions and outcomes from collaborations (Stewart et al, 2002, cited in Sullivan et al, 2006), which suggests that goodwill is needed from all collaborators. The hard budget decisions of the council will surely test the goodwill and patience of collaborators and staff. Wright's (2012) definition of power highlights that individual agents have the capacity to act and work together to deliver change. Theoretically, place-based working may have the potential to capitalise on this to deliver positive social change where common purpose exists, and may have the potential to overcome some of the criticisms of area- and people-based initiatives; however, in practice, and without resources, it is difficult to see how this potential can be realised.

Another aspect of the Thrive pledges concerns how any success can be measured, and this is considered in relation to poverty, inequality and employment. The pledges are broad and lack clarity, covering aspects of inequality (such as health inequality) and poverty (child, food and fuel poverty). Measuring poverty is a contested concept and there are a variety of measures, which could produce different results. There is no longer any official measure of poverty in the UK, though the Social Metrics Commission (2019) is developing a new approach that is recognised as promising and experimental statistics are due to be published by the Department for Work and Pensions in 2020 (Joseph Rowntree Foundation, 2020). For many people, poverty is not a fixed state as they may move in and out of poverty (Dermott and Main, 2018). Inequality measures the gap between different groups and there is not a linear relationship between poverty and inequality. Similarly, Gateshead's pledge to create sustainable opportunities for employment is laudable. However, if employment is low paid, insecure, with poor terms, conditions and progression (MacDonald and Marsh, 2005), it is not necessarily a route to well-being or out of poverty as 56 per cent of people in poverty have someone in the household in paid work (Joseph Rowntree Foundation, 2020). Therefore, employment could increase but the percentage of households in poverty may not fall.

This demonstrates the difficulties of assessing the Thrive pledges and place-based working's effectiveness in general, and ultimately, perhaps, whether such initiatives continue. If outcomes are unable to be effectively measured, will stretched organisations continue to support resource allocation for labour-intensive ways of working? The pressures for justification may come from distinct sources in different organisations (for example, senior managers and local politicians in the local authority, and the management boards of, and those who fund or donate to, charities) but the outcome of withdrawing support could generate the same outcome. To help overcome this, should evaluations consider implementation instead of outcomes (and so effectively be process evaluations) and extend beyond models of theories of change to reflect qualitatively on the experiences and contexts of the organisations involved, their capacity and their contributions (Sullivan et al, 2006) to place-based working? Instead of quantitative outcome measures that are difficult to establish and attribute, and that are often beyond the scope of the council to change, a qualitative process evaluation may represent a more plausible method and capture the views of stakeholders. This would enable a more detailed assessment of Thrive, the authority's implementation of austerity and how collaborative working can be developed in future – insights that may also help other organisations.

## Conclusion

This chapter described how Gateshead Council implemented place-based working in two policy areas to cope with austerity and as part of its anti-poverty strategy through the implementation of Thrive. Developing a collaborative approach is laudable and Thrive is a promising approach that focuses on community interests; however, it is being delivered during (and as a response to) austerity, when organisations are experiencing challenges in their operating environment. Thrive aims to improve people's lives and to contribute to social justice by reducing poverty and disadvantage. Engaging partners to improve engagement in and with communities in order to achieve better outcomes has the potential to contribute to social renewal. Gateshead's ambitious approach to Thrive demonstrated that diverse partners can be brought together to work towards common purposes in order to improve the lives of its citizens. Its success might be nuanced and take longer to achieve than was envisaged but its approach speaks of a council that cares. However, place-based working operates within existing structural inequalities. Consequently, its potential to contribute to social justice and social renewal and to deliver positive social change is constrained because of this.

## Acknowledgements

Michael Walker is a member of the Tackling Poverty in Gateshead Board and contributes to delivering the Council's wider strategic Thrive agenda. Mel Steer attended the Board's meetings during 2018 and 2019 during the chapter's development. Our thanks to other chapter authors and Mandy Cheetham for helpful comments on our chapter.

## References

Bailey, N., Bramley, G. and Hastings, A. (2015) 'Symposium introduction: local responses to "austerity"', *Local Government Studies*, 41(4): 571–81.

Beatty, C. and Fothergill, S. (2013) *Hitting the Poorest Places Hardest: The Local and Regional Impact of Welfare Reform*, Sheffield: Centre for Regional Economic and Social Research, Sheffield Hallam University.

Blyth, M. (2013) *Austerity: The History of a Dangerous Idea*, New York: Oxford University Press.

Cambridge English Dictionary. Available at: https://dictionary.cambridge.org/dictionary/english/food-poverty

Cheetham, M., Moffatt, S. and Addison, M. (2018) '"It's hitting people that can least afford it the hardest": the impact of Universal Credit in two North East localities: a qualitative study', Final report, November. Available at: www.gateshead.gov.uk/media/10665/The-impact-of-the-roll-out-of-Universal-Credit-in-two-North-East-England-localities-a-qualitative-study-November-2018/pdf/Universal_Credit_Report_2018pdf.pdf?m=636778831081630000

Child Poverty Action Group Scotland (2016) 'What is welfare reform and how is it affecting families?', May. Available at: www.cpag.org.uk/sites/default/files/CPAG-Scot-EWS-Welfare-Reform%28May16%29.pdf

Comptroller and Auditor General (2018) *Financial Sustainability of Local Authorities 2018, HC834, Session 2017–2019*, London: National Audit Office. Available at: www.nao.org.uk/wp-content/uploads/2018/03/Financial-sustainabilty-of-local-authorites-2018.pdf

Curtis, S. and Rees Jones, I. (1989) 'Is there a place for geography in the analysis of health inequality?', *Sociology of Health and Illness*, 20: 645–72.

DBEIS (Department for Business, Energy and Industrial Strategy) (2019a) 'Annual fuel poverty statistics in England, 2019 (2017 data)', 13 June. Available at: https://assets.publishing.service.gov.uk/government/uploads/system/uploads/attachment_data/file/808534/Annual_Fuel_Poverty_Statistics_Report_2019__2017_data_.pdf

DBEIS (Department for Business, Energy and Industrial Strategy) (2019b) 'HECA reporting 2019: forward guidance to local authorities on changes to Home Energy Conservation Act (HECA) report submission from 2019', January. Available at: www.gateshead.gov.uk/media/13837/Home-Energy-Conservation-Act-Report-May-2019/pdf/Home_Energy_Conservation_Act_Report_May_2019.pdf?m=636947412073300000

DCLG (Department for Communities and Local Government) (2016a) *Estate Regeneration National Strategy: The Role of Local Authorities*, London: DCLG.

DCLG (Department for Communities and Local Government) (2016b) *Estate Regeneration National Strategy: Better Social Outcomes*, London: DCLG.

Dermott, E. and Main, G. (2018) 'Poverty and social exclusion in the UK', in E. Dermott and G. Main (eds) *Poverty and Social Exclusion in the UK: Volume I: The Nature and Extent of the Problem*, Bristol: Policy Press.

Gateshead Council (no date) 'Making Gateshead a place where everyone thrives', Gateshead Council. Available at: www.gateshead.gov.uk/media/7200/Making-Gateshead-a-place-where-everyone-thrives/pdf/Making_Gateshead_a_Place_Where_Everyone_Thrives.pdf

Hambleton, R., Howard, J., Denters, B., Klok, P.-J. and Vrielink, M.O. (2012) *Public Sector Innovation and Local Leadership in the UK and the Netherlands*, York: Joseph Rowntree Foundation.

Hastings, A., Bailey, N., Bramley, G., Gannon, M. and Watkins, D. (2015a) *The Cost of the Cuts: The Impact on Local Government and Poorer Communities*, York: Joseph Rowntree Foundation.

Hastings, A., Bailey, N., Gannon, M., Besemer, K. and Bramley, G. (2015b) 'Coping with the cuts? The management of the worst financial settlement in living memory', *Local Government Studies*, 41(4): 601–21.

Hirsch, D. and Stone, J. (2020) Local indicators of child poverty after housing costs, 2018/19, Summary of estimates of child poverty after housing costs in local authorities and parliamentary constituencies, 2014/15-2018/19, Loughborough University. Available at: https://hdl.handle.net/2134/13169510.v1

HM Treasury and CLG (Communities and Local Government) (2010) *Total Place: A Whole Area Approach to Public Services*, London: CLG.

John, P. (2014) 'The great survivor: the persistence and resilience of English local government', *Local Government Studies*, 40(5): 687–704.

Joseph Rowntree Foundation (2020) *UK Poverty 2019/20: The Leading Independent Report*, York: Joseph Rowntree Foundation. Available at: file:///Volumes/NCL%201/jrf_-_uk_poverty_2019-20_report_4.pdf www.jrf.org.uk/report/uk-poverty-2019–20

Longlands, S. (2020) 'Now is not the time for Westminster to tighten its centralising grip', 25 March. Available at: www.themj.co.uk/Now-is-not-the-time-for-Westminster-to-tighten-its-centralising-grip/217130

Lowndes, V. and McCaughie, K. (2013) 'Weathering the perfect storm? Austerity and institutional resilience in local government', *Policy and Politics*, 41(4): 533–49.

Lupton, R. and Turok, I. (2004) 'Anti-poverty policies in Britain: area-based and people-based approaches', in U.-J. Walther and K. Mensch (eds) *Armut und Ausgrenzung in der 'Sozialen Stadt'*, Darmstadt: Schader-Stiftung, pp 188–208.

MacDonald, R. and Marsh, J. (2005) *Disconnected Youth? Growing up in Britain's Poor Neighbourhoods*, Basingstoke: Palgrave Macmillan.

Marmot, M., Allen, J., Goldblatt, P., Boyce, T., McNeish, D., Grady, M. and Geddes, I. (2010) *Fair Society, Healthy Lives. The Marmot Review: Strategic Review of Health Inequalities in England Post-2010*, February. Available at: www.instituteofhealthequity.org/resources-reports/fair-society-healthy-lives-the-marmot-review/fair-society-healthy-lives-full-report-pdf.pdf

Marmot, M., Allen, J., Boyce, T., Goldblatt, P. and Morrison, J. (2020) *Health Equity in England: The Marmot Review 10 Years On*, London: Institute of Health Equity.

McLoone, P. (2001) 'Targeting deprived areas within small areas in Scotland: population study', *British Medical Journal*, 323(7309): 374–5.

Munro, F. (2015) 'Place-based working', *Iriss*, 28 July. Available at: www.iriss.org.uk/resources/irisson/place-based-working

ONS (Office for National Statistics) (2018) 'Regional ethnic diversity', 1 August. Available at: www.ethnicity-facts-figures.service.gov.uk/uk-population-by-ethnicity/national-and-regional-populations/regional-ethnic-diversity/latest

ONS (Office for National Statistics) (2020) 'Labour market profile – Gateshead', Nomis Official Labour Market Statistics. Available at: www.nomisweb.co.uk/reports/lmp/la/1946157064/report.aspx?town=gateshead

Public Health England (2019) 'Place-based approaches for reducing health inequalities: foreword and executive summary', 29 July. Available at: www.gov.uk/government/publications/health-inequalities-place-based-approaches-to-reduce-inequalities/place-based-approaches-for-reducing-health-inequalities-foreword-and-executive-summary#executive-summary

Ramsey, S. (2018) *Budget Consultation 2019/2020, 20 November*. Available at: https://www.gateshead.gov.uk/media/10686/Budget-2019-20-report-to-Cabinet/pdf/Cabinet_Report.pdf?m=636783095582630000

Rees, G., Power, S. and Taylor, C. (2007) 'The governance of educational inequalities: the limits of area-based initiatives', *Journal of Comparative Policy Analysis*, 9(3): 261–74.

Shaw, K. and Robinson, F. (2018) 'Whatever happened to the North East? Reflections on the end of regionalism in England', *Local Economy*, 33(8): 842–61.

Social Metrics Commission (2019) 'Measuring poverty 2019: a report of the Social Metrics Commission. Chaired by Philippa Stroud, CEO of the Legatum Institute', July. Available at: https://socialmetricscommission.org.uk/wp-content/uploads/2019/07/SMC_measuring-poverty-201908_full-report.pdf

Stafford, M., Cummins, S., Ellaway, A., Sacker, A., Wiggins, R.D. and Macintyre, S. (2007) 'Pathways to obesity: identifying local, modifiable determinants of physical activity and diet', *Social Science and Medicine*, 65(9): 1882–97.

Sullivan, H., Barnes, M. and Matka, E. (2006) 'Collaborative capacity and strategies in area-based initiatives', *Public Administration*, 84(2): 289–310.

Taylor, M. and Buckly, E. (2017) *Historical Review of Place-Based Approaches*, London: Lankelly Chase. Available at: https://lankellychase.org.uk/wp-content/uploads/2017/10/Historical-review-of-place-based-approaches.pdf

Toynbee, P. (2020) 'Coronavirus will brutally expose the effect of a decade of public service cuts', *The Guardian*, 5 March. Available at: www.theguardian.com/commentisfree/2020/mar/05/coronavirus-epidemic-decade-austerity-public-services

Wright, E.O. (2012) 'Transforming capitalism through real utopias', *American Sociological Review*, 78(1): 1–25.

# 9

# City of Dreams: enabling children and young people's cultural participation and civic voice in Newcastle and Gateshead

*Ben Dickenson and Venda Louise Pollock*

## Introduction

City of Dreams is a long-term mission to make the conurbation of NewcastleGateshead the 'best place to be young' by enabling the local population of children and young people – 168,000 under 25s – to have the opportunity to engage with culture and creativity. As well as enhancing engagement with culture and the creative arts, it also aims to be a platform for children and young people's voice and to increase their influence in cultural organisations. Through this, City of Dreams seeks to support young people in becoming active and creative citizens who are able to improve their life chances. Established in 2018, City of Dreams is an initiative led by NewcastleGateshead Cultural Venues[1] (NGCV is a voluntary partnership of 10 organisations running 20 venues, archives and heritage sites across Tyne and Wear) and which has 53 affiliated organisations drawn from a variety of sectors including voluntary, community and social enterprise, and the arts. This broad base of support evidences the collective intent to create a transformational shift in the way the cultural sector, and indeed cities themselves, engage with young participants and audiences.

The ambition is both risky and brave: the longitudinal vision outstrips all partner organisations' funding cycles and the initiative has been instituted in a climate of austerity, starkly reflected in Newcastle City Council's announcement of a 100 per cent cut to its culture budget in 2013 (it has since worked with various agencies to address the situation). The Newcastle decision highlighted the immense pressure local authorities are under to balance their books, and the sharp impact on cultural provision. The early evolution of City of Dreams offers insights that can inform alternative approaches to operating in this context. It is a collective mission, pooling the resources, ideas and activity of cultural institutions in the city, rather than a formally constituted body. This approach embraces both ambition and challenge: as well as being drawn together for this shared vision, the constituent members of the collective are also, as independent organisations, competing for ever-dwindling funds. Moreover, in embarking on this transformational journey together, many of the implications for the organisations involved – for example, their modes of operation, programming, organisational structures and priorities – could not be predicted.

Fast-forward to September 2019 and a review of its first year involving NGCV stakeholders, affiliated organisations, a steering group of 16–25 year olds – called Young Champions – and a representative body of over 1,000 children and young people acknowledged that the initiative had rapidly become high-profile and strategically resonant, acting as a test bed for new approaches that broaden reach, deepen engagement, strengthen partnerships and provide evaluative insights. Partners understood it as a collective mission of change, rooted in practical activity, operating through consensus, collaboration and invention, and combining resources and ideas to create a whole that collectively achieves more than individuals and organisations could ever do working independently.

At this early stage, it is not appropriate to embark on an in-depth analysis of the impact of the mission on life in the city, or on the equity of children and young people's outcomes. Instead, after outlining the context in which City of Dreams emerged, the research findings thus far will be presented for the first time and we will show how they have shaped the City of Dreams theory of change and action plan. This is a study of a process. Ultimately, the chapter considers whether an initiative like City of Dreams can institute a culture change within the cultural sector and also impact on the city at large.

## Background and context

City of Dreams formally launched in September 2018, with the broadcaster Kirsty Lang advocating its importance within the context of a decline of opportunity for children and young people, particularly those attending state schools, to engage with the arts. The event was devised and chaired by young people's elected representatives from local youth councils and assemblies, and attended by key stakeholders from regional and national organisations, and local elected members. The culture sector leaders and young people laid out an ambition for NewcastleGateshead to be a national exemplar in young people's engagement in the arts. An extract from 'Where do we belong?', a dramatic performance by the Young Company of the regional producing theatre Northern Stage, highlighted the difficulties and choices facing young people growing up in contemporary NewcastleGateshead, and a poem written by over 300 young people from disadvantaged backgrounds offered a contemporary youth-relevant definition of culture. Thus, the event reflected the ethos of City of Dreams, which, from the outset, has had a close relationship with the political, educational and social context in which it was conceived. Indeed, a late 2017 briefing on these issues had been the point of departure for the development of a theory of change – the guiding strategic framework for the ten-year mission – underscoring its ambitions with a broader social philosophy.

The theory of change was co-developed through a series of workshops with the NGCV partnership, other partner organisations and young people, and it was clearly responding to a particular social and economic context. It has been reviewed and revised regularly in the same way as the initiative has evolved.

Evidence showed that while the different venues of the NGCV partners welcomed 89 per cent of schools in the 2016/17 academic year, and there were 1.8 million learning engagements by under-19s in Newcastle and Gateshead between 2014 and 2017,[2] following transition to high school, young people's engagement with NGCV organisations decreased by 60 per cent and under-19s in some of the most deprived wards in the city were at least 25 per cent less likely to attend subsidised arts activity than counterparts in wealthier areas. Although not wanting to assume any correlation or causation, it was noted that the postcodes of lower cultural engagement were also those with the greatest ethnic diversity and highest level of special educational needs statements. It was also recognised that while 70 per cent of Newcastle and Gateshead schoolchildren had good educational development in Year 6, 2017 general certificate in secondary education (GCSE)[3] results showed that 64 per cent achieved Grade 4 or above in English Language, 67 per cent in English Literature and 66 per cent in mathematics – all 5 per cent behind the English national average.[4] Of equal concern was the stark decline in young people's well-being, reflected in both *The Good Childhood Report* by The Children's Society (2019) and The Prince's Trust (2018) Macquarie Youth Index, the latter showing that 44 per cent of young people think there will be fewer jobs in the future and 21 per cent think their life will 'amount to nothing'. A further 28 per cent do not feel in control of their lives and 59 per cent are 'anxious' about the future in light of an 'uncertain political climate'. Set alongside the general downward trend in voting rates for 18–25 year olds – excepting the increased number of student voters at the 2015 general election – there is a growing sense that austerity has driven down expectations for the future, worsened emotional and psychological well-being, and created a civic confidence deficit. In this context, the agency of young people as social actors is being tested and reconstituted.

While there is no firm evidence to demonstrate a link between these statistics and education policy, the founders of City of Dreams did consider the introduction of the English Baccalaureate when developing their programme for change. The English Baccalaureate has created a perceived hierarchy of subjects in secondary schools and, as the proposed core subjects do not include any creative arts fields of study, a sense that arts are not as valued or valuable for children and young people. Building on the findings of the Warwick Commission (2015) that there had been a general drop in art-related GCSE uptake between 2003 and 2013 (for example, 50 per cent in design and technology, and 23 per cent for drama), in July 2019, the education think tank Education and Skills (EDSK) published 'A step baccwards' (Richmond/EDSK, 2019), which charted the decline in GCSE entries since the introduction of English Baccalaureate measures in 2010 for music (24 per cent), design and technology (63 per cent), dance (46 per cent), media studies (35 per cent), and art and design (6 per cent). According to the Fabian Society report *Primary Colours* (Cooper, 2018), 68 per cent of primary teachers in England felt that there was less arts education since 2010 and 49 per cent felt that the quality of what was provided was worse. As school budgets have become increasingly pressured, difficult decisions have had to be made as to where money is spent. Understanding this context is crucial to recognising why an ambition of City of Dreams has been to rationalise and coordinate resources of otherwise competing cultural organisations to provide affordable offers to local schools. In the 2018/19 academic year, this approach achieved engagement by 100 per cent of state-funded schools with performance, exhibition, learning and participation programmes offered by NGCV partners – with 68,145 students taking part and an average of 8.7 engagements per school. That these offers have been a mix of curriculum-linked creative learning and alternative provision demonstrates an innovative response to education policy. This was affirmed when City of Dreams was chosen as a case study in the Durham Commission on Creativity and Education (Durham University and Arts Council England, 2019), which advocated for creativity within and across education.

On a pragmatic level, the English Baccalaureate context has also raised significant concerns about the skills pipeline for culture and creative arts (see, for example, Busby, 2018), and a sense that the government's education policy is at odds with the lauding of the creative industries as a core contributor to the UK economy. The response from educationalists and the cultural sector, however, has focused more on the wider benefits to health and well-being, educational attainment across disciplines, transferable skills, social mobility, identity and community development, and employability that engagement in creative arts and creative learning can bring (Cultural Learning Alliance, 2017; RSC et al, 2018). It is the sector that has taken significant steps to lobby (for example, see 'Time to listen', a research-informed report from the Royal Shakespeare Company, Tate and Nottingham University [RSC et al, 2018]) and to intervene through prominent initiatives such as the Victoria and Albert Museum's DesignLab Nation, which seeks to engage secondary school pupils in design and inspire the next generation of designers. City of Dreams has therefore initiated a large programme of work, drawing together two-dozen arts organisations to promote and support creative careers, while piloting a new model of accelerating opportunities for skills and career development for disadvantaged 16–25 year olds called 'creative pathways'.

Thus, City of Dreams directly emerged from a particular set of social, political and societal circumstances, and actively seeks to respond to and change this context. Integral to informing the response has been a body of action research undertaken during the first 18 months of the programme in partnership with engaged organisations and with children and young people at its heart. This has led to the formation of the theory of change and City of Dreams framework to date.

## Underpinning research: institutions and the voices of children and young people

The first 18 months of City of Dreams was informed by action research with the intention that this would then inform the structure, focus and activity of the wider programme. The preliminary phase of research (conducted in late 2017 before the initiative began) took the form of semi-structured interviews with colleagues in operational, strategic and creative roles within NGCV organisations, as well as 34 engagements with people, organisations and groups outside of this partnership. Interview transcripts were then coded to identify common themes. The aim of this was to give a sense of the 'institutional' view of the existing activity, barriers and opportunities for working with young people.

A key finding was that while commitment to the vision of City of Dreams was high, there was a focus on the *how* – the operational level of activity – rather than the *why*. This was driven, in part, by the reporting expectations of funding regimes and an increasing need to generate income in a period when local authority subsidy had declined and Arts Council England investment had, at best, stood still. In some cases, it also revealed a lack of understanding about the experience of young people from the 'institutional' perspective. Conversations centred around learning and programming within organisations, as well as the delivery of activity, and less on the underlying motivation for activity, the nature of participation and the difference this was actually making. Given the social mission of NGCV partnership members – all of them charities with objectives for benefitting the lives of local citizens – this finding implied a disconnect between strategic intent and operational levels of working. It is interesting to note that voluntary and community sector partners, as well as local authority representatives, were more concentrated on the underlying motivations of City of Dreams, in particular, on ensuring that the programme was structured around an informed understanding of the knowledge and needs of young people. This echoed an awareness within the NGCV partnership that their engagement with under-25s, especially as audience members outside of targeted programmes, may be unevenly weighted to those with greater economic and cultural capital, and hence that perceptions about engagement with young people might not reflect the diversity of the youth population. This consolidated the already-recognised need for the programme to be shaped and directed by young people, with a suggestion emerging from the research of an annual young people's consultation process that would then inform decisions about cultural programming and activity. This led to City of Dreams developing the Big Culture Conversation and looking at how young people could be more actively engaged with organisations, including having a role in decision-making.

The research also highlighted what were perceived to be, from the perspectives of the NGCV partnership and other organisations, the barriers to engagement. Cost and logistics were recognised as prominent barriers – not only the cost of events themselves, but also transport (significant in a region with several rural hinterlands) – as was the short-term, project-based nature of the majority of activities (largely due to the means by which they were funded). This pointed very much to the need for an enhanced level of partnership working between sectors, something City of Dreams directly aims to facilitate, and also the potential for the partnership around City of Dreams to work to achieve meaningful life changes with and for young people that stretched beyond the culture sphere to within broader civic life, such as changes to transport.

From the outset, there was recognition that City of Dreams had to be shaped by young people, and as the initial conversations with organisations took place, the need for young people's voices to be present became ever-more apparent. The precise mechanism for this, however, remained undetermined. It was both necessary and a challenge for the consultation with children and young people to be representative, in particular, to reach audiences who would not normally engage and to ensure that those with protected characteristics were given the opportunity to shape the programme.

What emerged was the Big Culture Conversation, a cycle of consultation and participation specifically designed for young people to set the agenda for culture in NewcastleGateshead but that became a broader platform for consultation around the experience of young people growing up in the area. The first iteration took place in 2018 and had three stages: small group consultation with young people already engaged in structured cultural activities in up to 12 settings across the cultural sector; small group consultations with young people less likely to be engaged in cultural activities in up to 12 settings across the voluntary/community sector; and then a large-scale annual event co-produced with young people, drawing on the results from the first two stages of consultation and setting an agenda for the following year. Consultations were held in settings familiar to young people (for stage two, these included community centres, schools and youth projects) and often followed an activity the young people were taking part in. The sessions lasted between 10 and 40 minutes, depending on the setting and group, and adopted a 'participatory appraisal' method, based on simple tools. Support for the process was stronger than expected, and for the first two stages, over 652 young people were reached through the small group consultations and a further 296 young people were engaged in the large-scale event, bringing together a range of schools, groups and individuals.

Research participants accessed via the venues of the NGCV partnership covered all major art forms and science (the Centre for Life being a key partner), and were aged five to 25, with the average age being 15. A total of 58 per cent identified as female and 42 per cent as male, with 16 per cent drawn from a black, Asian and minority ethnic (BAME)[5] background and 2 per cent describing themselves as lesbian, gay, bisexual, transgender and queer (LGBTQ).[6] A total of 6 per cent of participants had a special educational need or disability and 5 per cent were looked-after children. Crucially, this represented a diverse range of young people and included groups often absent in standard data collected by venues. Thus, the range of views gathered came from a more representative sample of the broader demographic that City of Dreams sought to engage and pointed to the three-stage approach of the Big Culture Conversation being worth repeating. In 2019, while the demographic remained largely comparable, 71 per cent of 1,259 young people engaged in the consultation process were not regularly engaged with cultural organisations or programmes. In this instance, the geographic spread was focused on areas of high deprivation and lower cultural engagement, resulting in 57 per cent of participants coming from postcodes of higher child poverty. Sessions were extended to roughly one hour in length in order to include additional research activity exploring ambitions, careers and the support required to achieve desired life outcomes.

The headline findings from both years were encouraging, with 98 per cent of all participants having visited a cultural venue within the NGCV partnership during the previous year and 40 per cent feeling that they had learned something new during the visit. When digging into the details, however, the balance shifted. Those most engaged (stage one consultees) had, on average, experienced at least three different arts practices, and of those consulted in theatre, dance and visual arts settings, 80 per cent had been to another cultural venue in the previous year, over 60 per cent without the support of school. However, 63 per cent of those less regularly engaged (taking part in the stage two and three consultations) had experienced only one cultural activity in the previous year – with pantomime topping the bill and a visit to a local museum or science centre being next on the list, though this had been an activity arranged by school or parents in the majority of cases – which raises alarm bells given the decline of the presence of arts in schools. What this indicated was that those already taking part in regular activities with cultural venues were multiply and deeply engaged, while those involved less often were likely to be engaged through adult-brokered involvement. This is significant as when asked about how cultural organisations communicate with young people, 80 per cent of those under 12 said that they did not believe that adults in home or school knew what was on offer in venues or were supportive of their engagement. The majority of those aged over 13 preferred peer recommendation to venue social or print media, which highlighted significant challenges in communications that City of Dreams sought to respond to by, among other things, creating X-Culture ambassadors – a team of young people giving peer recommendations.

An analysis of what the young people considered talent development, what they had made and where they had learned provided interesting insight into their perceptions of engagement with cultural activity. While visits to some venues often involved making activities, children and young people largely saw these as 'seeing' experiences only; also, while over 50 per cent had visited galleries, museums or science-focused exhibitions (most often as part of a school trip), only a third considered these 'learning' activities. Moreover, when asked what was on offer for young people at cultural venues, only one in five could articulate what there was for them to do. When asked what they would like to do in the future, the overwhelming response from across the participant groups was to 'make things'. Through this kind of engagement in creative activity, the young people saw the potential for skills development and work opportunities, as well as for it to enable them to have a louder voice. These findings directly informed the development of two City of Dreams initiatives, #Make Something Brilliant and Our City Our Story (discussed later).

Interestingly, the biggest benefit identified was also one of the most stubborn barriers – confidence. The other significant barriers were travel and transport cost and – second highest in both years – adults whose negative influence deters young people from getting involved. Also significant in the 2019 conversation were young people's top ambitions for the future, primarily to 'just get a job' but second highest was to go to university or become a YouTuber/influencer. Creative career ambitions – musician, visual artist, actor and filmmaker – were individually lower than others but collectively the most popular. What young people felt they needed most to achieve their ambitions were transferable skills like time management, planning and budgeting, help to meet industry contacts, and support to find the resilience they thought they would need to overcome the difficulties they expected to face if they wanted to sustain a decent standard of living.

As a result of these consultations, the City of Dreams strategy and action plan were formed in 2018 and refreshed in 2019, working through an extensive theory of change process with NGCV and wider constituents (see Figure 9.1). The programme launched in 2018 with three central pillars: taking part; the voice of young people (this is both within cultural programming and organisations, and also about giving young people a stronger platform for their civic voice); and confidence skills. Through the programme, partners seek to: coordinate content, learning programmes and resources; develop long-term activities addressing the challenges faced by younger people rather than short-term, project-based activities; find new ways to engage the diversity

**Figure 9.1:** City of Dreams, theory of change, version 7 (2019)

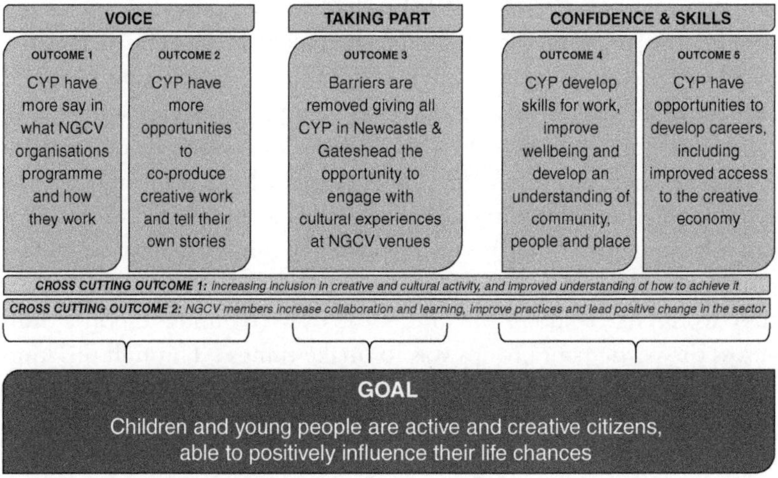

Note: CYP = children and young people.

Source: From City of Dreams Strategic Action Plan 2019–2022, courtesy of NewcastleGateshead Cultural Venues

of the local population; and promote children and young people's agency. Central to the City of Dreams framework are four elements:

- The Big Culture Conversation: the annual consultation event that seeks to engage a representative sample of young people across NewcastleGateshead so that City of Dreams responds directly to their needs and priorities.
- Our City Our Story: an annual showcase of creative activity, curated by a team of young curators, which uses creativity to enable young people's voices to be heard on issues directly relevant to their lives. This is accompanied by panel discussions hosted by young people with key stakeholders, many of whom are also in the audience.
- #MakeSomethingBrilliant: a coordinated summer programme offering largely free activities for young people in NewcastleGateshead that avoids venue-specific branding, which research showed deterred or meant little to young people.
- Twi-Lates: mirroring the format of 'The Late Shows', a weekend where venues put on special cultural events in the evening, with more content being scheduled from 4–7 pm to enable young people to attend.

To enhance resilience and increase opportunity, City of Dreams piloted the Creative Pathways programme, supported by the Guy

Redman Trust which involves placements with partners to provide experience and raise awareness of creative careers. A young ambassadors programme is also being trialled, as are buddying systems, to overcome issues of communication and help to attend to issues of confidence. A relatively recent development has been organisations appointing young people within their own decision-making structures, for example, as young trustees or young programmers. Naturally, City of Dreams' own management structure has been built around the need for engagement with young people, the wider constituency interested in engaging in the initiative and the NGCV partnership as the lead organisation. Strategic decision making resides with the chief executives of NGCV partnership organisations and this works alongside the City of Dreams Champions' Board, a body of advocates and affiliates drawn from the wider group of partners, and the Young Champions' Board, an equivalent body of young people that enables them to shape strategy and activity.

Newcastle University is the key research partner for City of Dreams – 'research facilitator' might be a more appropriate term as the university seeks to draw on its own research strengths as well as those of the other regional universities to support, and be a critical friend to, the wider mission. In these early phases, much time has been spent sharing information about the research strengths of the university and considering where they might intersect with the research interests of City of Dreams. A working group initially facilitated these conversations and this has now evolved into the City of Dreams seminar series, which brings together academics and wider arts, charity and other sectors working with young people to discuss topics of mutual interest, for example, the first event looked at 'youth citizenship and culture'. The hope is that these might spark research and practice projects across the City of Dreams partnership. At a strategic level, the university has also worked with City of Dreams around evaluation, first, developing an evaluation framework, and then working together to try to secure further support for longitudinal evaluation. It is a relationship of support, mutual challenge, commitment and advocacy.

## Discussion

Through a grounded, open process of consultation, reflection and iterative development, City of Dreams is exploring the role that young people can play in creating more equitable institutions and access to culture. As well as being committed to the ambition, the partnership is also aware of the risks – most recently, the NGCV partners have undertaken 'poverty-proofing', learning how to identify, understand and work to overcome the barriers that children from families with fewer financial resources face in order to ensure that the initiatives are accessible to all and not simply taken up by children from more advantaged backgrounds (Reay, 2004). In the symbiotic relationship between its findings and strategic development, there are echoes of 'social justice youth development', which 'examines how urban youth contest, challenge, respond to and negotiate the use and misuse of power in their lives, together with a common view of social justice' (Ginwright and James, 2002: 35), integral to which is young people being empowered to influence, and adults supporting young people's development and decision-making. It seeks for young people to become more critically conscious citizens through developing an awareness 'of how institutional, historical, and systematic forces limit and promote the life opportunities for particular groups' (Ginwright and Cammarota, 2002: 87). It is an approach that recognises the intersectional forces that impact young people's lives. While 'social justice youth development' places emphasis on the relationship between critical consciousness and collective action, in City of Dreams, this is mirrored in the relationship between critical consciousness and cultural expression, which is acknowledged in 'social justice youth development' as an integral part of collective action but, here, operates within the City of Dreams framework rather than independently. The ethos remains similar, however, Ginwright and Cammarota (2002: 87) (in discussing 'social justice youth development with youth of colour') reference the education scholar Paulo Freire in thinking about the relationship between critical consciousness and social action as 'what Freire calls "praxis: reflection and action upon the world in order to transform it"'.

Like 'social justice youth development', City of Dreams works to support young people to define their own problems and solutions. This might operate primarily through a cultural lens and in a cultural sphere but indicatively, particularly through the outputs of Our City Our Story, the cultural becomes a significant vehicle for both exploring and expressing young people's identity and their wider lived experience to influential stakeholders. The impetus is to get decision-makers not only to listen, but also to take action. Within cultural organisations, this has happened with young trustees and young programmers ensuring that young people are on the inside of institutional structures and decision-making bodies to act as advocates for their issues. It has also been visible in the collaborative programming model of #MakeSomethingBrilliant, the first initiative in the city to be jointly produced across NGCV members. City of Dreams has recognised, however, that it is not enough to place young people in these positions; rather, it is essential for them to be skilled to act, and it supports organisations and children and young people with training. In this way, City of Dreams is creating the necessary conditions for young people to be empowered to engage with and change cultural organisations, and their broader cultural and civic landscape.

## Concluding thoughts

From its outset, City of Dreams has been explicit in its desire to understand the conditions young people growing up in NewcastleGateshead face. In placing young people at the heart of its activity, it sees them as integral to and capable of transforming those conditions and contexts in ways that are *meaningful to them*. It is too early to say whether enabling young people's voice through culture will impact fundamental structural issues but it certainly provides a platform where their experience of these issues can be voiced. In striving towards its overarching goal – that children and young people are active and creative citizens able to improve their life chances – early progress indicators include a shift in pricing at cultural venues (with Live Theatre, Tyneside Cinema and Seven Stories all changing policy to enable poorer children and families to visit for costs as low as £1), the creation of #MakeSomethingBrilliant (representing a collective commitment to accessibility through a largely free programme of summer activity) and the creation of youth-led structures to inform organisational decision-making at Sage Gateshead, Northern Stage and Dance City, which may further suggest a shift in power balances. All ten NGCV partnership members received Investing in Children (IiC) status[7] in September 2019, giving recognition to attempts to increase the voice of young people in their organisations and suggesting that they are embracing children's rights.

Agency is perhaps the key word here. It is used liberally in the culture sector. Arts Council England aim to promote citizen agency through community arts in their emerging 2020–30 strategy. Developing 'community agency' and social capital was a key principle established during phase one of Calouste Gulbenkian's inquiry into the civic role of arts organisations (Calouste Gulbenkian Foundation, 2020). Fostering agency through arts engagement and entrepreneurship is also a priority in the inclusive economic vision of the North of Tyne Combined Authority (NTCA, 2019). It is not difficult to draw funding and policy lines between City of Dreams' partners and these bodies, as well as several others seeking to develop agency. The agency of the NGCV partnership in instituting and committing to the ambition and risk of City of Dreams, and the agency of the young people engaged, are forming a framework that they seek to make genuinely transformative. While what is presented here is indicative, what this case study intimates is the potential for collective, creative and civic intent to institute a city-wide culture shift towards the partners' shared vision of a more socially just city.

## Postscript

At the time of writing, the City of Dreams programme is in furlough due to the COVID-19 pandemic and lockdown. In response to this exceptional situation, the creative sector has been widely praised for, at a very human level, showing its love for audiences and participants. Whether through theatre streamed online, arts organisations or artists offering activities for young people to do at home, or illustrated books explaining what is going on in the wider world, in a myriad of ways, the creative sector is helping people through, offering both escapism and constructive challenge. Yet, the pandemic has also highlighted the fragility of the sector: while organisations, venues and artists have shown impressive agility in realising the potential of online platforms, we are enjoying much of this for free. That does not pay the bills or provide the essential support for the activities many organisations deliver for young people. It is unlikely that our cultural sector, one of the largest contributors to the UK economy, will emerge in the same form, and this has significant implications for young people, who will inevitably feel the impact of the pandemic in many aspects of their lives, including education and employment. Engagement with the arts will be crucial to getting through this crisis and to forging our collective future – we will need young people who are not afraid to think differently, to learn from failure and to take risks, and who can empathise. In the midst of, and as we emerge from, this moment, there is and will continue to be a core need for the space, connectivity, challenge, inspiration, hope, distraction, language and so much more that the cultural world enables. While NGCV remains wholly committed to its work with young people, how that will develop is, like much at the moment, uncertain.

### Notes
[1]   NGCV comprises the Baltic Centre for Contemporary Art, Sage Gateshead, Northern Stage, Theatre Royal, Centre for Life, Tyne and Wear Archives and

Museums (comprising nine heritage sites), Tyneside Cinema, Dance City, Seven Stories, and Live Theatre.

[2] See economic impact assessments, available at: http://gnculturalvenues.ning.com/

[3] The GCSE is one of the main groups of academic examinations in England taken by young people aged 15/16 years at the end of secondary schooling.

[4] See analytics, available at: https://analytics.ofqual.gov.uk/

[5] BAME is a UK demographic.

[6] LGBTQ is an initialism also abbreviated as LGBT or GLBT.

[7] IiC is a children's human rights organisation working in partnership with children and young people to exercise their rights and participate in decisions that affect them. Its membership award gives organisations national recognition for the good practice with and active inclusion of children and young people in dialogue that results in change (see: www.investinginchildren.net/what-we-do/membership-award/).

## References

Busby, E. (2018) 'Decline in creative subjects at GCSE prompts fears that arts industry could be damaged', *The Independent*, 2 August.

Calouste Gulbenkian Foundation (2020) 'Phase one: the inquiry', Calouste Gulbenkian Foundation, 10 March. Available at: https://gulbenkian.pt/uk-branch/our-work/the-civic-role-of-arts-organisations/phase-one-the-inquiry/

Children's Society, The (2019) *The Good Childhood Report 2019*, London: The Children's Society. Available at: www.childrenssociety.org.uk/what-we-do/resources-and-publications/the-good-childhood-report-2019

Cooper, B. (2018) *Primary Colours: The Decline of Arts Education in Primary Schools and How it Can Be Reversed*, London: Fabian Society. Available at: https://fabians.org.uk/wp-content/uploads/2019/01/FS-Primary-Colours-Report-WEB-FINAL.pdf

Cultural Learning Alliance (2017) 'The case for cultural learning'. Available at: www.culturallearningalliance.org.uk/evidence

Durham University and Arts Council England (2019) *The Durham Commission on Creativity and Education*, Durham: University of Durham.

Ginwright, S. and Cammarota, J. (2002) 'New terrain in youth development: the promise of a social justice approach', *Pedagogies for Social Change*, 29(4): 82–95.

Ginwright, S. and James, T. (2002) 'From assets to agents of change: social justice, organizing, and youth development', *New Directions for Youth Development*, 96: 27–46.

NTCA (North of Tyne Combined Authority) (2019) 'Home of ambition: North of Tyne'. Available at: www.northoftyne-ca.gov.uk/wp-content/uploads/2020/09/NorthofTyne_EconomicVision_webfinal.pdf

Prince's Trust, The (2018) *The Prince's Trust Macquarie Youth Index 2018*, London: Prince's Trust. Available at: www.princes-trust.org.uk/about-the-trust/news-views/macquarie-youth-index-2018-annual-report

Reay, D. (2004) 'Educational and cultural capital: the implications of changing trends in education policies', *Cultural Trends*, 13(50): 73–86.

Richmond, T. and Education and Skills (2019) A step Baccward: analysing the impact of the 'English Baccalaureate' performance measure. EDSK. Available at: www.edsk.org/wp-content/uploads/2019/07/A-step-Baccward.pdf

RSC (Royal Shakespeare Company), Tate and University of Nottingham (2018) 'Time to listen'. Available at: https://cdn2.rsc.org.uk/sitefinity/education-pdfs/time-to-listen/time-to-listen.pdf?sfvrsn=45b80921_2

Warwick Commission (2015) *Enriching Britain: Culture, Creativity and Growth*, Coventry: University of Warwick.

# 10

# Are we 'all in this together'? Reflecting on the continuities between austerity and the COVID-19 crisis

*Annette Hastings*

At the time of writing, in April 2020, the phrase 'We're all in this together' has returned to popular discourse. Once deployed with respect to post-'Global Financial Crisis' austerity, the trope has re-emerged with respect to the COVID-19 pandemic in an attempt to convey a sense of common suffering. However, evidence of the uneven social and economic impacts of COVID-19 has been quick to emerge, much as it was in relation to austerity. The *in it together* trope is clearly a fallacy, therefore. However, its re-emergence at this time is a signal that we would be wise to reflect on continuities between the two crises. The aim of the chapter is to begin this process of reflection. Responding to the book's themes, the chapter focuses on how the 2010–20 decade of austerity in the UK and the COVID-19 pandemic highlight common issues in relation to the unevenness of impacts on social groups, public services and civil society.

It is no surprise that the early evidence on who is affected most by the COVID-19 crisis mirrors pre-existing inequalities. The first evidence on death rates showed them to be twice as high in the most deprived places compared to the least deprived places (ONS, 2020) and much of the research on the effects of lockdown points to the vulnerability of those on low incomes, in precarious employment or inadequately housed. Three groups severely affected by austerity and COVID-19 – young people, women and front-line public sector workers – deserve attention.

Young people under 25 were acutely affected by the decade of austerity. Many will have experienced the impacts of budget cuts on children's centres, youth centres, libraries, schools and further education colleges. If they or their households did not directly experience the privations of welfare state retrenchment, they will nonetheless have witnessed growing levels of destitution and will assume that food banks are integral to the social safety net. The 'crisis cohort' that entered the labour market during the 2009 financial crisis have – a decade later – higher unemployment rates, lower pay and damaged career prospects compared to other youth cohorts (Clarke, 2019). The indications are that they have been hit hard by the COVID-19 economic lockdown and are highly vulnerable to its aftermath. Thus, employees under 25 are more than twice as likely as others to work in those sectors of the economy that were shut down, and more likely to report COVID-19-related job loss (Adams-Prassl et al, 2020). Crucially, the experience of the 'crisis cohort' is that labour market transitions during economic downturns are very challenging and that a period of unemployment as a young adult can have a long-term scarring effect on employment and careers.

The impacts on front-line public sector workers have been to the fore in debates about the pandemic, not least because of the numbers dying. Health workers, care workers and bus drivers are on an actual front line. The impacts of austerity on the front-line workforce are, however, less well known. In research on the impacts of austerity on local government, it was found that front-line workers were acting as 'shock absorbers' of austerity – through burgeoning workloads caused by rising needs, staff cutbacks and back-office savings, and through pay reductions and job insecurity (Hastings et al, 2015). As understanding of the effects of the pandemic develops, it will be important to assess how the impacts of the pandemic for these people were amplified by the austerity that preceded it.

Women are the majority of the front-line service workforce, thus ensuring that austerity and COVID-19 have gendered impacts. Austerity cuts to welfare and housing systems impacted heavily on female-headed households (Patrick, 2014); cuts to public services affect women not only because they use them more, but also because they tend to compensate for service gaps with their unpaid labour, especially for child- and eldercare (Gillibrand, 2020). Some of the biggest cuts were to services used more by women, such as children's centres and domestic abuse refuges. Further gendered impacts of COVID-19 include strained domestic abuse services and a doubling of the rate of women killed by men in the first weeks of lockdown (Grierson, 2020). While we do not yet know how the additional caring labour required by lockdown is being shared, gender-disproportionate burdens seem likely. We do know that women's paid work is in those sectors most acutely affected by lockdown (Joyce and Xu, 2020), affecting current earnings, debt levels and future prospects. Analysis of which workers are being laid off and, conversely, those that are being asked to work longer hours shows disproportionate impacts on the female workforce (Khurana and Stronge, 2020). Finally, we also know that three quarters of workers considered to be at 'high risk' in relation to contracting COVID-19 are women, a third of whom are paid below 60 per cent of median wages (Kikuchi and Khurana, 2020). Finally, the rate of confirmed cases of COVID-19 in Wales is around twice as high among working-age women as it is among men (Public Health Wales, 2020), suggesting, perhaps, the dangerous interaction of compromised immunity and high risk for these women.

The COVID-19 crisis has provoked sudden recognition of the need for properly funded, staffed and provisioned public services to sustain life, livelihoods and quality of life, most notably, of the NHS. During austerity, the NHS budget enjoyed 'protected' status but the pandemic has confirmed that this protection was relative rather than absolute and did not reflect rising needs. Local government, particularly in England, endured the most significant level of cuts of any public service (Hastings et al, 2017) but is enjoying its own (re)valorisation: it is now the 'fourth emergency service' and its staff are 'unsung heroes' according to the Local Government Secretary. Most obvious is recognition of the work of social care and of the fact that poorly protected, front-line social care staff are risking their lives for incomes that fail to meet the cost of living. In addition, the pandemic has highlighted the vital work done elsewhere in local government by refuse collectors, bus drivers, cemetery workers, social workers and housing officers, and emergency funding has been allocated to councils to help with additional spending pressures created by the pandemic.

New-found recognition should not, however, be mistaken for the end of austerity. Internationally, there are signs that neoliberal state rollback is already being identified as the means to pay for the costs of the pandemic. The Australian federal government, for example, has announced a public sector wage freeze, arguing that the public servants playing a 'critical part' in managing the pandemic should 'share the economic burden' and that tax cuts will be delivered as planned. In New York, a 'wartime' city budget will cut £2 billion from municipal services, including sanitation and policing, as well as the city's workforce. However, in Spain, city mayors are arguing loudly for the 'opposite' response to austerity to counter this crisis.

In the UK, it is apparent that austerity has rendered local government acutely vulnerable to the shock of COVID-19. This derives not just from budget cuts, but also from increased exposure to risk in relation to business rate income and strategies devised to diversify income, such as investment in commercial property markets (Taylor et al, 2020). Analysis by the Institute for Fiscal Studies of the initial emergency funding allocation to English councils showed that the additional costs of social care left almost no extra resource for other pressured services such as homelessness, domestic abuse, waste collection, environmental health and cemeteries (Phillips, 2020: 5). In mid-April, councils across England were warning of imminent insolvency as a result of increased demand and of collapsed council tax, business rates and other revenue, warnings that led to a second emergency fund considered by council leaders as sufficient to meet costs for 'a month or two'. More significant – in terms of the future treatment of local government by the UK government and in an echo of the international evidence – were reports from council leaders that they are expecting to be required to 'share the burden' (Butler, 2020). There is therefore little to suggest that COVID-19 will provoke a seismic shift from austerity politics in relation to local public services.

Finally, expectations of the role of charities, community groups and volunteers in relation to both crises are strikingly similar: to act as significant mitigators of social and economic impacts, and public service gap-fillers. A striking continuity is the extent to which both austerity and COVID-19 have responsibilised civil society with regard to food aid. While we might celebrate the bottom-up mutual aid movement, the broader expansion of charitable food aid responds to welfare state retrenchment. The burgeoning demand experienced by food banks during the COVID-19 crisis is as attributable to austerity-induced vulnerability as it is to the direct effects of the virus. Furthermore, as food banks have become central to the new normal of austerity, we need to be alert to further responsibilisation of civil society in relation to care work in the post-COVID-19 world.

Community organisations and charities are expected to respond quickly and flexibly to the demands created by the COVID-19 crisis. There are early signs that austerity cuts have impacted on their capacity to respond and that this has accentuated uneven capacity (Poverty Alliance, 2020). Austerity damaged the income streams of the charitable sector, 'hollowing' it out – particularly in more deprived areas, where charity survival rates are also lower (Clifford, 2017). Formal volunteering rates are higher in better-off quintiles and there are key differences in forms of social capital and access to power in different socio-economic contexts. Taken together, the impacts of austerity cuts undermine the capacity of the sector to be strongest where it is needed most at this time of crisis.

Reflecting on the community organisations discussed in this book, what is striking is the likely variation in their capacities to meet pandemic challenges. The story of the Glendale Gateway Trust suggests a socio-economic and organisational context likely to support resilience. Established in 1996, with the time and the professional skill base required to build an asset base and revenue stream, it responded to state retrenchment by filling service gaps. During the pandemic, it might therefore be expected to be able to provide effective local support and be one of its survivors. In contrast, the Byker Community Trust (BCT) was set up in one of the most disadvantaged housing estates of the UK, just as the challenges of austerity began to unfold. It has had to navigate a hostile funding environment from the outset and to attempt to meet its aims at the same time as the estate's population have been rendered more precarious and impoverished. It had become clear prior to the pandemic that substantial additional resources would be required if the BCT was to transform the prospects of the estate. Uncertain before the pandemic, more resources must now be highly improbable.

Thus, the vigour of civil society in response to the early phases of the COVID-19 crisis should not be taken to indicate a healthy resilient sector left undamaged by austerity. A survey of the immediate impacts of the pandemic on community organisations in Scotland in early April 2020 suggested significant challenges in terms of survival, income and meeting needs, which may only be exacerbated as the crisis proceeds (Poverty Alliance, 2020).

To conclude, this chapter has identified some of the ways future research may find that austerity has amplified the effects of the pandemic. It has responded to a potential danger that, over time, the social and economic effects of austerity and the virus will be elided. If this happens, we will lose sight of how austerity undermined the 'immune systems' of some social groups, of public services and of civil society, increasing their susceptibility to the virus and its immediate effects, and amplifying and intensifying its long-term consequences. Austerity was a political choice, whereas the COVID-19 crisis was not. However, decisions about the management, mitigation and aftermath of the virus *are* matters of ideology and politics, that is, of governmental and societal choice. By bringing the effects of austerity to the fore in relation to COVID-19, the intention here is to help counter emerging narratives in which a second wave of austerity is deemed appropriate for dealing with the costs of the COVID-19 crisis. A decade of austerity in the UK did not cause COVID-19, but it did contribute significantly to how it is being experienced, particularly by poorer and more vulnerable groups.

## References

Adams-Prassl, A., Boneva, T., Golin, M. and Rauh, C. (2020) 'Inequality in the impact of the coronavirus shock: new survey evidence for the UK', 1 April. Available at: https://abiadams.com/wp-content/uploads/2020/04/UK_Inequality_Briefing.pdf

Butler, P. (2020) 'English councils set for £1bn bailout as costs of Covid-19 hit them hard', *The Guardian*, 17 April. Available at: www.theguardian.com/society/2020/apr/17/english-councils-set-for-1bn-bailout-coronavirus-ravages-finances

Clarke, S. (2019) 'Growing pains: the impact of leaving education during a recession on earnings and employment', Resolution Foundation, May. Available at: https://mk0nuffieldfounpg9ee.kinstacdn.com/wp-content/uploads/2019/11/Growing-pains-final-report.pdf

Clifford, D. (2017) 'Charitable organisations, the Great Recession and the age of austerity: longitudinal evidence for England and Wales', *Journal of Social Policy*, 46(1): 1–30.

Gillibrand, S. (2020) 'The ideological dangers of austerity – and why women are bearing the brunt of it', blog, 17 February. Available at: https://wbg.org.uk/blog/the-ideological-dangers-of-austerity-and-why-women-are-bearing-the-brunt-of-it/

Grierson, J. (2020) 'Domestic abuse killings "more than double" amid Covid-19 lockdown', *The Guardian*, 15 April. Available at: www.theguardian.com/society/2020/apr/15/domestic-abuse-killings-more-than-double-amid-covid-19-lockdown?CMP=Share_AndroidApp_Gmail

Hastings, A., Bailey, N., Bramley, G., Gannon, M. and Watkins, C. (2015) *The Cost of the Cuts: The Impact on Local Government and Poorer Communities*, York: Joseph Rowntree Foundation. Available at: www.jrf.org.uk/report/cost-cuts-impact-local-government-and-poorer-communities/

Hastings, A., Bailey, N., Bramley, G. and Gannon, M. (2017) 'Austerity urbanism in England: the "regressive redistribution" of local government services and the impact on the poor and marginalised', *Environment and Planning A*, 46(9): 2007–24.

Joyce, R. and Xu, X. (2020) *Sector Shutdowns During the Coronavirus Crisis: Which Workers Are Most Exposed?*, IFS Briefing Note BN278, London: Institute for Fiscal Studies. Available at: www.ifs.org.uk/uploads/BN278-Sector-shutdowns-during-the-coronavirus-crisis.pdf

Khurana, I. and Stronge, W. (2020) 'What can we learn from the recent "Business Impact of Covid-19 Survey" (BICS)?', Autonomy, 13 April. Available at: https://autonomy.work/portfolio/covidfindingsfrombics/

Kikuchi, L. and Khurana, I. (2020) 'The Jobs at Risk Index (JARI)', Autonomy, 24 March. Available at: https://autonomy.work/portfolio/jari/?fbclid=IwAR0npzrfqHZV2JIfuDR6x5o4QubPrONrbkc_v6LEGRoKbM0S3SBwaDE6TR0#1585136754097-c3a84246-300f

ONS (Office for National Statistics) (2020) 'Deaths involving COVID-19 by local area and socioeconomic deprivation: deaths occurring between 1 March and 17 April 2020', ONS Statistical Bulletin, 1 May. Available at: www.ons.gov.uk/peoplepopulationandcommunity/birthsdeathsandmarriages/deaths/bulletins/deathsinvolvingcovid19bylocalareasanddeprivation/latest#local-authorities

Patrick, R. (2014) 'Working on welfare: findings from a qualitative longitudinal study into the lived experiences of welfare reform in the UK', *Journal of Social Policy*, 4(43): 705–25.

Phillips, D. (2020) *How Much Emergency Coronavirus Funding are Different Councils in England Receiving? And is the Funding Allocation Sensible?*, IFS Briefing Note BN282, London: Institute for Fiscal Studies. Available at: www.ifs.org.uk/uploads/BN282-How-much-emergency-coronavirus-funding-are-different-councils-in-England-receiving.pdf

Poverty Alliance (2020) 'Community organisations, activists and the coronavirus: Poverty Alliance briefing', 6 April. Available at: www.povertyalliance.org/wp-content/uploads/2020/04/Community-organisations-and-COVID19-PA-briefing-6-April-2020.pdf

Public Health Wales (2020) 'Rapid Covid-19 surveillance'. Available at: https://public.tableau.com/profile/public.health.wales.health.protection#!/vizhome/RapidCOVID-19virology-Public/Headlinesummary

Taylor, L., Haynes, P. and Darking, M. (2020) 'English local government finance in transition: towards the "marketization of income"', *Public Management Review*. Available at: www.tandfonline.com/doi/abs/10.1080/14719037.2020.1743343?journalCode=rpxm20

# PART II

# The civic university

# 11

# The civic university: introduction

*Liz Todd, Simin Davoudi, Mark Shucksmith and Mel Steer*

The relationship between the city and the university has ebbed and flowed since the early medieval universities became integrated into the cities. In the UK, the 13th-century 'town and gown' adversarial relationships, exemplified in the establishment of the University of Cambridge, are now often replaced by attempts on both sides to create fruitful collaborations (Madanipour and Davoudi, 2017). It has become clear that their fortunes are often tightly entwined, especially in smaller cities with large universities (Benneworth et al, 2010) such as Newcastle. Here, the city's 19th-century industrial origin of shipbuilding, mining, heavy engineering and agriculture provided the foundation for the disciplinary strengths of Newcastle University and its advances in the development of professional training in these fields, as well as newly emerging professional fields such as architecture, planning, teaching and arts. These earlier connections became less tangible and direct from the mid 20th-century for a number of reasons, notably, the globalisation of the higher education sector, the growing neoliberal emphasis on competitiveness in both student recruitment and research funding, and the encroachment of 'new public management' approaches to academic performance and university rankings. International academic publications trumped local civic engagement in the universities' order of priorities. It was not until the last decade or so that the latter began to be foregrounded, partly due to a change in the way universities' research excellence was nationally assessed, giving weight to its non-academic impacts as well as its academic excellence (Davoudi, 2015; Laing et al, 2017).

It is within this historical context that the concept of the civic university was promoted to capture not only a utilitarian ideal of mutually beneficial links between cities and universities, but also an ethical ideal of serving the cities in which universities are located and directly responding to the needs of local communities. Newcastle University was among the pioneers in adopting this approach and, since 2012, has become a torch-bearer of the civic university ideal. The case studies in this part of the book examine the *extent* to which this ideal has been materialised and *how*. To some extent, universities themselves have been cushioned by student fee income from the austerity experienced in other spheres, such as the public sector. It is therefore even more important to ask: what is the role of universities in turbulent and challenging times?

While all chapters in this book are co-written by university researchers and those working for organisations outside the university, the six case-study chapters in this part are written by co-authors who have also worked together on the initiatives described in the chapters. All chapters demonstrate different ways that university research is situated in various civic actions. Sometimes, the research led by the university partner has provided critical reflections on the case study; at other times, the researcher has acted as a facilitator or project manager in ways that might not resemble more traditional forms of research.

The chapter 'Reinventing a civic role for the 21st century' draws parallels between the journey of Newcastle Cathedral (previously known as St Nicholas's Cathedral) in rediscovering its roots through place making and interaction with the community and civic life, and the way that Newcastle University situates itself as a civic university. The chapter is about the cathedral's Common Ground in Sacred Space project to transform the cathedral into a distinct space for worship, civic events and activities. The authors demonstrate that the cathedral has had similar challenges to those experienced by civic universities in needing to integrate core functions. For the university, this is teaching, research and engagement. For the cathedral, this is the use of space for worship, the community and income-earning events. Other challenges for both include funding and that freedom to operate is constrained (in the case of the cathedral, by church structures and the building).

The chapter 'Realising the potential of universities for inclusive, innovation-led development' discusses the City Futures Urban Living Partnership projects, in which university-led consortia were developed to promote innovation in order to deliver inclusive future city growth. This chapter exemplifies the quadruple helix model, linking business, government, the third sector and the community, in bringing about social innovation. A total of 60 projects were developed using a range of participatory engagement approaches, including digital technologies. The authors show the importance of the innovative change agent approach that the project director, Professor Tewdwr-Jones, operated in focusing on impact first (rather than research). He acted as a bridge between different academic fields, industry, charities and the local authority. The chapter shows that there were challenges such as buy-in from the more formal city leadership structures and the time required for people to participate. Even the successful projects took a number of years. Not for the first time, academic time frames and those for other organisations were different and made joint working problematic. Within the university, the projects provided a way to assemble interdisciplinary teams to tackle development projects with community partners in innovative ways. Apart from the small number of projects that gained funding, there was a problem of sustainability. Once the initial pilot funding had been used, it was not possible for the project to continue. The projects contributed much to the future possible shape of the city and involved many people but could not be sustained long enough to deliver on more than a few of the projects.

The chapter 'Future Homes' is one of the City Futures Urban Living Partnership projects introduced in the chapter 'Realising the potential of universities for inclusive, innovation-led development'. The authors describe the journey of the Future Homes Alliance, a community interest company. The chapter explores how unheard voices can be drawn into housing design, how housing can respond to the challenges of ageing and social sustainability, and how learning cycles can be built into the development of housing. Some important points are made about place, in that commitment to place was a key motivating factor for the partners. Newcastle University was the only research body in the partnership, and other partners were Ryder Architecture, Zero Carbon Futures, Sustainable Communities Initiative and the Elders Council. The chapter raises interesting questions about university research since such research could not of itself create transformation; rather, what was important was the interplay between the different forms of knowledge. However, it was suggested that the university had a role in creating a place of trust for stakeholders to articulate ideas and was a catalyst for exchange and innovation.

The chapter 'The good, the bad and the disconcerting' shows how university expertise in learning and education is used to develop change in schools. It argues for the need for 'project-based learning' and 'community curriculum making' as a challenges to the current test-driven school curriculum. Project-based learning has students working in groups on investigative activities with community partners over extended periods of time, leading to realistic products or presentations. The 'Healthy Living' project originated from Newcastle University sports science contacts and involved a number of community partners and other university departments. Students liked working on independent projects and having a taste of university life. They enjoyed the activities and skills that they learnt. Going against the prevailing discourse of schools was not easy and there was a lack of preparation by the schools, suggesting a deficiency in buy-in from schools. The project has potential to enhance university participation and access by proposing a project-based model of learning to schools.

The chapter 'The containment of democratic innovation' reflects on two instances of street activism in the West End of Newcastle: the Fenham Pocket Park and Reclaim the Lanes projects. These projects demonstrate the limits that austerity places on social innovation. University researchers are key actors in the projects, along with community leaders. The Fenham Pocket Park sought to build a park in the back lanes. Reclaim the Lanes used fun, parties and environmental work to start local conversations about the environment. The developments were undermined by the marketisation of the third sector and the concentration of decision-making power in council structures. University research autoethnography was used to enable reflection on the projects. Research compared the projects and helped explore the relationships between them and their communities, environments and institutional partners. The authors show the fragility of community transformation and collaboration in a context of insecurity of funding, even for anchor institutions that have a central role in civic life. The chapter questions the role of the civic university in the community in a context where funding is scarce, and sees limits on the extent that the civic university can collaborate with the community in order to be transformatory.

The chapter 'Citizen power, the university and the North East', in contrast to the chapter 'The good, the bad and the disconcerting', suggests a key transformatory role for the university in its discussion of the achievements of the first four years of Tyne and Wear Citizens, a community-organising alliance. The alliance is not university-led, but the university provided key funding and is involved in a myriad of ways. After four years, many people from varied university roles are engaged in one way or another in Tyne and Wear Citizens, despite the citizens' leadership model not sitting easily alongside university hierarchies and despite the predominance of the neoliberal model of the university. However, engagement with Tyne and Wear Citizens is consistent with the civic university. Multiple opportunities are available for the university to engage with members of the community, put theory into practice and work for social justice in a real-life context. Tyne and Wear Citizens remained active throughout the COVID-19 response and the authors discuss its role in the societal response to the pandemic. They suggest that since there is not time in a crisis to start from the beginning, relationships and leaders that already existed in Tyne and Wear Citizens were central to what they achieved. They argue that given that the impact on the financial security of many civic organisations has been severely challenged by COVID-19, citizens' practices that foster and strengthen the ability of civil society to act through building relational power have never been more necessary.

Paul Benneworth's reflective piece ('So what is a university in any case?') is a critical perspective that usefully acts as a break on some of the hyperbole that can surround claims of the civic university. Certainly, all chapters demonstrate the challenges for universities in engaging with their local communities and organisations. However, they all also show that people from very different organisations have come together. Using different approaches and methods, they demonstrate various models of collaboration. They also reveal the potential for more joined-up thinking between universities and local policymakers and practitioners. Some of the cases are examples of ways in which universities can listen to the needs of communities, as demonstrated by the chapters on the Future Home Alliance and on Tyne and Wear Citizens. This is a much-needed role for universities if they are to engage seriously with their complex and varied set of communities. Projects that give universities the opportunity to really listen are rare and should be nurtured carefully. Other cases show universities trying to take leadership in societal change and acting in a collaborative manner, such as project-based learning in schools (as opposed to a curriculum led by testing) or inclusive further city growth in the City Futures Urban Living Partnership projects. Benneworth is ultimately hopeful that the cases in this book suggest that there are people who can provide the basis for a more civic approach to universities.

### References

Benneworth, P., Charles, D. and Madanipour, A. (2010) 'Building localised interactions between universities and cities through university spatial development', *European Planning Studies*, 18(10): 1611–29.

Davoudi, S. (2015) 'Research impact: should the sky be the limit?', in E. Silva, P. Healey, N. Harris and P. van den Broeck (eds) *The Routledge Handbook of Planning Research Methods*, London: Routledge, pp 405–14.

Laing, K.L., Mazzoli Smith, L. and Todd, L. (2017) 'The impact agenda and critical social research in education: hitting the target but missing the spot?', *Policy Futures in Education*, 16(2): 168–84.

Madanipour, A. and Davoudi, S. (2017) 'Multi-level governance und Stadtentwicklung', IBA LOGbuch No.1, IBA Heidelberg. Available at: https://iba.heidelberg.de/en/publications/essays/iba_logbuch-n1-madanipour-ali-davoudi-simon-multilevel-governance-and-knowledge-based-urbanism

# 12

# Reinventing a civic role for the 21st century: the cathedral and the university

*John Goddard and Lindy Gilliland*

## Introduction

This chapter explores how a long-established institution, St Nicholas's Cathedral (subsequently referred to as Newcastle Cathedral), has set about rediscovering its roots through place making and interaction with the community and civic life. It draws parallels between the journey of the cathedral and the university. The present cathedral was a medieval parish church for a mercantile city until 1882, when the regionally oriented northern part of the diocese separated from the Diocese of Durham, with its strong theological orientation, to become the Cathedral Church of St Nicholas for a new Newcastle Diocese serving the area 'between Tyne and Tweed'. Newcastle University had its origins in a School of Medicine and Surgery established in 1834, and Armstrong College, with a focus on applied sciences relevant to the rapidly industrialising North East of England, established in 1871. Together, they became King's College University of Durham in 1937.

In the early stages, philanthropy and the local state played a key role in the development of both institutions, for example, the corporation funding of the lantern tower on the church to guide ships into the River Tyne and merchants endowing the church to 'buy a place in heaven'. The college was named after the industrialist William Armstrong; it relied heavily on philanthropic endowments. During the late 19th century, alongside other civic bodies with their own premises, such as the Literary and Philosophical Society and Mining Institute, both institutions contributed to a vibrant civil society.

In 1963, King's College separated from the more academically oriented University of Durham to form the independent University of Newcastle upon Tyne. This was facilitated by the provision of land by the city council as part of a major redevelopment of the city centre. However, in the following decades, as higher education (alongside local government) was incorporated into the nation state, the university turned its back on the city. This disconnection became problematic after the turn of the last century, particularly following the 2008 financial crash as public austerity increased pressure on both institutions to plug gaps left by the shrinking local state at the heart of a region facing severe economic decline and social deprivation. In response, Newcastle University developed a role as a 'world-class civic university' seeking to mobilise its global intellectual capital for the benefit of the city and region. Newcastle Cathedral, through its project on making 'Common Ground in Sacred Space', has drawn upon the experience of the university in seeking to re-establish its civic role in the commercial as well as religious life of the city that dates back to the 15th century, with a particular focus on meeting the needs of the most deprived citizens.

This chapter outlines the theological and practical origins of the 'Common Ground in Sacred Space' (CGISS) project, its subsequent development, and a related initiative to meet the needs of homeless people. It then goes on to link this to the academic literature on civic universities, concluding with reflections on how these two types of civic institution might learn from each other. Both now face operating in a very different post-COVID-19 world, though one in which the contribution of both civic institutions to rebuilding local communities economically, socially and spiritually is vitally important.

## Cathedrals as spiritual capitals

Newcastle Cathedral has drawn on an aspirational model for cathedrals as set out in a major investigation into their role in society as 'spiritual capitals' (Theos, 2012). This report identifies a number of functions that cathedrals perform in addition to being places of worship and a tourist destination. They: provide a *venue* for civic, cultural and academic events; engage in social action, especially in response to social justice issues within their communities; offer leadership around interfaith issues, enabling the community to address community tensions and distress; act as a symbol of community identity; and contribute to the local economy and prosperity. Most significantly, the report focuses on the significance of cathedrals in terms of 'social capital', in particular, the much-in-demand 'bridging social capital'. It argues that few institutions manage to combine a clear identity with a public profile that allows them to connect disparate sections of (an often diverse) community but suggests that Cathedrals can be an exception. Almost universally recognised as *Christian institutions*, they can establish and maintain links both with and between 'others' within their communities, and beyond:

> This is part of an authentic Christian duty of hospitality, informed by the theological recognition of humans as irreducibly relational beings. In an age that celebrates – but is often vexed by – both individualism and diversity, and also contends that the public square should be neutral with regard to value and identity, this is clearly a highly significant role for cathedrals ... The challenge is how do cathedrals respond to the tensions, ambiguities and arguments that they are part of in the community? The risk is in being captured by the dilemmas and either taking sides or becoming paralysed. It seems to us that the cathedrals are able to hold the ambiguity of the dilemmas so that new meanings can emerge. (Theos, 2012: 45)

What does this ambiguity mean in terms of the leadership and management of the cathedral? Theos's (2012) report recognises that deans, together with other members of cathedral chapters, are faced with leading and managing a complex, multifaceted organisation with diverse expectations and demands for which they are ill equipped (chapters are responsible for managing cathedrals and are composed of a majority of independent clergy with some lay members). It suggests that it is all too easy for them to become caught up in the business of running a large historic building, a busy place of worship and a tourist destination, and the constant need to find funding, and to lose sight of opportunities to contribute to developing community well-being and supporting the mission of the diocese:

> The present and future of English cathedrals lies particularly in their ability to enable and sustain a range of connections – between the tourist and the pilgrim; between people and the traditions from which modern life cuts them off; between the diverse organisations and communities that share the same social and physical space and infrastructure yet never meet; and between a people who may be less Christian than their parents but are no less spiritual. (Theos, 2012: 61)

These challenges were picked up in a separate Church of England review of cathedrals prompted by recent failures of governance and management within a small number of cathedrals, particularly those undertaking major capital projects (Church of England, 2018). These projects highlighted vulnerabilities and weaknesses across the sector, many of which have a financial basis. The review made a series of recommendations to improve the governance and management of cathedrals 'in order to sustain and enhance the vital role that cathedrals play across the landscape of the Church's mission and public life' (Church of England, 2018: 6). The report notes that:

> Cathedrals 'do God' in ways that resonate uniquely with aspects of contemporary culture but the responsibilities and accountabilities of various cathedral bodies and roles are unclear or ambiguous under the current governance arrangements set out in the Cathedrals Measure ... without more robust financial management, the sustainability of cathedrals is at risk. Given their often-substantial outgoings and obligations, cathedral finances are under considerable pressure, and yet their management is often under-resourced for the tasks they need to undertake ... [In particular,] major buildings projects play a large part in the life of many cathedrals but represent the largest episodic financial risk that cathedrals face. Before embarking on major projects, chapters need to establish effective project governance and management structures and have access to high quality advice. (Church of England, 2018: 6, 7, 8)

## Common Ground in Sacred Space

Such challenges prompted the Newcastle Cathedral Council (an advisory body to the dean and chapter, which included one of the authors as a university representative) to develop a mission for the cathedral as 'common ground in sacred space'. The aim was:

> To bring 900 years of history into the 21st-century by reviving the medieval role of our unique building as a distinct space for worship, civic events and activities. The transformed cathedral will be a dynamic hub for engaging with the community and business as well as a special place of prayer and spiritual discovery. (Newcastle Cathedral, 2018: 1)

The council recognised that realising this vision required significant organisational change and, most particularly, additional financial resources that the cathedral did not have. More specifically, being run by the dean and clergy, and overseen by the chapter, it lacked operational management capacity. While the latter did include a small number of lay members with some business experience, the cathedral was operating at a loss and relying on dwindling investment income. Alongside the chapter, there was a charitable trust responsible for raising endowment funding. Therefore, two key initial steps were the recruitment of an operational manager with experience of running a heritage asset (Newcastle City Castle) and an initial project manager with experience of transforming parish churches. The aim was to prepare a bid to the national Heritage Lottery Fund for resources to take forward the vision in a clearly defined programme of work. A project board with a majority of external lay members was appointed to guide this work. The board was chaired by the Newcastle Cathedral Council member and the co-author of this chapter with experience of Newcastle University's development as a civic university. In preparing the bid, the board undertook a 'strengths, weaknesses, opportunities, threats' (SWOT) analysis of the capacity of the cathedral to fulfil this new mission (see Box 12.1).

---

## Box 12.1 SWOT analysis of the capacity of the cathedral

### Strengths and weaknesses

- The cathedral is located in the centre of Newcastle, with good local and national transport links. However, there is a lack of awareness and knowledge of its importance to the city's heritage. Many people do not know the cathedral. Despite being in easy walking distance from Newcastle Central Station, the medieval quarter of Newcastle is not the main visitor destination.
- A significant part of Newcastle's heritage, with stories connected to development of the city across a wide range of periods of history, can be found in its memorials, including saints connected to the early Christian heritage of the region. However, there is a lack of interpretation and what is available is cluttered because of limited space.
- The proximity of the cathedral (the church) to the castle (the state) and the Bigg Market (commerce) reinforces physical connection to where the story of Newcastle began. However, there is little sense of place in the areas between these sites.
- It is a unique building with awe-inspiring scale, high-quality architecture, detailed craftsmanship, unique acoustics and a calm, peaceful, spiritual interior.

However, apart from services or when the choir is practising, the space lacks dynamism (a wow factor), being dominated by pews.

- The iconic lantern tower provides some of the best views of the city but is not open to the public.
- The cathedral has a committed and passionate (albeit small) team of clergy, staff and volunteers but minimal operational and marketing capacity.

## Opportunities and threats

- There is scope to build on the unique scale, atmosphere and multidimensional heritage (including creative dimension) of the cathedral to encourage engagement and to reposition the cathedral as a modern, dynamic part of the city. However, there is competition for visitor time and money given the range of leisure and heritage venues across the city.
- There is scope to build connections with other historic venues in medieval Newcastle in order to become a 'must-see' part of a heritage visit to this part of the city, and to be a driving partner creating a dynamic and sustainable partnership of heritage venues whose stories link to the cathedral's heritage. However, competition with recent redevelopment of nearby heritage venues, most notably, the castle, could draw visitors away from the cathedral and inhibit collaboration.
- There is scope to increase the prominence of the cathedral's human stories in new permanent and changing interpretations and activity programmes for visitors of all ages and backgrounds linked to monuments, ledger (grave) stones, windows and banners. However, there are limited numbers of volunteers to ensure the sustainability of such programmes and a need to rely on other organisations for delivery.
- There is scope for new multipurpose performance space created by the removal of pews, with the opportunity for revenue generation. However, there is possible conflict with the cathedral's role as a place of sanctuary and refuge, offering a safe, neutral, welcoming space for a diverse range of local people to meet and share ideas.
- There is scope for a redeveloped retail and cafe offer to contribute both financially and in attracting a more diverse audience. However, there has been past failure to make this financially viable and an overall gap between the cathedral's income and expenditure.

Building on the SWOT analysis, and after many iterations, the following aims for a project to transform the cathedral into 'common ground in sacred space' were agreed:

- to open up the nave in order to create a stunning open and flexible space for modern worship and community events amid a historic backdrop;
- to preserve (by relocation within the cathedral), interpret and display the unparalleled collection of historic ledger (grave) stones in order to reveal their stories;
- to provide a radical welcome to an increased number of visitors and communities through an enhanced and empowered volunteer programme, and the creation of new visitor facilities in the Cathedral Hall complex;
- to reveal the history of the cathedral and its role in the city through the centuries via new, engaging interpretation and activities;
- to completely refresh the churchyards in order to create engaging spaces for relaxation, performance and activities;
- to provide a programme of activities and events that will involve all ages in journeys of learning and discovery;
- to stabilise and enhance the cathedral's fabric through the replacement of the current ineffective and obsolete heating system in the nave, and the relaying of the floor in that area;
- to develop partnerships in order to drive up awareness of, and engagement with, the heritage of the city of Newcastle and its wider environs, not least linked to the stories contained within the cathedral itself; and
- to develop a sustainable business plan for the operation of the cathedral based on an organisational step change to focus on resilience and management of risk.

Following funding for a preparatory study, the cathedral was awarded £4.2 million from the Heritage Lottery Fund to deliver a multifaceted transformational project that would create a financially sustainable institution embedded in the life of the city and region. In addition to a major capital programme, the Heritage Lottery Fund provided recurrent funding for:

- the development of new interpretations of the role of the cathedral in the life of the city and region through the ages;
- an activity programme for visitors, especially schools; and
- marketing to attract local and international visitors, as well as major paid-for events, to use the newly configured space.

For its part, the Cathedral Trust raised £1.3 million in matched funding from individual benefactors, trusts and foundations for the capital works.

## Strategic partnerships

Critical to the successful delivery of this ambitious project are partnerships with external organisations. Newcastle City Council, the Business Improvement District (NE1, where the cathedral is situated), the Newcastle and Gateshead Initiative (which promotes the city) and Tyne and Wear Archives and Museums are represented on the delivery board overseeing the CGISS project. Significantly, NE1's successful renewal bid for the next five years identified Newcastle as having the highest percentage of upper-classification listed buildings of any city outside London. NE1's work to date has started to shine a light on Newcastle's heritage. The organisation has committed to 'work with our partners on supporting further investment in the city's historic core (cathedral, castle keep, Black Gate, Lit and Phil Library and Mining Institute) together with a coordinated approach to marketing and promotion of this area of the city' (NE1, 2019). The CGISS board has recognised that Newcastle has a large number of other heritage assets from medieval times onwards that have been undervalued as community resources and visitor attractions. With the support of Heritage Lottery funding, the cathedral has led the way in bringing these actors together in a Newcastle and Gateshead Heritage Forum with 20 members. The forum offers practical support and peer guidance on issues such as marketing, training volunteers and digital presence.

Both Newcastle University and Northumbria University are members of the forum and also work directly with the cathedral. In the case of Newcastle University, the cathedral provides volunteering opportunities for students and has research and teaching links in the fields of archaeology, classics, music and the digital civics team in computer science. Recent discussions between the cathedral and Newcastle University's engagement manager have identified a number of mutually beneficial activities, ranging from 'widening participation' and science, technology, engineering and mathematics (STEM) engagement programmes, to collaboration on social justice engagement programmes and advisory networking.

The cathedral also has a long-standing relationship with Northumbria University, including a six-year-old strategic partnership featuring a 'music consultancy agreement'. The cathedral's assistant director of music acts as part-time director of campus music at Northumbria University during term time to develop extra-curricular music provision. A full-time PhD by practice student in strategic heritage management assists the cathedral in challenging itself when developing its strategy for the management of heritage activities, as well as when plans are being developed to increase the cathedral's capacity to curate exhibitions, stage large events, support school visits and attract the student audience. Both universities work with schools and local communities across the region, and recognise that through the Newcastle Diocese, the cathedral has a regional role, not least through a network of 236 churches in 172 parishes and an education department that provides expertise and advice to all regional church schools.

## Releasing spiritual capital

Another key set of partnerships are with the community and voluntary sector through the 'Lantern Initiative' project, which runs alongside the heritage-focused GCISS. This initiative seeks to engage with homeless and other vulnerable people who visit Newcastle Cathedral, offering them time to talk and a safe space to help meet their practical, emotional and spiritual needs, while linking in with the wider specialist services across the city (for example, the cathedral liaises closely with the charities Crisis, Changing Lives and Street Zero). The project title recognises the fact that cathedral's lantern tower originally housed a beacon to help guide ships up the Tyne to safe haven in Newcastle. The initiative likewise seeks to bring light into darkness, offering welcome rather than rejection, connection instead of isolation and hope in place of despair. It will dovetail with the CGISS focus on heritage visitors in a number of ways:

- Trained welcomers: providing welcome to all at the cathedral irrespective of who they are but with personal qualities and specific training that will equip them to engage in an inclusive, non-judgemental way with vulnerable people who come into the building, for example, homeless, those with mental health problems, those fleeing domestic violence, those with addiction problems and asylum seekers.
- Practical support: helping make life easier for homeless people – a place to sit and rest or get shelter from poor weather, access to toilets, tea/coffee, phone-charging points, and so on.
- Signposting and referral: building relationships with services and identifying link persons to ensure people needing help actually get it.
- Progression: people who have progressed along the road to recovery will be offered opportunities to volunteer in roles around the cathedral, such as gardening and tea/coffee making. Those with

lived experience who have moved on will be offered opportunities as welcomers. The trust placed in them as volunteers and improved self-esteem through volunteering will help them to continue their progress.

- Spiritual nurture: by means of interactive exhibitions, groups, activities and conversations, the initiative will provide spiritual interactive displays/exhibitions about spiritual issues, such as forgiveness and hope. Activity sessions using singing, art, photography, music, food and so on will bring people together. Some of these will target homeless people but some activities will involve other visitors to the cathedral that day, which helps to build connection and reduces the stigma and 'separateness' of homelessness.

- Advocacy and social justice: offering a 'prophetic voice' where it sees discrimination, barriers to services and wider injustices faced by homeless and vulnerable people. The cathedral has a position of power and influence in the city and will raise concerns through the dean to challenge wrongs and injustice.

This initiative recognises that, as Baker (2009) and others point out, spiritual capital is not the sole preserve of citizens attending religious institutions, but also, in terms of its properties as a value system and moral vision, a motivating force for those outside formal religious affiliation in the form of secular spiritual capital. The 'Lantern Initiative' is a key area where faith and non-faith actors are coming together, with the cathedral providing a formal institutional setting where bridging spiritual capital can be built. As Chapman (2012: 28) suggests in a report for the Local Government Association on *Faith and Belief in Partnerships: Effective Collaboration with Local Government*, the cathedral can be a place to 'develop strategies where councils, statutory bodies, VCS [voluntary and community sector] and other faith groups meet each other with a view to building understanding, trust, relationships, information sharing and collaborative working'. Therefore, in Newcastle, the dean chairs the Council of Faiths.

The 'Lantern Initiative' is a clear and distinctive response to one of the key challenges facing the city. It is one of the three pillars of the dean's vision for the cathedral: 'empowering worth'. The other pillars are the core functions of 'inspiring worship' and 'radical welcome' – the focus of the CGISS project. All three pillars are interdependent, for example, the multiple roles of volunteers, music as part of the radical welcome and commercial activities generating the resources needed to underpin support for the dispossessed.

## Cathedrals and universities as anchor institutions

The cathedral's SWOT analysis suggested that it was in the city but not part of it. In the context of the ongoing globalisation of the economy and society – a process in which higher education is an active player – questions are being asked in many circles about the contribution that universities can make to the public good, not least in the places where they are located (Brink, 2018). In his book – in this context, significantly titled *The Soul of a University: Why Excellence Is Not Enough* – Chris Brink (2018) (the former Vice Chancellor of Newcastle University) argues that universities must be based on the twin principles of excellence and purpose: a 'good' university must be good as in *virtuous* as well as being good as in *excellent*. More specifically, this regards not only what a particular university is 'good at' in terms of the quality of its research and teaching (as perversely reflected in national and international league tables and the higher education marketplace), but also what it is 'good for' in terms of its active contribution to the wider society, globally and locally. In a new mission statement for Newcastle University, Brink (2007) notes that:

> The combination of being globally competitive and regionally rooted underpins our vision for the future. We see ourselves not only as doing high quality academic work ... but also choosing to work in areas responsive to large-scale societal needs and demands, particularly those manifested in our own city and region.

This required considerable institutional change in the way that the core functions of teaching and research were organised.

The Newcastle experience has been documented in research that looks into the university from the point of view of the city (Goddard and Valance, 2013) and the internal challenges of combining excellence and purpose (Goddard et al, 2016). This work led to the development of a normative model: a civic university. This, in turn, has influenced the transformation of Newcastle Cathedral through an informal process of knowledge exchange, with the present authors being involved in the life and work of both institutions. Goddard et al (2016) argue that the ideal civic university must:

- have a *sense of purpose*, understanding not just what it is good at, but what it is good for;

- be *actively engaged* with the wider world, as well as with the local community of the place in which it is located;
- take a *holistic approach* to engagement, seeing it as institution-wide activity and not confined to specific individuals or teams;
- have a strong *sense of place*, recognising the extent to which its location helps to form its unique identity as an institution;
- be *willing to invest* in order to have impact beyond the academy;
- be *transparent and accountable* to its stakeholders and the wider public; and
- use *innovative methodologies* such as social media and team building in its engagement activities with the world at large.

Central to this civic role is the idea of the university as an anchor institution – a concept that is equally relevant to the cathedral. Anchor institutions might be characterised as not just in the place, but of the place. The UK think tank The Work Foundation has defined anchor institutions as:

> Large locally embedded institutions, typically non-governmental public sector, cultural or other civic institutions that are of significant importance to the economy and the wider community life of the cities in which they are based. They generate positive externalities and relationships that can support or 'anchor' wider economic activity in the locality. Anchor institutions do not have a democratic mandate and their primary missions do not involve regeneration or local economic development. Nonetheless their scale, local rootedness and community links are such that they can play a key role in local development and economic growth representing the 'sticky capital' around which economic growth strategies can be built. (2010: 3)

This could equally apply to cathedrals.

While a university is a much larger and more complex organisation than a cathedral, working together, the authors have been able to exchange experience around common challenges:

- appropriate leadership and management structures (academic, religious and functional);
- funding and sustaining social action (business models);

- relations with funders/regulators (diocese, church commissioners and central and local government);
- external accountability (the general public, media, business, government and civil society organisations);
- the role of intermediary organisations (voluntary and community sector and business organisations);
- the role of philanthropy (trusts and foundations);
- the role of volunteers (staff and students); and
- transforming and managing spaces (opening out the campus and cathedral to the city).

## Conclusion

Interconnecting the different functions of the cathedral on the completion of the project will not be without its challenges, not least in terms of the delay caused by COVID-19. In terms of leadership and management, there will inevitably be tensions between the use of space for worship, community engagement and income-earning events – the cathedral is not a museum. While funding bids for capital have been successful, most trusts and foundations focus on individual beneficiaries and are reluctant to contribute to the substantial overheads of running a cathedral should the commercial function not deliver enough surplus. Notwithstanding its stake in the cathedral, Newcastle City Council has not had the resources or mandate to provide recurrent funding and could be even more cash-strapped as a result of the COVID-19 crisis (the adjacent castle owned entirely by the city council has operated as an independent trust charging visitors, while the cathedral remains free). To overcome these barriers, the cathedral will have to find ways of enhancing its accountability to external stakeholders and work with a range of other organisations, which have their own performance metrics. At the same time, its freedom to operate is constrained by church legislation enshrined in law and by Church of England bodies that oversee even minor changes to the fabric.

In facing these challenges, a growing 'civic university movement' suggests pathways that cathedrals can learn from. Civic universities are becoming better at integrating their core functions of teaching and research with their engagement with society so that it is no longer an inferior 'third mission'. Work-based learning and volunteering, not least with cathedrals, are examples of this. They are opening out their campuses to the cities so that they are part of the public realm and no longer 'cloistered' spaces (Bender, 1998). As discussed elsewhere in this volume, public accountability is being enhanced by a wide range of community engagement activities in response to rising socio-economic disparities and the popular disenchantment of many people with established institutions like universities.

The civic university movement in the UK reflects a growing resistance to the marketisation of higher education and is reflected in the work of the Civic University Commission, which has been supported by a charitable foundation (UPP, 2019a). In response to one of the commission's key recommendations, 55 university vice chancellors across the country have publicly committed to co-create 'civic university agreements' with other local anchor institutions, guided by the following principles:

- As a place-based institution, we are committed to attaching a high-priority to the economic, social, environmental, and cultural life of our local communities.
- Our civic role will be informed by an evidence-based analysis of the needs of our place, developed collaboratively with local partners and informed by the voice of our local community.
- We will collaborate with other universities and anchor institutions and form partnerships to overcome the challenges facing our local communities.
- With our partners, we will be clear about what we do and how we measure it, so we can say with confidence what we have achieved – and how we might do better in the future. (UPP, 2019b: 8)

Many of these universities are in cities with cathedrals and both could learn from the process of experience sharing documented in this chapter, not least in terms of how to build a better future for their communities after a crisis that has severely hit the most disadvantaged. University scientists and laboratories have contributed to combating the disease and, though closed, churches have continued to provide hope and guidance through virtual means to bigger 'congregations' than when they were open. For both institutions and society at large, it has been not only the worst of times, but also the best of times in terms of community solidarity, a recognition of the importance of the state locally as well as nationally, and a recognition of the community and voluntary sector in coping with the immediate effects of the virus. Going forward, the role of the social sciences and humanities in supporting the civic role of universities as described in this chapter will be more important than ever. While churches have emptied in an increasingly secular world, Charles Taylor, in his treatise on the secular age, has argued that they are still valued in towns and cities, partly because they are spaces that are holders of ancestral memory. They have also provided a source of comfort and orientation in terms of individual rites of passage and in the face of collective disasters like that now being witnessed (Taylor, 2007), and contribute to surrounding places. In this regard, the full reopening of Newcastle Cathedral on completion of the CGISS project will bear witness to its role through the centuries in addressing local and national challenges, building civil society and 'making the place'. It should be a moment of great celebration for the whole city, and one in which the universities and other stakeholders referred to in this chapter will no doubt participate, signalling a renewed spirit of community cohesion that has been engendered by the crisis.

## References

Baker, C. (2009) *The Hybrid Church in the City: Third Space Thinking*, London: SCM Press.

Bender, T. (1998) *The University and the City: From Medieval Origins to the Present*, Oxford: Oxford University Press.

Brink, C. (2007) 'What are universities for?', public Lecture, 27 November, Newcastle University.

Brink, C. (2018) *The Soul of a University: Why Excellence is not Enough*, Bristol: Bristol University Press.

Chapman, R. (2012) *Faith and Belief in Partnerships: Effective Collaboration with Local Government*, London: Local Government Association.

Church of England (2018) *Report of the Cathedrals Working Group*. London: Church of England.

Goddard, J. and Vallance, P. (2013) *The University and the City*, London: Routledge.

Goddard, J., Hazelkorn, E., Kempton, L. and Vallance, P. (2016) *The Civic University: The Policy and Leadership Challenges*, Cheltenham: Edward Elgar.

NE1 (2019) *Business Improvement District Renewal Business Plan*, Newcastle upon Tyne: NE1.

Newcastle Cathedral (2018) *Common Ground in Sacred Space: Second Round Application to the Heritage Lottery Fund*, Newcastle upon Tyne: Newcastle Cathedral.

Taylor, C. (2007) *A Secular Age*, Harvard: Harvard University Press.

Theos (2012) *Spiritual Capital: The Present and Future of English Cathedrals*, London: Grubb Institute.

Universities Partnership Programme (UPP) (2019a) *Truly Civic: Strengthening the Connection between Universities and their Places, Final Report of the Civic University Commission*, London: UPP Foundation.

Universities Partnership Programme (UPP) (2019b) *A Guide to Preparing Civic University Agreements*, London: UPP Foundation.

Work Foundation, The (2010) *Anchoring Growth: The Role of 'Anchor Institutions' in the Regeneration of UK Cities*, London: The Work Foundation Alliance Limited.

# 13

# Realising the potential of universities for inclusive, innovation-led development: the case of the Newcastle City Futures Urban Living Partnership pilot

*Louise Kempton and David Marlow*

## Introduction

Universities are increasingly seen as key actors in their local innovation systems and important catalysts of inclusive growth. This has accelerated since the financial crisis in 2008 and through the subsequent decade of austerity, with significant cuts to public sector budgets hollowing out much of the UK's regional level of institutional capacity and resources. At the same time, universities are seen to have gotten off lightly. Indeed, many have emerged in an even stronger position financially following the increase in the tuition fee cap to £9,000 in 2012. Meanwhile, the disparities in economic performance between London/the Greater South East and the rest of the country have continued to grow, and many analysts expect the effects of COVID-19 to impact more negatively on people and places that have historically been less resilient to economic shocks. The Brexit vote in 2016 has been cited as an illustration of the disconnect between many universities (which, as a sector, strongly argued for remain) and the leave-voting communities in which they are located or adjacent to. It is therefore unsurprising that the government has tried to pull a range of policy and funding levers in recent years in an attempt to encourage universities, not least those that are considered to be nationally and globally 'excellent', to play a more proactive role in contributing to the economic and social development of the places in which they are located.

One of these programme levers was the Urban Living Partnership pilot funded by UK Research and Innovation,[1] which aimed to 'harness

UK research and innovation strength to help cities realise a vision of healthy, prosperous and sustainable living' (Future Urban Living, 2021). The Urban Living Partnership pilot programmes provided a vehicle for preliminary investigation into how university-led consortia can promote innovation that progresses the challenges of delivering inclusive 'future city' growth. In 2016, Birmingham, Bristol, Leeds, Newcastle-Gateshead and York were selected as the five pilots, led by these cities' Russell Group[2] universities.

The Newcastle-Gateshead pilot was Newcastle City Futures (NCF), originally initiated by Newcastle University in 2014 to create shared opportunities to shape the future of places through research, engagement and innovation. The NCF Urban Living Partnership pilot was initially funded for 18 months (from August 2016 to January 2018), with a further extension of six months to July 2018.

From the outset, NCF adopted a 'quadruple helix' and 'disruptive innovation' approach by creating and facilitating spaces for partners in the quadruple helix sectors (that is, the public, private, voluntary/community/social enterprise and academic sectors) to engage without the usual expectations for time-bound, specific and measurable outputs. It took a challenge-based approach to identifying potential collaborations and utilised a range of innovative methods to engage with partners and the public at large.

While NCF had its ups and downs, and successes and failures, it has become a transformational, learning-by-doing initiative with valuable insights for other universities and their partners in place-based innovation. An independent review has analysed and synthesised this learning into some key insights that we believe have resonance for other places in the UK and internationally in defining the role of their universities in challenging and turbulent times. Our experience suggests that places seeking transformational change require inclusive and diverse local leadership teams that cut across and beyond traditional institutional boundaries.

## Universities as civic actors for inclusive growth: the theoretical and policy context

Public funding for teaching and research activities is under scrutiny, putting universities under increasing pressure to demonstrate their non-academic impact and societal value. Local communities and taxpayers facing tough economic conditions might question the value of universities, especially in economies where the direct benefits are less apparent (for example, low levels of local recruitment, graduate retention and so on). The national and international political and policy environment over recent years has placed increasing expectations on universities to be proactively engaged in supporting their local areas (Cochrane and Williams, 2013) beyond the passive direct and indirect effects of their presence (Power and Malmberg, 2008). This trend can be expected to accelerate as local authorities, businesses and communities grapple with the impacts and aftermath of the COVID-19 crisis. Over the past decade, successive UK national and sub-national policymakers, through a range of initiatives – from government reviews to independent inquiries (for example, the Civic University Commission[3]) – have contended that places should make better use of the assets and capabilities of their local universities. This can be further evidenced through the recent emergence of a range of funding levers in which universities are increasingly expected to be at the vanguard of driving inclusive growth and development in the places in which they are located. The current development of civic university agreements[4] between many UK universities and their local places is the latest manifestation of these trends, and this has taken on a new urgency as universities consider how these (and other) local agreements can provide a platform to coordinate local responses to the COVID-19 crisis in their economies and communities.

Goddard describes the civic university as:

> one which provides opportunities for the society of which it forms part. It engages as a whole with its surroundings, not piecemeal; it partners with other universities and colleges; and is managed in a way that ensures it participates fully in the region of which it forms part. While it operates on a global scale, it realises that its location helps to form its identity and provide opportunities for it to grow and help others, including individual learners, business and public institutions, to do so too. (2009: 5)

These concerns with society more broadly, the importance placed on a connection with place and the need for an institutional (and institution-wide approach) to engagement provided a new perspective that built on the more general concept of the 'engaged' university (Watson et al, 2011). It also offered a counterpoint to the entrepreneurial university model (Clark, 1998) that became the prevailing model for higher education management policy during the early 2000s, which focuses on universities' links with industry through technology transfer and commercialisation of intellectual property.

The civic university perspective argues for engagement with a much wider range of organisations and sectors, using mechanisms that mobilise people and units across the institution for reciprocal, mutual benefit. The vision set out by Goddard (2009: 4) calls for 'an institution-wide commitment … [that] has to embrace teaching as well as research, students as well as academics, and the full range of support services'. This can be seen as a challenge to the discourse on a 'third mission' (Gunasekara, 2006), where activities involving links with external, non-academic partners are seen as separate and distinct from (and, by definition, less valued than) the 'core' mission of teaching and research, to be delivered by specialist (usually non-academic) staff or units rather than embedded across all areas of institutional operations (Goddard and Vallance, 2013).

The implicit assumption behind civic university participation in place-based programmes is that as part of local leadership teams, they can assist in the assessment of interventions and in designing and even delivering their roll-out. However, expert scepticism, and a sense that powerful metropolitan elites represented by large anchor institutions act in their own, rather than wider societal, interests, has increased during the austerity decade. In this world view, the university's membership of the local leadership team and its own institutional requirements will often trump wider interest in local well-being and redressing disadvantage. Evidence suggests the track record of universities as critical anchors is highly inconsistent, ranging from instrumental engagement (that is, only willing to get involved to satisfy their own self-interest) to indifferent place-blindness (for example, working with the best partners to further their agenda, regardless of where they are located). Even where a university does strive to demonstrate a genuine willingness to contribute to the development of its place, in reality, this is often confined to a portfolio of individual interventions rather than a coherent place-based agenda co-designed and agreed with diverse, inclusive place-leadership teams. NCF is one approach to these issues, and is discussed by Vallance et al (2019) in terms of the specific project and as part of future urban leadership and governance. The rest of this chapter will present the origins and evolution of NCF, the findings from the review, and the lessons learned that can be applied in other places seeking to maximise the contribution of their universities to inclusive, innovation-led development.

## NCF: background and approach

The origins of NCF can be traced back to the appointment of Mark Tewdwr-Jones as Professor of Town Planning at Newcastle University in 2012. Professor Tewdwr-Jones already had an established interest and reputation in working with innovative forms of stakeholder engagement and using futures research[5] methods for foresight and planning. The then Vice Chancellor, Professor Chris Brink, who championed the (re)positioning of Newcastle as a civic university, tasked Tewdwr-Jones soon after his arrival to look at ways to try and join up the range of activities happening across the institution that were relevant for the city. In 2013, a delegation of civil servants from the UK Government Office of Science (GOS) visited Newcastle to discuss the possibility of a foresight project focused on future cities. This provided the impetus to bring together a range of academics and other city stakeholders to discuss the future of Newcastle. The following year, with support from the Vice Chancellor's Strategic Fund and the Newcastle Institute for Social Renewal (NISR), Tewdwr-Jones led a three-week-long public exhibition and series of events to engage citizens and local actors in a conversation about the long-term future of the city, which was titled Newcastle City Futures. At the same time, a GOS grant funded a piece of foresight research to develop a set of potential scenarios for the city over the coming 50 years, the output from which was the *Newcastle City Futures 2065* report (Tewdwr-Jones et al, 2015).

The success of the exhibition and the publication of the *Newcastle City Futures 2065* report created an appetite in the city council (led by the then deputy chief executive and supported by the leader) and the university (led by the vice chancellor and NISR) to continue the conversation. In 2015, at the behest of Newcastle City Council, the City Futures Development Group (CFDG) was established to look at the longer-term future of the city, with representation from the city council, local enterprise partnership, Northumbria University, Newcastle University and other interested parties. Tewdwr-Jones was appointed as chair of the CFDG and given the title of Director of NCF. The evolution of this collaboration around the future of the city, driven by Professor Tewdwr-Jones's particular interests in foresight and engagement, and supported by the university, city council and wider city partnership, meant that Newcastle was ideally positioned to respond to a call for proposals for funding for Urban Living Partnership pilots when it was opened by the UK research funding council in September 2015. Indeed, it was a testament to the initiatives and investments that had happened over the preceding two years that the NCF proposal was not only one of just five awarded nationally, but also ranked first out of the 44 proposals submitted.

NCF sought to establish ways in which universities can help citizens and businesses in cities and regions to 'diagnose the complex and interdependent challenges' to thinking about change and imagining the future.[6] The focus of NCF was the development of a shared long-term vision for Newcastle and Gateshead[7] as an age-friendly, sustainable urban area. Working together with local authorities and other public sector actors (for example, the NHS), businesses, communities, and universities, NCF developed new projects (more than 60 in total, some examples of which are shown in the following figures) across the city using participatory engagement, digital technologies and photography.[8]

Some of the more citizen-focused projects identified by partner organisations and facilitated by NCF included Metro Futures and Transforming Northumberland Street. The former sought to encourage residents and businesses to get involved in designing the next fleet of Metro trains in order to develop inclusive mobility. The latter is about creating opportunities to 'redesign and green' the high street in Newcastle city centre, using digital retailing that links customers to businesses. Other initiatives focused on intergenerational work and included creating digitally enabled sustainable homes for an ageing society (Future Homes, discussed by Gilroy et al in this volume) or encouraging children to design their own future city (The Big Draw). An overview of these projects can be found in Box 13.1.

---

**Box 13.1 Newcastle City Futures project examples**

**Metro Futures: digital train design for an inclusive society**

Tyne and Wear Metro is one of the UK's busiest light-rail systems, carrying 40 million passengers a year across the five local authorities that constitute Tyne and Wear – the cities of Newcastle and Sunderland, and the metropolitan boroughs of Gateshead, North Tyneside and South Tyneside. However, after nearly 40 years of service, its train fleet needed to be replaced. As the new fleet will be around for decades to come, Nexus wanted to ensure its design reflected the aspirations and needs of people across the community and throughout their lives. Nexus partnered with Open Lab – a leading research group in human–computer interaction and ubiquitous computing based at Newcastle University – and NCF to work with people across Tyne and Wear to understand their needs and develop proposals for future Metrocars through pop-up labs and an interactive website.

These insights were used to inform the designs for new trains that were developed with suppliers in 2018/19. This helped inform a successful £337 million bid to the Department for Transport to upgrade the Metro's rolling stock. There were more than 24,000 visits to a website set up for the project and over 3,000 ideas were submitted by the travelling public.

### Future High Street: transforming the Northumberland street area

NCF worked with Newcastle City Council to engage with other partners around plans for the redevelopment of the main shopping street and surrounding area in Central Newcastle. The focus of this collaboration was to create opportunities to redesign the high street using the creative arts, digital retailing linking customers to businesses and blue-green infrastructure to enhance the place and shopping experience for citizens. The Northumberland Street Advisory Group was established by Newcastle City Council in 2016. With strong support from the local partnership a £3 million+ master plan was approved by the council cabinet in November 2017.

### The Big Draw: engaging young people in city futures

One weekend in October 2016, NCF took over Seven Stories, the National Centre for Children's Books, based in Newcastle's Ouseburn Valley for a weekend of Big Draw Festival activities, which encouraged children and families to design and build their future city. More than 540 people visited Seven Stories and built homes, cultural, sports and science venues, businesses, hotels, transport systems, power stations, and several bridges. In fact, the children organically created pretty much everything you would need in a future city. The event formed part of the 2016 Big Draw Festival, which aimed to inspire illustrators everywhere to explore creative innovation, enterprise, digital technologies and the arts through drawing. It also led to the development of Jigsaudio, a new engagement tool in the form of a digital jigsaw that allows children to learn and interact with the future city by recording their views in a fun and interactive way, and the spin-out of Little Inventors, a charity to support innovation and creativity among schoolchildren.

The operating model of NCF was to work as a 'quadruple helix', linking together government, businesses, communities and the academy to generate test-bed demonstrator projects. It aimed to deliver four objectives (simultaneously if possible): excellent research; business growth; public expenditure savings; and citizen engagement. NCF aimed to link existing university initiatives and funded research projects to new audiences and opportunities in a 'hub and spoke' approach, drawing together academic research projects focused on the region with user groups from policy, businesses and communities. New project initiatives were identified by partner organisations, working together but facilitated by NCF. Projects were required to entail multi-sector, multi-partner involvement, and to use digital, visualisation and/or engagement methods. Projects that were supported for further development were presented to the CFDG, a special-purpose Newcastle City Council committee, for comment and endorsement.

One of the most important features of the pilot has been the continuous development of the innovative engagement model, led by the particular interests and expertise that Professor Tewdwr-Jones brought to the project. NCF saw itself as a neutral broker, or a bridge between different academic fields and industry sectors, and policy and organisations. Operating 'at arm's length' from both the university and city council, it sought to turn the traditional research process on its head by finding potential areas of impact first and then developing activities to influence policies that result in empirical data and further research.[9] While this allowed a greater methodological flexibility, it also enabled the researchers to bridge some of the cracks between disciplines and subjects by using a quadruple helix approach. Using a wide range of methodologies and systems analysis to visualise scenarios, combined with expertise in computing, mapping, spatial analysis and urban planning, this approach allowed for a stronger understanding of the interdependent challenges confronting the city and the region.

## The NCF review and key findings

As NCF's Urban Living Partnership pilot programme phase drew towards its end in the summer of 2018, a review was undertaken in which the NCF approach was tested as a type of civic university contribution within emerging approaches to place-based strategies. To this end, a policy development exercise to consider the roles and impact of universities in place-shaping, city leadership and inclusive growth was commissioned. A new framework (see Figure 13.1) was deployed against which NCF was assessed.

Analysis using this framework suggests that large anchor institutions (like Newcastle University) overwhelmingly tend to structure their civic activity towards the bottom right-hand quadrant of the matrix. However, in places with major socio-economic challenges and pressures for transformational change, there is a need for universities to act much

**Figure 13.1:** The Newcastle City Futures review framework

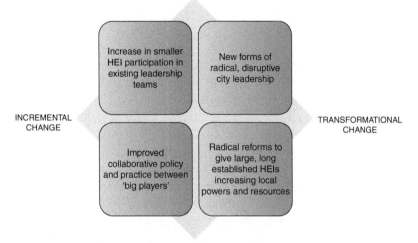

UNIVERSITY ACTS AS A 'LOOSENER'

INCREMENTAL CHANGE

Increase in smaller HEI participation in existing leadership teams

New forms of radical, disruptive city leadership

TRANSFORMATIONAL CHANGE

Improved collaborative policy and practice between 'big players'

Radical reforms to give large, long established HEIs increasing local powers and resources

UNIVERSITY ACTS AS AN ANCHOR

Source: Authors' own for Marlow et al (2019: 21)

Note: HEI = higher education institution.

more as a disruptive challenger to local incumbent elites and their traditional ways of doing things.

The assessment sought to establish how far NCF (as an initiative within a large anchor) could play and had played 'challenger'/'catalyst' roles in promoting and championing new approaches to place-shaping and city leadership. The process included a literature review, desk research on NCF and Urban Living Partnership documentation, a survey of role players, and some comparative analysis of NCF with experiences in the Birmingham, Bristol, Leeds and York Urban Living Partnerships. In addition, interviews were conducted with key individuals from organisations across the quadruple helix partnership, which explored: the motivation for, roles of and impact of NCF; what worked well and less well; strategic and operational learning from the NCF experience; key relationships; and direct and more subtle influences on city leadership and management.

The overall question that the review sought to answer was to what extent NCF (and the Urban Living Partnership pilots more generally) provided a viable, replicable model for large civic university anchors to transcend their position as members of the local incumbent elite and promote radical, disruptive change at scale should this be required. The review found that NCF was seen as playing a range of roles and functions in place-shaping and (inclusive) city leadership. While these can be seen as distinctive, they are related and potentially complementary and synergistic. They can be broadly summarised as follows:

- Providing a neutral space for 'visioning' and discussing 'difficult issues': many NCF participants – even the local authority officers – recognised gaps in formal leadership structures and processes. NCF was seen to play a role in filling these in a relatively unthreatening way. To some extent, the CFDG was a forum for deliberative exchanges on 'wicked issues' faced by the city and its surroundings. However, there was scepticism of the actual traction the group had with more formal city leadership structures and processes.
- A way for generating and incubating novel ideas and partnerships: NCF acted as an 'ideas factory', with small amounts of pump-priming expertise and sometimes resourcing for experimental and pilot projects. NCF generated and incubated literally hundreds of ideas and grew from an initial partnership of 22 to more than 180 partners at its peak (for a breakdown by sector, see Figure 13.2). The challenge came in scaling up.
- An 'accelerator' for demonstrating ideas: a small number of the ideas sought major resources to be scaled up. Some made progress, for instance, Newcastle Future Homes (see the chapter 'Future

**Figure 13.2:** Newcastle City Futures partners by sector

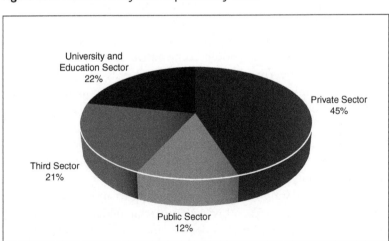

Source: Authors' own for Newcastle City Futures (2018)

Homes'), which has realised its early ambition to be an estate-level regeneration demonstrator. However, even the success stories took several years to incubate and evolve.

- A quadruple helix project/programme and potentially policy developer: the use of co-design and co-production tools and techniques was a methodological approach integral to NCF (and all its Urban Living Partnership partners). It is also one where universities potentially have capabilities that are relatively scarce in mainstream public and private decision-makers and investors. As the centre of expertise and referral gateway to this expertise, NCF played a distinctive role.
- A university facility for promoting pan-university interdisciplinary collaboration and getting local involvement in academic work: NCF was seen within the university as a convenient way of assembling interdisciplinary and particularly inter-faculty/school teams to tackle research and development projects, and city or community challenges, in holistic and innovative ways. Correspondingly, it was welcomed by non-traditional collaborators with the university as a highly accessible, easy way to mobilise bespoke university support for their needs.

As well as identifying a range of roles and functions played by NCF during the life of the project, the review also highlighted a number of challenges faced by NCF in realising its goal of contributing to inclusive, placed-based leadership. First, the transactional costs of participation were considered very high, especially for smaller companies and organisations in the voluntary, community and social enterprise sector (and even, at times, for the austerity-struck local authorities). This is a chronic issue for many such interventions led by or including large anchor institutions. Second, as NCF evolved over time, it became increasingly difficult for latecomers to understand the NCF story, its relationships and how they could leverage them most effectively. A more explicit induction process might have helped. Third, some participants considered the co-identification/design tool of choice (the 'mash-up') to not be their preferred operating style. A portfolio of approaches might have worked better. Fourth, there was a mismatch between academic and business/local authority time frames, with academics much more comfortable with longer-term interventions where the outcomes might remain unclear for some time compared to the more immediate and urgent priorities of other stakeholders. Finally, NCF struggled internally with the lack of university incentives and even systems for pan-school, interdisciplinary working that takes engagement and impact as a starting point (rather than an outcome) for academic research.

There were also a number of institutional and external factors beyond the project that impacted on NCF's ability to design and secure a longer-term legacy. The lapsing of the national funding, combined with uncertainty of future university commitment to the model, inevitably led to a waning of influence and dynamism. It is increasingly clear that it is unrealistic to expect short-term, low-cost pilots to develop and deliver solutions to the challenges of university contributions to inclusive future urban living. Long-term commitment and resourcing from university, place and government is important. At the same time, there is a definite renewed and heightened interest in civic university models and practice. This culminated in the February 2019 Civic University Commission's (2019) report *Truly Civic: Strengthening the Connection between Universities and Their Places*. This proposed, among other things, a new generation of civic university agreements to capture this relationship and its shared agendas. Newcastle University was in the first tranche of institutions that signalled a commitment to a civic university agreement. Therefore, the relevance of lessons from NCF is current and important.

## Learning: conceptual frameworks that can be applied in other places

In its first two phases, NCF was a relatively short-life institutional arrangement: first, for the *Newcastle City Futures 2065* visioning and scenario-planning exercise; and then as the host for an Urban Living Partnership pilot programme. The review sought to understand how successful NCF has been as a challenger for disruptive change in the city's leadership and management, and how far it has catalysed new behaviours within the university, with other anchors and with 'loosener' participants in planning and managing change.

It makes sense, therefore, to return to the framework for the preliminary learning from the assessment in considering the roles NCF played (and some of the challenges faced) within each of the four quadrants (see Figure 13.3). As can be seen, for such a (relatively) low-cost, short-life pilot, NCF's impact is impressive, with specific deliverables in each of the quadrants of the framework. However, what undoes all these potential benefits is precisely the short-life character of the initiative, and the lack of commitment to a legacy and learning programme within the university, the city and the government/UK Research and Innovation.

**Figure 13.3:** Findings from the Newcastle City Futures review

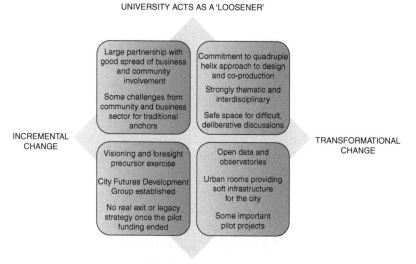

UNIVERSITY ACTS AS A 'LOOSENER'

INCREMENTAL CHANGE

Large partnership with good spread of business and community involvement

Some challenges from community and business sector for traditional anchors

Commitment to quadruple helix approach to design and co-production

Strongly thematic and interdisciplinary

Safe space for difficult, deliberative discussions

TRANSFORMATIONAL CHANGE

Visioning and foresight precursor exercise

City Futures Development Group established

No real exit or legacy strategy once the pilot funding ended

Open data and observatories

Urban rooms providing soft infrastructure for the city

Some important pilot projects

UNIVERSITY ACTS AS AN ANCHOR

Source: Authors' own analysis, after Marlow et al (2019)

If large anchors wish to be genuinely civic in their values and impact, they need to encourage and embrace the small, flexible disrupters that can challenge and catalyse radical change. NCF has had some success in this regard but it needed long-term commitment and resourcing if it was to be more than a flash in the pan. All large anchors can establish equivalent arm's-length change catalysts to NCF, and/or welcome small specialist universities and other valuable third sector challengers to the leadership top table.

The comparative analysis with the other four Urban Living Partnership pilots has identified a set of approaches and design principles that may be applicable, relevant and scalable in many places across the UK and beyond. There is a sensible menu of roles, responsibilities and activities that future NCF-type entities can assume for a city or other economic geography. This is illustrated later in the Urban Living Framework and, the authors argue, is a precondition for enduring sustainable inclusive future growth in any ambitious place.

Defining civic-ness has to increasingly be determined by the place – rather than the university itself. Part of the NCF-type entity's 'neutral space' role might well be to enable that discussion to take place between all relevant partners, for example, in determining what a local civic university agreement might comprise. If the NCF experience within the Urban Living Partnership pilot has national or international relevance, it is to demonstrate how important it is that governments and their research and innovation arms recognise the benefits of national endorsement for new radical models of university civic-ness. This requires a further, extended and better-resourced programme across a much wider variety of geography, governance regimes and university configurations to test and develop these propositions.

## Conclusion

The UK has enduringly extreme and growing place-based disparities in performance and outcomes within a highly centralised system of political leadership. Place-blind strategies are likely to exacerbate the problems they are trying to address. Universities are critical anchors in the places in which they are located, both directly as employers and purchasers of goods and services, and indirectly through the impacts of their research, teaching and public engagement. This is even more acutely felt in institutionally 'thin' places, which tend to be most economically fragile and dependent on universities beyond mere generators of knowledge and graduates.

The NCF experience illustrates fundamental limitations to policy assumptions that universities' place-based contributions to inclusive, innovation-led development are inevitable consequences of increasing university civic engagement. Improvements in traditional large anchor university collaboration locally may contribute to innovation-led development of some scale. However, the typical outcomes of these improvements will most likely overwhelmingly benefit incumbent local elites – whether public or business sector. There is no guarantee that these benefits will be shared inclusively – let alone prioritise marginalised and 'left-behind' communities and places.

The key recommendation of the Civic University Commission (2019) was that universities should develop civic university agreements with the places in which they are located. While this is a welcome development in encouraging universities to contribute more explicitly to the leadership of place, our research suggests that the implied civic university question – 'What can the university do for its place?' – should be turned on its head. Instead, the question is: 'What do places need from their universities?'

Where places are facing existential challenges requiring disruptive transformation, universities are well placed to catalyse policy responses. For the large anchor university, there is a menu of roles, responsibilities and activities that they need to assume in order to make a genuine and significant contribution to their place (as illustrated in the Urban

**Figure 13.4:** The Urban Living Framework – role for universities in supporting inclusive leadership in place

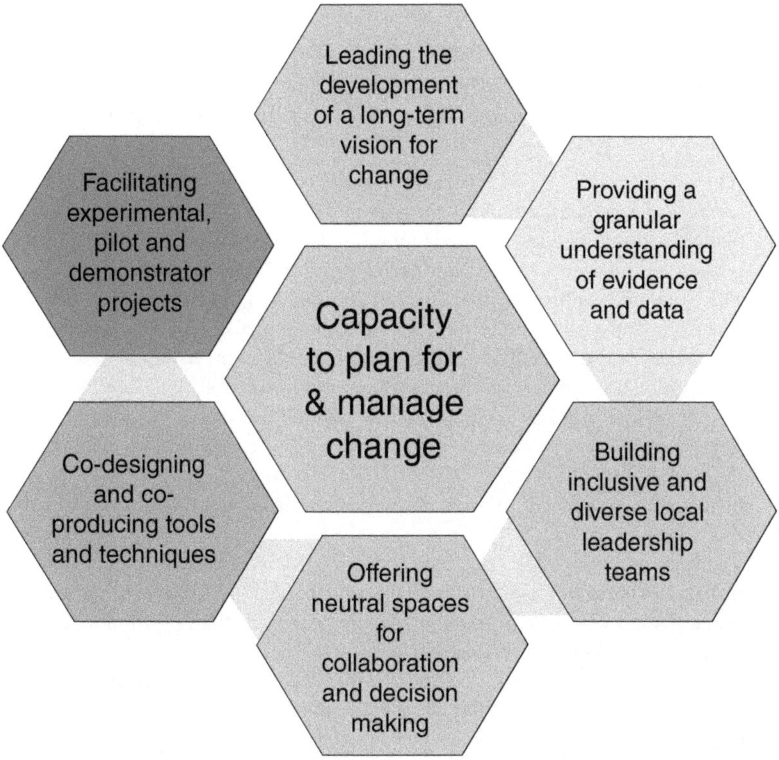

Source: Authors' own for Marlow et al (2019: 19)

Living Framework) (see Figure 13.4); indeed, the authors would argue that this is a precondition for enduring, sustainable and inclusive future growth. However, this needs to encourage and support a suite of arm's-length challenger arrangements, smaller specialist universities and community-based anchors that can interrogate and test the approaches of incumbent anchors and trial new intervention strategies.

NCF did attempt to do this – with relatively impressive, albeit short-term, results. Consequently, one of the findings of the review was to propose a much better-resourced and longer-term successor to the pilot, which recognises that realising the potential is both complex and a long-haul undertaking. What is certain from the NCF case, however, is that recognising and managing this complexity is a more honest and, most likely, a more effective strategy than those offered by civic university quick fixes, a lesson that is especially pertinent as regional economies seek to recover and rebuild after COVID-19.

This exploration of universities' role in place-based leadership through the NCF lens suggests that places seeking transformational change require inclusive and diverse local leadership teams that cut across and beyond traditional institutional boundaries. Defining the role and contribution of public institutions in local leadership must be determined by the place rather than the institutions themselves.

## Notes

[1] UK Research and Innovation is a quasi-autonomous non-governmental organisation of the UK that directs research and innovation funding, funded through the science budget of the Department for Business, Energy and Industrial Strategy.

[2] The Universities of Birmingham, Bristol, Leeds and York, and Newcastle University.

[3] The Civic University Commission was established in 2018 to gather evidence and report on the nature of civic engagement in the UK's universities.

[4] Civic university agreements are agreements developed collaboratively with local partners that set out how universities will help support their local communities.

[5] The aim of futures research is to help inform perceptions, alternatives and choices about the future.

[6] Newcastle City Futures, 'About us'. Available at: www.newcastlecityfutures.org/about-us

[7] The geography for NCF covers the Functional Urban Region of Tyneside, an area that extends beyond the administrative boundaries of the city council and encompasses Newcastle, Gateshead, North Tyneside, South Tyneside and the southern part of Northumberland.

[8] See 'Shaping innovation for city futures'. Available at: www.newcastlecityfutures.org/wp-content/uploads/2017/01/ncf_brochure_web.pdf

[9] Louise Kempton, presentation at the 'Urban development and change in the age of austerity' roundtable at the 'Co-creating Cities and Communities' event, 12–13 July 2017, Bristol.

## References

Civic University Commission (2019) *Truly Civic: Strengthening the Connection Between Universities and their Places. Final Report*, London: UPP Foundation.

Clark, B. (1998) *Creating Entrepreneurial Universities: Organizational Pathways of Transformation*, New York: Pergamon.

Cochrane, A. and Williams, R. (2013) 'Putting higher education in its place: the socio-political geographies of English universities', *Policy and Politics*, 41(1): 43–58.

Future Urban Living (2021) 'The urban living partnership'. Available at: https://urbanliving.ukri.org/

Goddard, J. (2009) *Reinventing the Civic University*, London: NESTA.

Goddard, J. and Vallance, P. (2013) *The University and the City*, London: Routledge.

Gunasekara, C. (2006) 'The generative and developmental roles of universities in regional innovation systems', *Science and Public Policy*, 33(2): 137–50.

Marlow, D., Kempton, L. and Tewdwr-Jones, M. (2019) *Inclusive Future Growth in England's Cities and Regions: Realising the Transformational University Dividend*, Newcastle upon Tyne: Newcastle City Futures.

Newcastle City Futures (2018) *Final Report of the Newcastle City Futures Urban Living Partnership Pilot*, Newcastle upon Tyne: Newcastle City Futures.

Power, D. and Malmberg, A. (2008) 'The contribution of universities to innovation and economic development: in what sense a regional problem?', *Cambridge Journal of Regions, Economy and Society*, 1: 233–45.

Tewdwr-Jones, M., Goddard, J. and Cowie, P. (2015) *Newcastle City Futures 2065: Anchoring Universities in Urban Regions through City Foresight*, Newcastle upon Tyne: Newcastle Institute for Social Renewal.

Vallance, P., Tewdwr-Jones, M. and Kempton, L. (2019) 'Facilitating spaces for place-based leadership in centralized governance systems: the case of Newcastle City Futures', *Regional Studies*, 53(12): 1723–33.

Watson, D., Hollister, R.M., Stroud, S. and Babcock, E. (2011) *The Engaged University: International Perspectives on Civic Engagement*, Abingdon: Routledge.

# 14

# Future Homes: developing new responses through new organisations

*Rose Gilroy, Dominic Aitken and Philip Miller*

## Introduction

This chapter explores the journey of the Future Homes Alliance (FHA), a community interest company in Newcastle, built from a cross-sectoral partnership of university, local authority, industry and third sector groups that developed innovative housing models to respond to social renewal and social justice. From a conversation in 2016, there is now a development proposal that has been submitted to Newcastle City Council for planning approval. The chapter explores three issues:

- How can we draw more unheard voices into housing design?
- How should housing respond to the challenges of ageing and social sustainability?
- How do we build continuous learning loops that allow for organisational growth and project replication?

It concludes by considering what deeper lessons can be drawn from the FHA that can be more widely applied.

## The housing policy context

Although the UK discourse is dominated by tenure, in the context of an ageing population, what is most important is the quality of the home and design that is 'future-proofed' to meet individual life changes (Habinteg, 2019). Design specifications with greater inclusivity have been established in a variety of developed countries (Habinteg, 2016; CMHC, 2017; Lifemark, 2019; Livable Housing Australia, 2019). These homes are often aimed at people across the life course but designed to be inclusive of people with disabilities and 'future-proofed' for easier adaptation as the needs of occupants change. Adaptability is highly correlated with space standards but these have fallen in the UK as central government has shifted the emphasis from mandatory to discretionary standards. The 1961 report of the UK Ministry of Housing and Local Government (1961), *Homes for Today and Tomorrow* (known as the Parker Morris Report), reflected a high point in thinking, with additional floor space given the highest priority as a long-term investment in the dwelling and the family. These standards were mandatory for social housing but, in practice, their influence extended into the private sector as developers recognised that aspiring families were demanding more from their dwellings. Parker Morris standards were abandoned in the 1980s, leaving the UK, at the time, as the only country in Western Europe with no minimum space standards for housing (Park, 2017).

Current UK government guidance (DCLG, 2015) has introduced optional and discretionary cross-tenure technical standards to address mobility changes. These are incorporated in Part M of the Building Regulations, which specifies the legal standards that new buildings need to adhere to for access and use of amenities by people with disabilities. All dwellings need to conform to M4(1) to be visitable by a disabled person. It is a matter of local discretion whether the local plan demands dwellings to be designed to M4(2), specifying step-free access, turning circles in living space, the minimum width of stairs and an accessible lavatory, making the dwelling usable by a wide range of older and disabled people. Design to M4(3), that is, wheelchair adaptable or immediately wheelchair accessible, is, again, discretionary. The adoption of M4(2) and M4(3) standards are expected to be supported by evidence of need, and all, to date, have been objected to on cost and viability grounds by the developers' representative body, the Home Builders Federation. The developers state that if accessibility was important, then the government would make such standards mandatory – and we might ask why this step has not been taken. It seems very clear that building to M4(2) would allow immediate and continued accessibility, promoting opportunities to age in place. Depressingly, very few homes are currently accessible. Only 1.7 million, or a mere 7 per cent of English dwellings, have the accessible features listed in M4(2). Issues of poor access standards and lack of resources to repair or adapt result in greater spending in the NHS, where the cost of dealing with older people's illness and injury resulting from poor housing is at least £634 million per year (Garrett and Burris, 2015).

With the appetite for housing in London matched by an almost guaranteed opportunity to make large profits in market-based housing, the London planning authorities have far greater power to demand cross-sector adherence to higher standards as material conditions for planning consent. London now outstrips the other English regions in standards of new-build housing. A three-bedroom home in London is 25 square metres larger than a three-bedroom dwelling in Leeds, Scarborough or York (Crosby, 2015). The London housing strategy includes a demand that 90 per cent of new dwellings are designed to M4(2) and the remaining 10 per cent to M4(3). The London Plan asserts that 'Every home should be flexible enough to accommodate a range of possible changes in circumstances. Flexibility is the potential for rooms in a home to be used in a variety of ways without altering the building fabric ... In practice, this means making individual rooms large enough' (Mayor of London, 2020: 53). The requirement for flexible room use has, perhaps, acquired a different significance during the COVID-19 outbreak, where home schooling is currently mandated, where people who are able to are instructed to work from home, and where people in the same home may need to socially isolate from each other. There are now different demands on the need for adaptable space and either a larger number of rooms or a larger size of rooms.

Conversely in the North East, lower land values and low or no competition to build housing leads to greater impotence in the planning system to demand better. These issues are not simply out of step with population trends, but a brake upon the prosperity of the region. The Watson Burton report *Solving the Housing Conundrum* (NECC and Watson Burton LLP, 2014: 10) concludes that 'houses unresponsive to changing housing needs, such as demographic change is a disproportionately greater issue in the North East'. It suggests that 'housing developments are regarded as failing to deliver for the customer when it comes to adequate space within homes, accessibility and house size and build quality' (NECC and Watson Burton LLP, 2014: 20). It was against this background that the FHA formed to question whether a better offer was possible.

## Case study description

### Beginnings

In early 2016, there was a considerable feeling of new possibilities in Newcastle. The city council had committed to become an age-friendly city (see WHO, 2007); Newcastle City Futures was developing new ways of generating engagement and participation across a range of partners (see Tewdwr-Jones et al, 2015); and Newcastle University had secured substantial funds for the building of the National Innovation Centres for Ageing and Data. Buoyed up by this tangible new optimism, this chapter's lead author invited named representatives of local stakeholder organisations to join her to consider the current housing offer and explore what could be done.

Table 14.1 lists the stakeholder organisations that were invited to come to the table. They map onto the quadruple helix model, bringing together the academy, local government, business/industry and the social/community sector. This model is based on the compelling idea that by working together, we can understand societal issues more deeply and offer more inventive responses with a broader array of finance than any one organisation can do alone.

Groups form and flourish because the people bond with and learn to trust each other, knowing that they have something to contribute and to gain. Despite the reputation that Newcastle has for being an enviable place of formal and informal business and cross-sector collaborations, few attendees knew each other. Early meetings were spent pulling out ideas for what housing was needed and, through this exercise of sharing and listening, gaining an appreciation of each other's expertise.

From the first meeting came an agreement that the group would go beyond research to build housing that was sustainable, self-sufficient, resource-efficient, tenure- and age-neutral, intelligent, and desirable. While conscious of the boldness of the ambition, the group were protected, to an extent, by setting a goal of building five demonstrator dwellings. The concept of demonstrators was important in giving us permission to test, make mistakes and learn. It also suggested that, at this early stage, each group member saw the collaboration as probably time-limited. Karbon (the registered social landlord) was able to secure development finance and the city council offered a site at nil consideration, adjacent to the Newcastle Helix development (see Newcastle Helix, no date). This is a new, 24-acre city neighbourhood, owned by Newcastle University and Newcastle City Council, which is being regenerated as an innovation quarter in the city centre, encompassing international technology and science businesses, as well as residential areas and community spaces.

Drawing on the early organisational commitment to be an open learning platform and to recognise the value of expertise, it was clear that the design of the dwellings should be developed from a democratised process that could draw on the rich knowledge base in

**Table 14.1:** Stakeholder organisations in the Future Homes Alliance

| Organisation | Summary |
|---|---|
| Business: Innovation Super Network | A vehicle under the North East Local Enterprise Partnership[a] to create, enhance and systematise innovation dialogue and flows of information within the region, ensuring that opportunities for innovation engagement, business development and inward innovation investment are not missed. |
| Business: Ryder Architecture | Founded in 1953 as Ryder Yates, Ryder Architecture has a global reach from its Newcastle base, encompassing offices in London, Glasgow, Liverpool, Hong Kong and Vancouver. Their design expertise spans civic buildings, healthcare, infrastructure, leisure, manufacturing, offices, residential and educational buildings. |
| Business: Karbon Homes | Karbon Homes is a registered housing provider and is funded by Homes England.[b] Karbon Homes develop and manage homes for rent and shared ownership. They have stock of more than 24,000 units and a turnover in excess of £130 million. In the Future Homes Helix project, they are the investor and developing agent. |
| Business: Zero Carbon Futures | Grown out of the regional development agency, Zero Carbon Futures was set up in 2011 as an independent consultancy specialising in low-carbon vehicle technologies. The company works with businesses, universities, government bodies and sector agencies to ensure that the UK can maximise the benefits. |
| Academy: Newcastle University | A Russell Group university with breadth and depth in research across all disciplines. Newcastle has the biggest concentration of researchers in Europe working on aspects of ageing, together with international expertise on data, energy and cities. |
| Third sector: Newcastle Elders Council | With roots in a 1997 Better Government for Older People project, the Elders Council has been working since 2001 to improve the quality of life for older people in the city by bringing older people's voice into policy and practice arenas. The Elders Council's work was key in supporting the city council's intention to become an age-friendly city, signalled by signing the Dublin Declaration in 2011. On this project, the Elders Council is coordinating engagement with older people and the broader community. |
| Third sector: Sustainable Communities Initiative (SCI) | The SCI was incorporated in July 2012. It conducts work encompassing social, economic and environmental aspects of sustainability and community-led local development. |
| The local authority: Newcastle City Council | Acting as planning authority. A partner in the regeneration quarter, Newcastle Helix. |

Notes: [a] In England, a local enterprise partnership is a voluntary partnership between the local authority and businesses to set local economic priorities. [b] Homes England is the government body responsible for increasing the number of new homes that are built in England (including affordable homes and homes for market, sale or rent), improving existing affordable homes and bringing empty homes back into use as affordable housing. A Homes England grant aided the development partner Karbon Homes.

the region. This commitment to open processes has been as important as developing new products.

## Co-designing the Future Homes and developing knowledge exchange

The programme began with three workshops initiated by Newcastle University and funded by the university's Institute for Ageing, which brought together Ryder Architecture and in-community health professionals, including occupational therapists, psychologists and rehabilitation workers for visually impaired people. The aim was to gain greater insight from those working with individuals and families whose changing needs had jeopardised comfort, safety and dignity in their homes. Over the course of three workshops, participants took part in seven separate activities designed to tap into their understanding and expertise, and to develop effective means of recording their thoughts.

To start the process, the participants were asked to write down their thoughts on problems they encountered in housing design and display them together on a wall. Following the presentations, everyone voted for the challenges and ideas they most identified with (see Table 14.2). The next activity focused on five specific activities: bathing, cooking/ dining, living, movement and sleeping. Participants were split into professionally diverse groups that used discussion-point sheets as a basis to write out their thoughts. The notes were collated around common themes and the groups rotated to the next table until they had explored three activities.

Votes for individual themes were tallied and collated to produce tables for each key space, from the most popular to the least popular theme. Votes were colour-coded on a heat-map basis, where light blue indicated the fewest votes and red the greatest number. Following this workshop, two forms of data collation and analysis were undertaken. All the key words and phrases from the workshop were processed into a word cloud for each key space and overall.

In the second workshop led by Ryder Architecture (see Figure 14.1), the Future Homes team provided feedback on the ideas raised, preferences and overall theme hierarchies. The participants reviewed the themes and their rankings, focusing on whether they felt the ranking was correct or should be reordered. A notable change was the reduction in importance of risk. Although it remained highly placed in both bathing and cooking/dining, it became a less critical issue when other key themes were addressed, such as good lighting, colour contrast, accessibility and removal of door thresholds.

**Table 14.2:** Cooking/dining themes in order of importance

|  | Theme | Votes |
|---|---|---|
| 1 | Risk/safety | 17 |
| 2 | Adaptability | 15 |
| 3 | Storage | 14 |
| 4 | Lighting | 12 |
| 5 | Technology/fixtures and fittings | 12 |
| 6 | Accessibility/thresholds/level change | 8 |
| 7 | Colour tactile contrast | 0 |
| 8 | Comfort | 0 |
| 9 | Consider whole family needs | 0 |
| 10 | Function and movement through covert design | 0 |
| 11 | Functionality | 0 |
| 12 | Green space, views | 0 |
| 13 | Materials | 0 |
| 14 | Orientation | 0 |
| 15 | Personalisation | 0 |
| 16 | Relationship with bathroom | 0 |
| 17 | Sensory | 0 |
| 18 | Sound and vision | 0 |
| 19 | Space (use/amount) | 0 |
| 20 | Structure/pre-build design/layout | 0 |
| 21 | Water | 0 |

Source: Reproduced courtesy of Ryder Architecture

The participants next considered two variations of a typical room layout of a bathroom, kitchen/dining room, living room and bedroom. One layout was from a social housing new-build typology currently available in the North East and the other was a deliberately contrasting layout based on several of the key themes derived from the previous workshop. The second layout generally received more positive feedback and there was a consensus on a more open, flexible (short-term) and adaptable (long-term) configuration for all the room layouts.

Movement on foot and with a walking aid or wheelchair was critical. As important, though, were access to daylight, connection with outdoors, accommodating 'normal' family life and the relationship to other functions within the house.

**Figure 14.1:** Collating the data

Source: Image reproduced courtesy of Ryder Architecture

In the last workshop, by drawing on the final heat map of overall themes, participants developed a written brief for the Future Homes team that would act as a concise document to aid in the development of the housing concepts. They critiqued two whole-house layouts taken from existing developments within the North East, one from a social housing provider and the other from a volume house builder. The final activity asked groups to review a live Ryder Architecture project that was exploring how a family home could be adapted to meet the special needs of two children and whether the level of adaptation could be kept to a minimum to improve the affordability of the works required. This final exercise brought the focus back to the participants' acknowledged expertise.

After each session, Ryder Architecture recorded and collated the information and feedback into a series of engagement packs. They act as a permanent and predominately graphic-based account of each workshop, building a body of work to be referred to as the Future Homes house types developed. These packs were circulated within the Future Homes team and used as the basis for other team members to conduct their own engagement sessions. Three workshops with older people run by Elders Council raised issues of how accessibility could be maintained in the home; two workshops with parents of younger children placed an emphasis on storage in order to make spaces that promote family fun that can then be transformed into adult-only rooms. In these sessions, there was a range of income levels and household diversity, providing uncommon opportunities for a broad group of people to be acknowledged as experts by experience. One workshop with social housing managers raised issues of affordability and the need to develop a community as well as dwellings. Seven parallel day-long

**Figure 14.2:** Timeline of co-design and public involvement

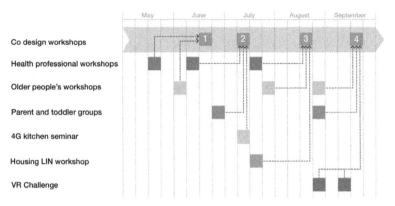

Source: Image reproduced courtesy of Ryder Architecture

sessions with the steering group explored how these various strands of expert views might be woven together (see Figure 14.2).

The process of engagement with a broad base of stakeholders can seem an obvious methodology to develop something as ubiquitous as housing. However, for many, if not all, participants, it was their first opportunity to discuss ideas with architects in an arena where their views could be recorded and acted upon. The standard approach to design is locked into a silo, and part of our innovation is demonstrating that more open approaches are worth the investment of time and money and that knowledge exchange can be longer-term. Interviews with health professionals following the workshops confirmed the positive lessons that they had learned from each other and from working with the architects:

> 'I think it is knowing the language architects use. It's how they design. I like the fact they use tracing paper to do changes. You can see how they can change things so easily and how they approach things. That gives me confidence to be able to communicate with them more on the same level as them ... I think I would have been a bit more intimidated [beforehand] to be honest.' (Participant 1)

> 'People feeding back to me about ideas and thinking, "Actually, that's something I can add to my daily work if I'm thinking about that." I think particularly some of the behavioural things and sensory sides. We often rush in and rush out and attend to the main problem but might miss

a few of the other little bits ... So I think it just makes you take a more holistic approach to what we're doing.' (Participant 2)

Additionally, from the architects' perspective, there was a validation of design principles that might be contested or questioned on cost grounds:

'You could use that opinion to make the arguments that you need to improve the design of the building rather than the architect sitting there going, " 'I know best." To be able to say, "I've asked 30 people who know about this, the consensus view is that that's the right solution." I think that's ... much better ... in helping us make those arguments ... using consultation and engagement more is definitely something that I will do. I think we should be promoting across the broader practice as well.' (Architect)

While the principles arrived at were not necessarily unexpected (Figure 14.3), the discussions around these topics raised notable issues of detail, which supports the use of rotating guided conversations (World Cafe method) and Delphi processes that allow the review and revision of previous answers and the tracking of decision-making in an iterative manner.

## Making a longer-term difference

As the partnership has matured, there has been an increasing sense of confidence and a feeling that the work can potentially contribute to developing new industry standards. When it became clear that the demonstrator site was not viable because of ground conditions, FHA was able to negotiate the development of a much bigger site on Newcastle Helix (see Newcastle Helix, no date). The larger Future Homes development now encompasses more than 60 dwellings, while the concept of demonstrator units as learning labs has been retained, but recast, as five dwellings interspersed within the estate that will offer opportunities for major industry players. These dwellings will be fitted out with products and services that have passed 'proof of concept' stage from which they, and FHA, can learn.

The resultant development will be a multigenerational community with one- and two-bed apartments and two- and four-bed houses, embracing the single-person household of any age and families, both

**Figure 14.3:** Principles of Future Homes design

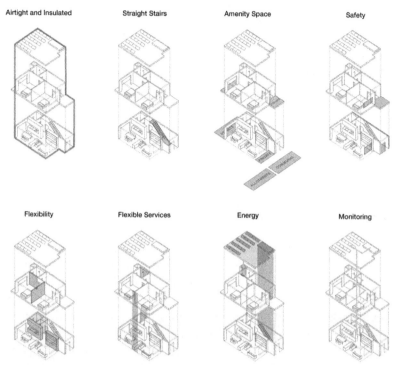

Source: Image reproduced courtesy of Ryder Architecture

nuclear and extended. Dwellings have built-in expandable zones that allow for easy adaptation, with bathrooms and kitchens made larger or bedrooms altered in size as life's requirements change. Matters of sustainability are addressed through an emphasis on the building fabric ensuring that domestic fuel use is kept to a minimum, satisfying both the carbon emissions agenda and fuel poverty. There will be a renewed emphasis on community – not just building units, but creating places that foster neighbourliness through biodiverse green spaces for quiet and active enjoyment and encourage local food growing, which addresses health and affordability. Additionally, if COVID-19 lockdowns are not unique events for 2020, access to local biodiverse green areas – important for physical and mental well-being anyway – is particularly important for those without gardens during any periods of lockdown, when shared green spaces need to be large enough to accommodate social distancing practices. Rents are governed by Homes England and are therefore set at affordable levels.

The residents of the development will provide experiential views of the comfort of and ease of living in their home through regular surveys, as well as being recipients of data about energy usage and generation intended to help them make more sustainable choices. In the social rented sector, considerable efforts are made to develop mutually beneficial relationships with tenants but Future Homes will go beyond this in seeing residents as mutual learners and contributors to change.

In 2018, FHA took the important step of becoming a community interest company, with seven organisations, including Newcastle University and third sector and industry partners, signing up to be shareholders. The aim was to formalise our intention to be a thought leader, developing housing models and ensuring that they are not only superior homes to live in, but also learning loops for researchers and industry to guarantee that further developments are continuously improving.

## Reflections on working in social renewal

Reflecting now three years later, it is clear that organisations chose to come together for multiple reasons. The presence of the university gave reassurance to several actors and raised credibility, which speaks to the understanding of the university as a respected anchor institution (Tewdwr-Jones et al, 2015). The opportunity to act rather than simply take part in research was a strong motivator for the Elders Council, whose own history demonstrated that real-world projects are empowering to individuals and reputation-enhancing to their organisations. The opportunity to think freely outside the constraints of their own organisations has been frequently praised by group members and is testimony to the trust that the partners have in each other. In the invitation letter, there was an appeal to a shared place attachment and a desire to see the city become a better place to live and work. This deep-seated love of place has frequently been used by North East organisations. The now-defunct regional development agency[1] known as One North East used the strapline, 'passionate places and passionate people'. For those in the city region, this is much more than a marketing tool; it is deeply felt, drawing people together for what is perceived to be a greater good. Knowing what values are shared is clearly salient in bringing strangers together.

The group is still together, bound by a strong sense of shared purpose that has developed new housing designs for people at all stages of the life course. This is the product that FHA are working towards, with a tangible output; however, deeper than that is a shared knowledge that we are in pursuit of something important. This has been enhanced by the widespread confidence that others have shown in us: design and industrial challenge finance from a major financial institution;

financial support from a local building society[2] for our events in the Great Exhibition of the North[3] (in the summer of 2018); invitations to speak at national and international events about Future Homes; and finance to employ a business adviser to make us investment-ready.

The power of the quadruple helix model is the diversity of partners that it draws in, with opportunities to acknowledge different forms of expertise drawn from experience, as well as those that draw on research. This new form of collaboration challenges all the partners to build new cultures and develop meaningful partnerships based on equality and respect. The founder takes pains not to claim any special authority for the university, but to emphasise the contribution of all. While it might be understood by those external to the partnership that Newcastle University is the research body, in FHA, the university is *one* of several research partners, alongside Ryder Architecture, Zero Carbon Futures, SCI and the Elders Council, all of whom are active within, and beyond, the partnership in building new knowledge.

Research alone does not necessarily create transformation; rather, it is the interplay between different forms of knowledge, policymakers and practitioners that can lead to change. In its roles as planning authority and implementer of a housing strategy, the city council has been critical, as has Karbon Homes, which, as the developer, has been able to commit considerable finance, without which there would be no buildings.

Our theory of change is that a quadruple helix can lead to four-point success: research excellence coupled with community voice can lead to business innovation that can be tested through further research with residents, generating business growth and, in some cases, savings to the public purse. When the dwellings are completed and occupied, FHA will then move into a testing and dissemination phase that allows continuous improvement. The challenge will be to scale up from a first project, taking the learning to new communities.

It is interesting to consider whether this could have happened in a place other than Newcastle. Scale is surely significant, with Newcastle being a city large enough to deliver innovation but small enough for participants to share an understanding of place. It may be that the economy of our city and its greater reliance on Newcastle University for new entrants to the labour market has been helpful, or even that the geography of Newcastle, with the close proximity of the university and the civic centre in what a previous city leader termed 'the ideas quarter', has helped forge close relationships. The strength of the third sector and the reputation within the city of the lead author may all have contributed to our success. What may be transferable is the university as an institution that can create a place of trust for stakeholders of all kinds to articulate ideas. While much may be context-specific, all universities have the potential to be a catalyst for exchange and innovation.

## Summary

This chapter has considered the work of FHA, which has become a strong organisation based on shared values, high levels of empowerment and transparency. It has demonstrated that a commitment to open processes has led to bold new designs and transformative knowledge exchange within and beyond the partnership. Deepening trust has created virtuous circles, where partners feel increasing commitment to each other and the project, seeking out new ways of increasing its value and reputation. This reflection comes at a time when our development has been submitted to Newcastle City Council for planning approval. Should this be successful, there will be a start on site late in 2020 and first occupation by early 2022. There is a great feeling of optimism and an excitement that FHA are going to build something different, something of which we can be proud. Our purpose has been to challenge the poverty of housing design by enriching processes in order to develop new environments that bring beauty, innovation and social sustainability within the reach of all households, re-emphasising that everyone is entitled to high-quality housing, irrespective of income or life stage.

### Notes

[1]   In the UK, the nine regional development agencies were non-departmental public bodies (NDPBs) established for the purpose of development, primarily economic, of England's government office regions between 1998 and 2010.

[2]   A building society is a financial institution owned by its members as a mutual organisation. Building societies offer banking and related financial services, especially savings and mortgage lending.

[3]   The Great Exhibition of the North was a two-month exhibition, celebrating art, culture and design in the North of England, held in Newcastle and Gateshead between 22 June and 9 September 2018.

### References

CMHC (Canada Mortgage and Housing Corporation) (2018) 'CMHC FlexHousing™ Checklist: Homes that adapt to life's changes'. Available at: https://assets.cmhc-schl.gc.ca/sf/project/cmhc/pubsandreports/pdf/61943.pdf?rev=f878a1d2-d51b-43a5-9e20-6c8d0c5a26e9

Crosby, M. (2015) *Space Standards for Homes: #HomeWise*, London: Royal Institute of British Architects.

DCLG (Department for Communities and Local Government) (2015) *Housing Standards Review: Summary of Responses*, London: DCLG.

Garrett, H. and Burris, S. (2015) *Homes and Ageing in England, Briefing Paper, Building Research Establishment and Public Health England*, Watford: BRE Trust. Available at: www.bre.co.uk/filelibrary/Briefing%20papers/86749-BRE_briefing-paper-PHE-England-A4-v3.pdf

Habinteg (2016) *Accessible Housing Standards 2015*, London: Habinteg.

Habinteg (2019) *A Forecast for Accessible Homes*, London: Habinteg.

Lifemark (2019) 'Design for life: for homes with space in the right place'. Available at: www.lifemark.co.nz/

Livable Housing Australia (2019) 'Championing safer, more comfortable and easier to access homes for everybody, everyday, at all stages of life', LHA. Available at: www.livablehousingaustralia.org.au/59/about-lha.aspx

Mayor of London (2020) *London Plan: Module C – Pre-consultation Draft. Housing Design Quality and Standards Supplementary Planning Guidance*, London: Greater London Authority. Available at: www.london.gov.uk/sites/default/files/hdspg_2020_module_c.pdf

Ministry of Housing and Local Government (1961) *Homes for Today and Tomorrow, Report of the Parker Morris Committee*, London: Ministry of Housing and Local Government.

NECC (North East Chamber of Commerce) and Watson Burton LLP (2014) *Solving the Housing Conundrum: A 3-Step Approach to North East Housing Policy*, Durham: NECC.

Newcastle Helix (no date) 'About'. Available at: https://newcastlehelix.com/about

Park, J. (2017) 'One hundred years of housing space standards: what now'. Available at: https://levittbernstein.co.uk/site/assets/files/2682/one_hundred_years_of_space_standards.pdf

Tewdwr-Jones, M., Goddard, J. and Cowie, P. (2015) *Newcastle City Futures 2065: Anchoring Universities through Urban Foresight*, Newcastle upon Tyne: Newcastle University.

WHO (World Health Organization) (2007) *Global Age-Friendly Cities: A Guide*, Geneva, Switzerland: World Health Organization.

# 15

# The good, the bad and the disconcerting: a week in the life of university project-based learning for schools

*David Leat, Ulrike Thomas, Kirsty Hayward and*
*Anne de A'Echevarria*

## Introduction

This chapter explores whether 'project-based learning' (PBL) combined with 'community curriculum making' (CCM) (Leat and Thomas, 2017), referred to as PBL/CCM, can provide more critically engaged, confident and informed citizens, and be a catalyst for developing a localised place-based culture and infrastructure of learning opportunities with some of the characteristics of a 'Learning City'. These potential outcomes of PBL/CCM are explored through the focus of a particular project undertaken in June/July 2018. PBL is a student-centred pedagogy in which students learn through active exploration of real-world challenges and problems. CCM is about making use of place in learning. It involves engaging with the local context and resources, including schools and other stakeholders, to design learning that meets the needs of both students and local communities.

In this chapter, there is an outline of the evolution of PBL/CCM work in the context of the performative culture that has moulded the school curriculum in England over the last 30 years. The chapter discusses how a national curriculum contrasts with a more localised curriculum. There then follows an account of a case-study PBL/CCM week, including an outline of the partners involved. There is a consideration of the good, bad and disconcerting outcomes of the week, which reflect both pragmatic issues and much deeper issues about working towards social justice. The conclusion broaches some wider issues about the role of universities in compulsory education and uses CCM as a lens for considering Tyneside (and its surrounds) as a 'Learning City'.

## Policy context: two metaphors of learning

Anna Sfard (1998) articulated two metaphors of learning: *acquisition*, in which direct instruction and memory are centre stage, as evident in traditional models of curricula; and *participation*, in which experience and participation are the source of learning. Sfard makes the point that whereas the proponents of each camp claim supremacy, there is a danger of choosing only one metaphor as we need both. Since the Education Reform Act 1988, England has had a 'national curriculum', which largely exemplifies the acquisition metaphor. Initially, this was achieved through specifying taught content but the government has increasingly switched to control by school exam performance. Consequently, in English secondary schools, the driving imperative and accountability metric is exam results, resulting in a highly performative culture, reinforced by the Office for Standards in Education (Ofsted) inspection regime and its grading system: inadequate, requires improvement, good and outstanding. The negative consequences are detailed by a range of authors (Berliner, 2011; Wrigley, 2018). Wrigley (2017) argues strongly that the present policy emphasis on canonical knowledge particularly disadvantages students in poorer communities through the erosion of the place of everyday, vernacular knowledge. A national curriculum generally offers uniform curriculum content, organised in traditional subjects, and that uniformity invites resourcing through textbooks that deliver the required uniform knowledge. There may be choices of content expressed in a national curriculum but some of these will be overridden by purchasing a textbook which makes that choice. Curriculum elements that are more localised in children's communities are more likely to be interdisciplinary as local topics or issues do not map so readily onto one subject. They also, naturally, require local resourcing and planning, which implicate more work for teachers and collaboration with local partners. However, a more localised and thus more participatory curriculum is more responsive to the needs and interests of both students and communities. Nevertheless, the perceived danger for schools is that through such localised elements, students will fail to successfully *acquire* the necessary subject knowledge to pass exams, on which the reputation and fortunes of the school will rest. The professional discourse in schools is saturated by terms such as 'unit test', 'progress', 'target grade' and 'intervention'. Teaching is therefore very pressured, and with increasing workloads, many teachers have left the profession. In 2016/17, 19.9 per cent of teachers left the workforce, compared to 9.2 per cent of the workforce in 2010/11 (Worth, 2018).

With educational budgets not keeping up with educational sector inflation, austerity has obvious effects on curricula in limiting choice and experimentation. A textbook-resourced, subject-structured, classroom-based curriculum is, in school accounting terms, cheaper to deliver than one where students 'go places, meet people and do and make things'.

Projects are, as Thomas (2000: 1) concludes, 'complex tasks, based on challenging questions or problems, that involve students in design, problem solving, decision making, or investigative activities; give students the opportunity to work relatively autonomously over extended periods of time; and culminate in realistic products or presentations'. CCM is a variation of PBL. One additional element introduced by the CCM dimension is that, where possible, projects are developed with a community partner. While community is hard to define precisely, digital technology allows that such partners do not have to be within a set distance of the school. Significant antecedents and influences are service learning (Butin, 2010), area-based curricula (Thomas, 2012) and the work of High Tech High in California (Patton and Robin, 2012). PBL/CCM addresses social justice by giving students opportunities to adopt a more agentic role in their education and by supporting teachers and schools to create more critical and empowering learning environments (Hackman, 2005) in which social, environmental, economic and political issues are explored and acted upon (Freire, 1972; Westheimer and Kahne, 2004).

Over a number of years, the researchers involved have therefore advocated, supported and researched CCM to help redress the balance in curriculum provision and provide opportunity for young people to learn through participation as they go places, meet people and do and make things in their locality and beyond. Consequently, the intention is to keep alive an alternative vision of achieving both qualifications and wider learning outcomes. Some of our regular partners and contacts have included the Great North Museum, Hexham Beekeepers, School Grounds North East, the Newcastle University Library, Open Lab (a human–computer interaction research centre), Leading Learning and Thinkwell (educational consultancies), Seven Stories (National Children's Literature Archive and Museum), English Heritage, and the Dove Marine Laboratory.

The case presented in this chapter has implications for two aspects of PBL/CCM: one relating to the community providers, such as museums, companies, local societies and university staff; and one relating to the outcomes for students. For the providers, there is recognition that they are going against the grain of educational policy and practice. Providers do valuable work as individual actors but the greater the density of community network connections between them, the greater the scope for concerted action. This partly comes as the providers create bilateral links for particular projects but they can also begin to feel that they are part of something bigger, with a web of resources to draw upon through other contacts. This raises the question of whether the Tyneside area might begin to show characteristics associated with 'Learning Cities' (Facer and Buchczyk, 2019), which is a United Nations Educational, Scientific and Cultural Organization (UNESCO) designation covering a network of global cities seeking to encourage citizens to take advantage of a wide array of learning opportunities throughout their lives. The 'Learning Cities' designation aligns with a conceptualisation of learning that is not the responsibility of schools alone, but results from the 'practices of cultures, communities and places' (Facer and Buchczyk, 2019: 169) to create a spatially networked learning culture. A networked learning culture would stand in contrast to the effects of austerity, which has seen an erosion of adult learning provision and a predominant focus on narrow vocational qualifications as the social and communitarian ambit of educational providers shrank (Smith and O'Leary, 2013). Facer and Buchczyk (2019) advance the case for focusing on the infrastructure of 'Learning Cities', which they equate with the material, discursive, social and technological mechanisms that enable the flows of knowledge, information and opportunities, as well as the agency, of relevant social actors. Can PBL/CCM contribute to realising aspects of a 'Learning City' on Tyneside and to transforming the way in which education is understood, thus ensuring better life chances for more young (and older) people? Strong infrastructures demand better network connections, create expectations and new models, and encourage better progression when people move between learning opportunities (Hodgson and Spours, 2013).

## Case study

The work on which this case study is based was funded by the North East Collaborative Outreach Programme (NECOP) as a special project for PBL/CCM 'pop-ups' in which a week-long activity of PBL/CCM on campus for secondary students was organised. They were hosted by some combination of university staff and outside facilitators. The focus for the week was healthy lifestyles and the students were given the following brief: 'Given the information (nutrition, exercise and health) provided during the week, plan an idea either using an app or "bootlegger" which would encourage people to change their behaviour'. 'Bootlegger' is a film-planning and directing app that can be deployed with collaborators using mobile phone video technology. The project took place in July 2018 and most of the planning and organisation within the university was undertaken by Ulrike Thomas, who acted as a vital broker between schools and the project facilitators.

The 'Healthy Living' project started through Ulrike Thomas finding contacts in the university in sports science who wanted to raise the profile of the new degree programme. It was an attractive topic given current concerns about mental and physical health, as well as its relevance to a variety of subjects. Planning started in November 2017 and required a series of meetings between Ulrike, Kirsty Hayward from the community partner Success4All and the facilitators from different university departments, namely, sports science, nutrition and Open Lab (part of computing science), in which much brokering was undertaken. The final group was composed of 16 Year 10 students (age 15) from one school and six Year 12 students (age 17) from a further three schools. One of the more disquieting aspects is that one school did not contribute to planning or send any staff with the students, making communication and linkage to the curriculum much harder. Therefore, the 16 Year 10 students arrived with little knowledge about the content and purpose of the week, despite the best efforts of the planning team, which had some repercussions during the project. Before discussing outcomes, key partner organisations are described.

One of the partners of the PBL/CCM was Success4All, an educational charity that has been based locally within the North East for over 12 years. The charity evolved to fill the gap between home and school experienced by many children and young people from disadvantaged areas. This is a gap where lack of access to a computer, the Internet, a safe and relaxed place to work, and someone to offer support and guidance might make all the difference in their engagement and enjoyment of education. Success4All provides this support by creating 'learning hubs', which provide after-school clubs with volunteer tutor befrienders. Success4All also offers summer schools to provide a wide range of activities, such as practical science, coding and programming, digital art, social action issues, languages, music, poetry, and manga drawing. In recent years, Success4All has partnered with the university in an EU project exploring self-organised learning environments (SOLEs), so there is a good level of mutual understanding. Kirsty Hayward from Success4All was contracted to be the lead facilitator for the week.

Anne de A'Echevarria, contracted to conduct an evaluation of the project, is from Thinkwell, an education consultancy that operates in the UK and the Netherlands, primarily with schools, colleges and professional development providers. It explores how best to develop communities of enquiry, creativity and creative learning. The related concepts of voice, agency and dialogue are central to their work. With schools, for example, Thinkwell engages pupils and teachers in developing clearer learning identities and in changing classrooms and school communities. To this end, the key focus is on pedagogies that develop critical and creative thinking, collaborative enquiry, and the capacity to be metacognitive (Leat and Lin, 1998) – to reflect on the thinking, attitudes and behaviours that help build community. A particular feature of Thinkwell's work has been the use of story and storytelling as an enquiry method and agent of both personal and organisational change. Previous involvement with Newcastle University has included contributing to secondary and primary initial teacher training and master of education courses in diverse areas.

## The outcomes of the week

### Some obvious good

The week-long programme demonstrated strong relational links within the university and with Success4All and Thinkwell, which is testimony to a common understanding about the power and importance of networks and brokerage. Kirsty and Anne were therefore able to cope with the less than ideal preparation and the lack of orientation on the part of the students.

By the end of the week, many of the student participants provided very positive feedback. It was evident that many from both Year 10 and Year 12 *experienced* the difference between their normal *acquisition* mode of learning and the *participation* that the week offered:

'I appreciated "being like a uni student", getting a feel for what it's like at university.' (Year 12 student)

'I thought it was going to be bad but I've really enjoyed the independence: being able to go off and do our project without being watched the whole time.' (Year 10 student)

'This project makes it more likely that I would apply to university in the future because it gives you a sense of what it would be actually like.' (Year 10 student)

'I liked being trusted to do our project with no one following you. It's really independent and I liked the freedom.' (Year 10 student)

'It's a good taster of university life – better than open days as you spend longer in the environment getting familiar with different tools and equipment used.' (Year 12 student)

For others, the experience of being pushed into new behaviours brought the sense of a transformation: "I was soooooooo scared of doing the presentation as I hate doing it but Duncan [a facilitator] made me and I did it!!!" (Year 10 student). The content and activities of the week also drew some approval:

'I liked getting input from university students and staff from different faculties. It seemed relevant and current – not old lecturers talking about something from decades ago!' (Year 12 student)

'Actually, I found the first-day lecture really interesting and useful, eg, how different nutrients react in a male or female. Science is not so good in school 'cos of bad behaviour so it was great to be able to learn and take something away.' (Year 10 student)

'I enjoyed the interviewing activity linked to behavioural psychology. It was good to plan questions then actually use them in real life to actually help people.' (Year 10 student)

For many young people, what is likely to shift them onto new life-course trajectories is the experience and the development of various forms of capital (such as social, cultural and science) (Nomikou et al, 2017), being given responsibility and being trusted, meeting potential role models and finding one's talents (Moll et al, 1992; Stanton-Salazar, 2001), and developing human capability. This is part of what private education does so well.

## *Some of the bad*

Planning this project took six months, not all day, every day, but it demanded serious lead-in time. When starting projects from scratch, everything takes time. You cannot assume anything and there is little that you can take on trust with parties that are unknown. When people who are busy do not reply to emails, and if this is part of a critical path of action, everything is stalled. You cannot write briefings for participants or ethics permission forms without a clear outline of the project, and when details from project leaders are not forthcoming. Consulting presenters on what they can offer and schools on what they expect or want takes time as you inch the parties together. In one instance, a school sent back consent forms for only some of the expected students and some were not signed, perhaps because of language difficulties. Some students were ill prepared for starting activities since they had not been well briefed. In addition, there was a little suspicion among the student group about collective motivation and capability. All this crops up in the following written comments:

> It would have been better if it had been all Year 12 students because the Year 10s create distractions and don't work on the same level as the rest of us. (Year 12 student)

> There has to be a better way of learning than lectures! Why do they use lectures to teach you things? They make me want to scream! (Year 10 student)

> It felt like the programme ended up having to be pitched at the level of the youngest to keep them engaged. (Year 12 student)

> We were told this was a work experience thing and it wasn't, it was all classroom learning. (Year 10 student)

> I would like it to link more with my A level course as I don't really see the connections – could these be made clearer? (Year 12 student)

One might be excused for thinking that you cannot please all of the people all of the time. The more serious issue here, which is developed in more detail later, is the importance of common understanding between students and between them and educational providers. Tackling social justice can feel like rolling a stone uphill.

## The disconcerting

Often, the more obvious positive and negative aspects of experiences are relatively predictable, and it is more subtle aspects that disconcert and require deep thought. There is a focus on three aspects: the first is what the week tells us about learning infrastructure; the second concerns the lack of a meta-language about learning among school students; and the third concerns issues of power and control, and the validity of some of 'good' and 'bad' issues.

Learning infrastructure refers to the organisations in a local area working in loose partnership with various bridging ties, intermittent communication and collaboration, and therefore constituting a network with overlapping aims. Although there are signs of an emerging infrastructure to support PBL/CCM, which served the projects well in a largely successful week, the situation is far less rosy in the wider compulsory education system. Local authorities are greatly diminished in their capacity to connect parts of the system. Government agencies are largely concerned with control, evaluation and accountability. University education departments have been undermined by the switch to a mainly school-led training system, which means that university teacher training is often staffed by part-time staff, recently retired or seconded from schools. School exam boards have become commercial operations. The tendons that might attach one part of the educational body to others are missing. Thus, despite six months lead-in and a catalogue of meetings and notes, there were still significant gaps in preparation. Some students arrived uncertain and poorly informed, and took time to warm to the week. This is not surprising. While there are a host of organisations such as universities who offer engagement and enrichment activities, it is not routine that these are integrated into the curriculum. The activities can be for careers guidance, reward or an antidote to the normal curriculum offering but much less often are they planned into a teaching sequence or module of work because that requires a degree of joint planning that the systems do not commonly allow. To overcome such bumps in the road, you need brokers working in a supportive infrastructure (Leat and Thomas, 2018). Without such infrastructure, there can be frustrations on both sides of the partnerships when expectations are not met. The nature of the apprehension stems from the scale of the challenges faced. While PBL infrastructure grows and new partners respond to the logic of PBL/CCM in addressing weaknesses in formal educational opportunities, it is dwarfed by the infrastructure and resource mobilised by the Department for Education and the schools they effectively control. You can choose your own metaphor – 'shouting in the wind', 'swimming uphill' or 'taking on the juggernaut' – advancing the case of PBL/CCM and greater social justice is daunting. Although the purpose of the project was made clear to an initial point of contact in the schools, it appeared to get rather lost in translation for some of the students concerned and probably led to elements of the poor motivation and indifferent behaviour displayed by some of the Year 10 students early in the week. Some arrived with little preparation and were initially unable to see its value, particularly where they had been told they were going on work experience. If we refer back to UNESCO's 'Learning Cities' concept, one of the defining features is a city that 'effectively mobilizes its resources in every sector to promote inclusive learning from basic to higher education'. Mobilisation is not passive; it requires human action to make connections and introductions, persuade, support, and follow up as necessary. In its efforts to manifest itself as a 'Learning City', Bristol puts a premium on brokerage to connect up disjointed infrastructure.

The second and related issue is that young people do not have a rounded view of what constitutes learning. Although there are ongoing debates about learning, it is still invaluable for young people to have some framework to understand the full range of outcomes that can be classified as learning and how, broadly, they can be achieved. School can be bizarrely isolated from everyday experience (Jay et al, 2017). Learning can become equated with completing subject schoolwork, focused on knowledge retention, in order to pass exams. There is iconic research by Phelan et al (1998), whose ethnographic study detailed the struggles faced by young people moving between the worlds of school, peers and family, with varying degrees of skill. This can be understood through the concept of boundary crossing, elaborated for school education by Akkerman and van Eijck (2013). Through the use of dialogical self-theory, they argue that young people need to be seen as whole people, participating in multiple sites and practices (for example, class work, swimming, making videos about clothes and caring for the family dog), continuously negotiating the demands and practices of each, and, at times, hybridising knowledge. Without an informed language of learning, they are disabled in taking full advantage of learning opportunities.

The third issue is over how to give students power and control in the PBL/CCM. The difficulties and contradictions in aiming to do this were evident in how the students responded to being asked to evaluate their experience of the PBL/CCM. Anne's intention to ask the students about PBL was immediately revised on finding that they had not apprehended that PBL was the essence of the week. Demonstrating commendable adaptability, which partly reflects the strength and common understanding of the PBL/CCM network, she changed tack. Anne brought a new angle to the week by choosing a web-based evaluation tool. The 'Consider.it' tool has previously been used to provide the opportunity to engage in public dialogue on important local or societal issues where it was difficult or inappropriate to bring the intended participants together physically. The value of 'Consider. it' for this project was in generating feedback that was potentially more revealing. Its use was ideal with participants who were not ready to provide reflective face-to-face comments with other students or the researcher (Anne), as well as where time for evaluation was short. 'Consider.it' was chosen for its potential to spark curiosity about the views of others (the evolving range of views is displayed as a visual graphic) and therefore potentially generating dialogue between the participants themselves, both within and across projects. It was also effective in encouraging participants to reassess attitudes, step outside their own 'group' to read and recognise points made by those with a very different stance, and ultimately to acknowledge the importance of comments made on both sides of the 'debate'.

The students were prompted to reflect on the nature of learning they had experienced, as well as the impact of the project on their future post-school plans, their likely university participation, their awareness of possible employment opportunities and so on. One or two students engaged with 'Consider.it' in their own time, though most took part while on campus. It was interesting to see how the location of the laptop influenced their comments and engagement with the tool, as well as the likelihood of relevant face-to-face conversations that took place in its vicinity before/during/after its use. When placed in seminar rooms, students were more inhibited and tended only to engage when reminded, particularly when session organisers were nearby. However, when placed in rest areas/common rooms during lunch breaks, there was longer engagement, more commenting on comments and more deliberation. When in this location, the tool also sparked some hoped-for richer, face-to-face dialogue between participants rather than the fleeting comments made in seminar rooms with adults nearby – the message seeming to be that if you want dialogue, you should attempt to generate it in places where talk is more likely to occur. Anne's perceived neutrality enabled students to be somewhat more relaxed about her presence, though they still seemed more prepared to be candid with her about the tool than about the project. One group agreed to be recorded and transcribed:

'You'd get more out of me if I could do it on the bus.' (Year 10 student)

'You wouldn't really get chatting about something unless it was a conversation you actually wanted to have.' (Year 10 student)

'It's a good way of gathering views though ... I was curious to see what other people were thinking ... and when you see people think along the same lines as you, it makes you more likely to share. And it's clear that people are disagreeing so it makes you more comfortable about sharing whatever view you have. There's a whole range.' (Year 12 student)

'And it gives you time to think about what you think. If we'd just been asked straight out in a discussion or whatever at the end of the day, I wouldn't have said a thing! This got more out of me.' (Year 10 student)

'But the people who've been running it, we can see ... we've been with the sorts of people who will read it ... so we're careful what we say. If you found something like this online, you might not be so careful.' [Interviewer asks: 'More honest?'] 'A bit more and *how* you say it might be different!' (Year 10 student)

'But this isn't public, it's just for the university people isn't it? It's anonymous. So I think I've been more honest as there's no comeback, nobody to fall out with! Social media is public, you're always thinking about how you come across.' (Year 10 student)

Several students double-checked whether their responses would be anonymous and some asked who would be looking at what they wrote. Fears generally centred on whether negative comments would be interpreted as 'ungrateful' or even 'bad behaviour' by their school, or even held against them if they ever applied to Newcastle University. (For information, students' login to the closed forum established on the site was anonymous and password-protected, with no identifying information. They were also able to delete their involvement at any time during or following the project.)

The use of the 'Consider.it' tool has potential to offer student participants decision-making power – active rather than merely 'responsive' participation and joint decision-making. However, partly because of the faulty communication with schools and thus the students, consultation did not feed into shaping the project, leaving the organisers and partners retaining power over the content and sequencing of the project. One Year 12 student commented that "an ideal project would be to create a redesigned programme based on all these comments". It would certainly align better with the principles of ownership and co-creation that underpin the CCM/PBL ethos. The evaluation generated some interesting dialogue and positive feedback; however, it remains a contradiction that despite seeking feedback through a useful consultation tool, our perceived need to have overall control and accountability limited our openness to student voice. This raises the question: as CCM develops and evolves, how much control do we give school students? The obvious disadvantage of giving students more control is that teachers need to check what is learned against subject knowledge course requirements, and student voice might complicate this process, especially when the new Ofsted framework demands rich subject knowledge. The obvious advantage is to offer greater scope for engagement and opening conversations that they 'actually want to have'. In addition, it could provide a formal mode for teachers to obtain feedback that would help shape the project and identify critical moments that might indicate learning thresholds. Such documentation should advise other teachers about what might need reflection-in-action as they work with students.

## Conclusion

PBL/CCM has intrinsic merit as a balance to a test-driven curriculum that reifies the acquisition metaphor. It is worth doing. The larger question is whether it can provide a catalyst for developing a localised discourse, culture and infrastructure of learning opportunities with some of the characteristics of a 'Learning City'. The social justice argument is clear. As Perry and Francis (2012) conclude, the social class gap in attainment is partly driven by an education market in which the wealthy have purchasing power. They recommend 'philanthropic' approaches characterised by engagement with and ownership by disadvantaged young people, emphasising collectivist rather than individualist approaches (see Boaler, 2008) that only target higher-achieving students, valuing the existing knowledge of working-class young people, and offering greater parity between vocational and academic pathways. A more promising way forward is not just more of the same, as in the acquisition of subject content-based curricula, but a pragmatic strategy to balance this with more learning experiences that influence self-worth, identity, motivation and social capital.

The network of committed actors is evolving slowly and the local enterprise partnership (LEP)[1] is pivotal as it promotes PBL/CCM in pursuit of better careers guidance and labour market supply. Currently, the LEP, the Great North Museum (a local museum of natural history), Open Lab (university computing science department) and the first two authors as university staff offer a variety of support, including networking to interested schools. There are also consultants, including Thinkwell, and organisations from civil society, such as Success4All, who provide further valuable support. A guide to CCM (Leat and Thomas, 2016) has been produced (soon to have a second edition), which draws together some of our common knowledge. There is a flow of knowledge, information and opportunities, at least in this specialised domain, and Open Lab provide magnetic attraction through their digital technology specialism, which can be irresistible to some teachers. There is further networking to do as it is clear that other organisations, such as the City of Dreams initiative, have overlapping ambitions. Currently, the researchers are funded by the Edge Foundation to develop, trial with a school, document and archive 30 reusable PBL/CCM projects, which other schools can adapt to their contexts, and are providing free continuing professional development to teachers to strengthen this approach.

Inequalities in access to learning have been exacerbated by the COVID-19 lockdown, with differences in access to technology, space at home and adults that can support learning. The lockdown exposes the weakness of a system that over-relies on schools as the site for education. Anderson-Butcher and colleagues (2008) argue that schools are 'walled in', thus walling out a significant array of resources and expertise in the community that is more likely to engage young people. When schools are effectively disabled, the community cannot immediately fill the vacuum. There is emerging evidence that some schools are losing contact with many students, predominantly from poorer homes, suggesting that the attainment gap between rich and poor will grow further. Much of the work being provided by schools is very traditional in purpose and design, aiming to maintain progress in an exam-led, metric-focused system. However, some of the principal advocates of PBL, such as High Tech High, are taking the opportunity to circulate materials to challenge current assumptions about the curriculum.[2] This is an opportunity to widen our conception of how education is offered to young people, though time will tell whether the moment is seized.

A hinge point in the PBL/CCM collective endeavour is the role of Newcastle University, in particular, but also other universities in the region with a civic ambition. Indeed, as universities are often cited as anchor institutions, significant both in scale and lifespan, this is an appropriate time for some attention being given to their wider role in regional learning landscapes. Without assuming too much patronage, there is scope for universities to develop learning manifestos in collaboration with other educational actors that begin to bring some greater coherence and explicitness to learning pathways in the city and beyond. Hodgson and Spours (2013) have made the case for a 'high opportunity progression ecosystem' (HOPE) that has the promise of greater benefit for all young people in a locality, not least those who face the greatest barriers.

## Notes

[1]  LEPs are voluntary partnerships between local councils and businesses to help plan local economic development and labour market priorities.

[2]  See: https://hthgse.online/?page_id=2355

## References

Akkerman, S. and van Eijck, M. (2013) 'Re-theorising the student dialogically across and between boundaries of multiple communities', *British Educational Research Journal*, 39(1): 60–72.

Anderson-Butcher, D., Lawson, H.A., Bean, J., Flaspohler, P., Boone, B. and Kwiatkowski, A. (2008) 'Community collaboration to improve schools: introducing a new model from Ohio', *Children and Schools*, 30: 161–72.

Berliner, D. (2011) 'Rational responses to high-stakes testing: the case of curriculum narrowing and the harm that follows', *Cambridge Journal of Education*, 61(2): 151–65.

Boaler, J. (2008) 'Promoting "relational equity" and high mathematics achievement through an innovative mixed-ability approach', *British Educational Research Journal*, 34(2): 167–94.

Butin, D.W.P.M. (2010) *Service-Learning in Theory and Practice: The Future of Community Engagement in Higher Education*, New York: Palgrave Macmillan.

Facer, K. and Buchczyk, M. (2019) 'Understanding Learning Cities as discursive, material and affective infrastructures', *Oxford Review of Education*, 45(2): 168–87.

Freire, P. (1972) *Pedagogy of the Oppressed*, Harmondsworth: Penguin.

Hackman, H. (2005) 'Five essential components for social justice education', *Equity and Excellence in Education*, 38: 103–9.

Hodgson, A. and Spours, K. (2013) 'Tackling the crisis facing young people: building "high opportunity progression eco-systems"', *Oxford Review of Education*, 39(2): 211–28.

Jay, T., Rose, J. and Simmons, B. (2017) 'Finding "mathematics": parents questioning school-centred approaches to involvement in children's mathematics learning', *School Community Journal*, 27(1): 201–30.

Leat, D. and Lin, M. (1998) 'Developing a pedagogy of metacognition and transfer: some signposts for the generation and use of knowledge and the creation of research partnerships', *British Educational Research Journal*, 29(3): 383–415.

Leat, D. and Thomas, U. (2016) *A Schools and Partner's Guide to Community Curriculum Making through Enquiry and Project Based Learning*, Newcastle upon Tyne: Newcastle University.

Leat, D. and Thomas, U. (2017) 'Productive pedagogies – narrowing the gap between schools and communities?', *Forum Special Edition on Freedom to Learn*, 58(3): 371–84.

Leat, D. and Thomas, U. (2018) 'Exploring the role of "brokers" in developing a localised curriculum', *Curriculum Journal*, 20(2): 201–18.

Moll, L., Amanti, C., Neff, D. and Gonzalez, N. (1992) 'Funds of knowledge for teaching: using a qualitative approach to connect homes and classrooms', *Theory into Practice*, 31(2): 132–41.

Nomikou, E., Archer, L. and King, H. (2017) 'Building "science capital" in the classroom', *School Science Review*, 98(365): 118–24.

Patton, A. and Robin, J. (2012) *Work That Matters: The Teacher's Guide to Project Based Learning*, London: Paul Hamlyn Foundation.

Perry, E. and Francis, B. (2012) *The Social Class Gap for Educational Achievement: A Review of the Literature*, London: The RSA.

Phelan, P.K., Davidson, A.L. and Yu, H.C. (1998) *Adolescents' Worlds: Negotiating Family, Peers and School*, New York: Teachers College Press.

Sfard, A. (1998) 'On two metaphors for learning and the dangers of choosing just one', *Educational Researcher*, 27(2): 4–13.

Smith, R. and O'Leary, M. (2013) 'New public management in an age of austerity: knowledge and experience in further education', *Journal of Educational Administration and History*, 45(3): 244–66.

Stanton-Salazar, R.D. (2001) *Manufacturing Hope and Despair: The School and Kin Support Networks of US–Mexican Youth*, New York: Teachers College Press.

Thomas, J.W. (2000) *A Review of Research on Project-Based Learning*, San Rafael, CA: The Autodesk Foundation.

Thomas, L. (2012) *Learning About, By and for Peterborough*, London: RSA.

United Kingdom National Commission for UNESCO (undated) 'Education: learning cities'. Available at United Kingdom National Commission for UNESCO.

Westheimer, J. and Kahne, J. (2004) 'What kind of citizen? The politics of educating for democracy', *American Educational Research Journal*, 41(2): 237–69.

Worth, J. (2018) 'Latest teacher retention statistics paint a bleak picture for teacher supply in England', NFER, blog, 28 June. Available at: www.nfer.ac.uk/news-events/nfer-blogs/latest-teacher-retention-statistics-paint-a-bleak-picture-for-teacher-supply-in-england/

Wrigley, T. (2017) 'Canonical knowledge and common culture: in search of curricular justice', *European Journal of Curriculum Studies*, 4(1): 536–55.

Wrigley, T. (2018) ' "Knowledge", curriculum and social justice', *The Curriculum Journal*, 29(1): 4–24.

# 16

# The containment of democratic innovation: reflections from two university collaborations

*David Webb, Daniel Mallo, Armelle Tardiveau, Caroline Emmerson, Mark Pardoe and Marion Talbot*

## Introduction

This chapter develops a comparison of two projects based in the West End of Newcastle, both of which involved university–third sector collaborations focused on place-based action. Both of the projects began in 2015 and before the general election of that year, in a policy environment that combined severe cuts (from a relatively high base in terms of urban policy) with a multifaceted emphasis on public service innovation. One was the Fenham Pocket Park and the other was the Reclaim the Lanes project. The authors are David Webb, Armelle Tardiveau and Daniel Mallo (university researchers), and Caroline Emmerson (former Youth and Community Manager at the CHAT [Churches Acting Together] Trust), Marion Talbot (Newcastle City Councillor) and Mark Pardoe (Friends of Fenham Pocket Park Secretary). The projects took place at a time when the government was reforming public services amid a rhetoric of 'localism', which was perceived by many commentators as a way of focusing public attention on alleged top-down control under the earlier New Labour government and away from the real causes of austerity (Kisby, 2010; Levitas, 2012), while driving a broadly conceived privatisation agenda (Myers, 2017; Findlay-King et al, 2018). Nevertheless, in this chapter, we offer some empirical reflections on our efforts to take localism at its word and, by working within the envelope of this policy agenda, to extend democracy to communities and to everyday life.

Our core argument here relates to the tensions that arise from the simultaneous pursuit of localism and austerity. These tensions are also contextualised by the marketisation of the third sector and by the concentration of decision-making power within council structures.

These conditions, we will argue, have important implications for the form of democratic innovation we were able to achieve, as well as, ultimately, the outcomes arising from the projects. In combination, their effect was to undermine and contain efforts at democratic innovation that might otherwise have come closer to the populist policy rhetoric of achieving 'a radical shift of power from the centralised state to local communities' (HM Government, 2010: 2). Through the two projects, we explore the limits that austerity places on social innovation and the implications these may have for the civic university agenda in a future that is likely to be defined by a post-pandemic economic agenda.

## The policy context for the two projects: localism and decentralisation

'Localism' can be understood as an attempt to manage two competing agendas. The 'Red Tory' agenda pushed by, among others, Phillip Blond and his think tank ResPublica centred on the need to rebuild community relationships as the basis for a good society and a 'politics of virtue' (Blond, 2010a: 35). This appealed to the tradition of shire-based compassionate conservatism. It influenced funders in the community and voluntary sector, most notably, the Big Lottery Fund, but also a number of piecemeal funding pots that the government attempted to draw together in a 'regeneration toolkit' (DCLG, 2012).

In contrast with the Red Tory agenda, which criticises both social and economic liberalism for focusing too much on the individual, the Department for Communities and Local Government's publication *Decentralisation and the Localism Bill: An Essential Guide* (DCLG, 2010) couched its ideas in what was described elsewhere as a 'muscular liberalism' (White, 2011). In practice, the interest in community politics and the Big Society were drawn into a more familiar neoliberal impulse to externalise the delivery of public services (see, for example, Miller and Rose, 2008). David Cameron pledged to 'create a new presumption ... that public services should be open to a range of providers competing to offer better services', ideally local initiatives (Stratton, 2011). Ultimately, the Department for Communities and Local Government's response incorporated elements of Blond's agenda but only to the extent that they fitted into a broader policy of public sector austerity that resulted, for local government, in the 'worst financial settlement in living memory' (Hastings et al, 2015: 601).

## The projects: Reclaim the Lanes and Fenham Pocket Park

In the university sector, government support for localism and public service reform was matched by a continued commitment to rewarding academic institutions able to demonstrate impact arising from their research, as well as through initiatives by the Economic and Social Research Council and the Arts and Humanities Research Council that supported co-creation and knowledge exchange. It was this combination of 'impact' with an interest in the politics of justice and democracy surrounding place-based action that provided the backdrop for the two projects discussed here. Both Reclaim the Lanes and Fenham Pocket Park were funded by Economic and Social Science Research Council impact grants that enabled work in partnership with local organisations. Reclaim the Lanes was developed and delivered with CHAT Trust, an outreach third sector organisation engaging with hard-to-reach young people and the wider community. The collaboration explored how the community could be involved in co-designing and co-delivering environmental services aimed at environmental cleanliness and pride (Webb, 2017: 62). Fenham Pocket Park was a collaboration with Sustrans, the sustainable transport charity, whose remit is to redesign streets and neighbourhoods with people to improve walking and cycling. Coming from an urban design standpoint, the research also sought to stimulate the co-design and co-delivery of services and changes in the area by adopting a 'socially engaged' approach to temporary urbanism (Tardiveau and Mallo, 2014).

A shared starting point for both of the projects discussed here was curiosity about whether localism really could do what it seemed to suggest: provide opportunities for local direction of the way place problems might be addressed. Indeed, Greg Clark, Minister of State for Decentralisation, opened his foreword to the government's *Decentralisation and the Localism Bill: An Essential Guide* with the following quote: 'If central government is everywhere, then local decision-making is nowhere – everything is subject to national politics, with nothing left to community leadership' (DCLG, 2010: 1). Localism therefore implied making room for at least some degree of political autonomy from the centre as a means of loosening top-down control. The Fenham Pocket Park project tested this through a series of temporary interventions that brought a group of residents together with the council in a supporting rather than driving capacity. For Reclaim the Lanes, the idea was also to develop a community with their own sense of ground-level knowledge, which might be brought to bear on issues of street litter, fly-tipping and care of the local environment.

## Reflecting on the projects: action research and autoethnography

The enhanced role of universities brought with it the need to consider more deeply the fact that academics were likely to be caught up in the very policy environment they were seeking to understand. Being engaged in 'impact' in this way involves normative, ethical and inescapably political motivations for action, grounded in a changing sense of the social, political and institutional context for impact work (Ferdinand et al, 2007).[1] This changes the relationship between researchers and project partners, making research as much about action and self-reflection as it is about studying the behaviour or accounts of others (Holman Jones et al, 2013).

As a means of reflecting on our projects, and for the purpose of this chapter, we adopted a particular form of autoethnography. We invited the central collaborator from Reclaim the Lanes to join a discussion with all three academics involved in both projects. We then repeated the process, inviting the central collaborator from the Fenham Pocket Park project to a discussion aimed at identifying cross-cutting issues. We sought to draw out commonalities and differences in our experience and recollection of both projects, developing a contained base of evidence with which to put our own autoethnographic reflections into context.

## Austerity and community action

Both projects reacted to the local impact of austerity, with Reclaim the Lanes occurring in an area that had been considered at risk from housing market failure but had still seen huge cuts to local environmental services. Fenham Pocket Park sought to put something back in the context of cuts to community services. One of our interviewees, who was a local councillor until recently, explained the experience of these cuts for local authority officers, which had brought the loss of years of experience and connections built up in the community:

> 'The individual officers who had been there for a long time could see a difference in the role that they were doing from the role that they had done. And for some of them, it was quite sad ... Officers were finding themselves doing things that were not positive, admirable or enjoyable. Whereas this [Fenham Pocket Park] actually was something that was very good as it was real, a physical intervention, it was

something you could see and gave people pleasure. People walked passed it and smiled, it made a difference. Quite many of the officers that were engaged in it just found it a positive thing to be engaged with. It was a bit different from the other work they were doing because it is hard to constantly have to do things with less. Whereas [Fenham Pocket Park] seems to counteract and capture people's imagination.' (Participant 1)

In a similar way, Reclaim the Lanes drew on the help of a digital artist in residence funded by the local authority. Both projects brought an element of positivity and fun to a period where local authority officers felt redundancies and residents felt service cuts.

The intention of the academics involved in the Fenham Pocket Park was to use a series of innovative participatory methods, including temporary interventions, to seek out a community of residents able to generate and trial their own ideas about the built environment. Daniel (one of the researchers) described this as "using physical change to generate community energy" or a "change in how the space started to be perceived and used … more the social aspect than the physical change". The hope was that "the temporary interventions might become anchor points and visual references for the community. And they will become little moments … of empowerment, you know, this is something that they've made, they feel proud of and I think that's something that's really powerful."

Reclaim the Lanes adopted a similar ethic, using street parties and environmental work to begin local conversations about the council's approach to delivering environmental services and to find out if young people could be encouraged to take pride in their local environment. Caroline (formerly at the CHAT Trust) thought back to a European research project she had been involved in with the council called Global Awareness in Action (GAIA): "The council and the GAIA project had been trying to do this and we were actually doing it. The council had been trying to impose community sparks top-down and that hadn't worked … it's got to be bottom-up." Over time, however, the issues covered by Reclaim the Lanes, as well as its approach to community knowledge, would prove to be controversial, with street-level knowledge of inequalities and deficiencies in service provision emerging at a time when the council's environmental team was struggling to deal with cuts. As Daniel suggested: "So, with environmental services, you were treading on their territory." Caroline continued: "It was the environmental services that caused the problem not the communities section. The problem was that the council was working in chimneys." The environment was made worse by central government's decision to impose significant budget cuts on local authorities year by year, without proper planning or forewarning local authorities.

## Democratic renewal and the promotion of 'better services'

Both projects, in their own ways, sought to gain a particular kind of community knowledge that could be directed towards the co-design and co-delivery of services. Fenham Pocket Park was about engaging the local residents in envisioning alternatives to what was perceived as a dreary urban landscape. A series of temporary interventions opened up the community to experiment and experience positive ways of living in the street despite it being dominated by cars. The research mobilised an active community group in the neighbourhood, who drove the co-production process. Reclaim the Lanes shared the interest in community mobilisation to gain, in the words of Dave (one of the researchers), "a causal picture of what was happening on a day-to-day basis". This knowledge was then directed towards service providers through informal discussions with officers, attempts at dialogue with the cabinet member, publishing a report and holding a workshop, with the aim of promoting a democratic approach to service delivery (Webb and Greening Wingrove, 2017). However, when the funding started to dry up, "that sort of chunk of knowledge all disappeared" and anecdotal reports from residents became more important. There was a feeling that more council resources had to be spent on clean-ups that could have been avoided with the benefit of services informed by better community knowledge.

Despite having a starting point centred on community input into service co-delivery, both projects were affected, albeit very differently, by a default mode of council decision-making that is often labelled 'decide–announce–defend'. Reclaim the Lanes had viewed terraced back lanes as underused spaces with community potential. However, the council decided to permanently locate large, 'communal' bins there instead, effectively reclaiming the spaces for waste storage and undermining engagement with residents about bringing in wheeled bins. The roll-out of the communal bins came in the face of numerous practical concerns and substantial opposition from residents, and led to the total collapse of the household recycling system, undermining much of the progress on behavioural change that had been achieved by Big Lottery investment in the area.

In the context of Fenham Pocket Park, 'decide–announce–defend' was experienced in the way cuts impacted the swimming pool, library and housing office adjoining the park. A university-based student project sought collaborative ways to consolidate these uses. However, as space became free, pressure arose to fill it and council decision-makers seized on a time-limited opportunity to house a drug and alcohol recovery support service in the buildings. A meeting was held to inform residents, prompting strong local criticism, while those involved in the Friends of the Pocket Park group were much more positive. Armelle (one of the researchers) explained that:

'The Friends of the Pocket Park received the information like everyone else: "This is going to happen." And they heard through the neighbourhood people, generally against it, pretty much what they lamented was the process rather than the outcome, and through a discussion with them, it turned out it was an opportunity to actually strengthen the Pocket Park, involve the volunteers.'

One issue that emerged through reflections in the interviews was the huge variation in local people's understanding of the issues affecting them. As Marion, reflecting on her experience canvassing as a local councillor, noted: "anything that goes on in any area is perceived as the council's responsibility or fault. Often, it really isn't, but that's not what people what to hear." There were differences in the demographics of those involved with Fenham Pocket Park relative to the wider area but, nevertheless, one of the benefits of building a community around the park appeared to be a better understanding of the constraints affecting council decision-making, as well as a sense of being able to affect some decisions. Both Daniel and Armelle speculated that these factors may have been crucial to the Friends of the Pocket Park's ability to develop a positive response to the drug and alcohol recovery support service.

## Time-limited funding and differences in local 'resources in kind'

There was a recognition that the social position of the residents who eventually constituted the Friends of the Pocket Park was different to those involved in Reclaim the Lanes. Friends of the Pocket Park were keen to address local issues of concern to them, such as cars parking on the pavement and obstructing pedestrians, and viewed the public realm as an important space for social interaction. As Armelle explained: "Through the process, we realised that they have meaningful social and cultural capital, as well as strong convictions about what they can contribute to the community." They also had strong institutional support at the community level. As Caroline pointed out:

> 'I noticed you've got Fenham Association of Residents involved now, [a name] has been doing an awful lot of work out with the community for years so you do have your key community players in there as well who, he's paid obviously to be there, they have an allotment, he has an awful lot of knowledge and expertise he can contribute to the group if he needed to, if he was called upon, and they've all got a vested interest in making the area look better.'

Daniel agreed: "That's absolutely true. I think Fenham Association of Residents was really helpful in the very beginning [to move the community] towards collaboration with the council rather than simply receiving an asset transfer." Every year, the Friends of the Pocket Park are able to access a small amount of money, maybe £1,000, to sustain the maintenance of the area.

The social context for Reclaim the Lanes was more challenging, partly because the population was more transient, more likely to be in poverty, less likely to speak English and more likely to be getting to grips with living in an unfamiliar country, but also because the route into that community, mainly working through young people, was more resource-intensive. As Dave noted, while working across the community, to a large extent, "we came in through young people who didn't speak English, or some of them spoke English". With the use of a translator, local people from the Roma community were encouraged to put on activities and paid small amounts to cover time and materials. As Caroline noted: "That's kind of where we were going, where it wasn't reliant on us to (a) provide the activity and (b) pay someone to do it"; "But it needed the funding for the link worker to make that happen", Dave interjected. A key characteristic of Reclaim the Lanes was also the need to understand and connect with those who took part. The strongest connection was around young people, with parents keen to see their children perform and to get outdoors and engaged in arts and social activities. Where place was central to all involved in the Fenham Pocket Park, the relationship of Reclaim the Lanes with place differed markedly among those involved, with more immediate needs often taking precedence. A key advantage of employing a link worker would have been that those needs could have been better understood and responded to.

## The containment of the projects

> 'A lot of people, I think, feel disenfranchised, feel that they don't have a voice.' (Caroline)

Both projects sought democratic innovation principally in a changed relationship between those within communities and the local authority, modelled along more communitarian lines. It was Caroline who laid out this vision most clearly. Drawing on her own extensive history of youth and community work, she reflected that:

> 'Slowly and slowly, the council took more control: "Oh, you can't do that, we'll sort it." They employed the people to then run it and they disempowered community. And what we're doing is going back the other way, and you can't just turn round one day and "Oh, you've now got to do it because we don't have the funding." You've disempowered communities for so long, you've taken control from them and now you're expecting them to just go back 30-odd years. That's not going to happen. You need to build it back up again and then you can't complain once you re-empower people that they have a voice because once you give power, once you cede it, you can't then pick and choose who you want to listen to when.'

This communitarian ethos was similar to Phillip Blond's (2010b) call for a 'politics of relationships'. In the case of Reclaim the Lanes, it led to the encouragement of community debate and action on environmental issues. However, both projects would be affected by the two 'evils' of social and economic liberalism, which Blond confronted in his book but was unable to challenge within public policy.

The impact of social liberalism was felt in utilitarian and relatively top-down approaches to managing local authority service delivery, while cutbacks to local government funding and funding for small community organisations reflect the economically liberal agenda of championing the individual over the state. Between us, as academic activists, the culture of top-down decision-making posed a moral dilemma. On the one hand, it can be associated with a Thatcherite legacy of centralised control and audit but, on the other, it also brings with it a commitment to universality in service provision. Daniel and Armelle advocated most strongly for local involvement and agency. As Daniel reflected: "People were not simply recipients of things; they were changing things themselves. There is a question whether the council is interested in pushing collaborative approaches or whether they are happy to just deliver what they can." As Armelle explained: "We are trying to walk a line between council and citizen to change the culture in how services are delivered. Citizens could be involved in delivering and shaping, and the council could, instead of trying to [always] seek for a solution, have more of a role of an enabler." There was a shared hope that this approach would address what Marion saw as a "lack of place-based pride". However, she also acknowledged that the situation was not simple: "People want a solution to the problem they are facing, and actually sometimes we haven't got the solution, but they don't necessarily want to be part of the solution. So, when you talk about co-production, some citizens just want somebody to do it for them." Dave held a similar view: "With Wingrove, when we talked about litter, some were saying: 'Well, that's council responsibility.' You can call it 'dependency culture' but that's a legitimate way of looking at things."

In terms of the projects' relationship with economic liberalism, the differing social environments led to different degrees of dependence on community sector funding and institutions. Reclaim the Lanes had relationships with three institutions – Greening Wingrove neighbourhood cooperative, The Time Exchange and the CHAT Trust – all of which fed time and resources into the events, and were anchor institutions supporting community activity. However, in 2018, they were all suffering from sharply declining funding and a lack of security around their future existence. The CHAT Trust, which was the key partner involved with Reclaim the Lanes, suffered most and was forced to close its doors in the autumn of 2018.

The organisations that supported Fenham Pocket Park also changed dramatically. The project was initially developed with Sustrans and supported with time-limited funding. The Friends of the Pocket Park then leaned on the swimming pool to maintain the park on a daily basis. However, in 2019, the swimming pool closed down due to a combination of reducing grant funding and structural damage resulting from lack of maintenance. The extension of the park, due to be completed in the summer/autumn of 2020, is now partially supported by Public Health England via the drug and alcohol recovery unit located in the library. The future of the part of the Fenham Pocket

Park adjacent to the swimming pool is uncertain as the pool has now closed permanently, is beyond repair and could be pulled down. As a result, the maintenance and life of the Fenham Pocket Park is entirely reliant on the continued commitment of the Friends of the Pocket Park.

## Conclusion

For both the projects, we highlight significant areas of innovation, which encouraged and brought together new groupings of local citizens around positive, place-based change. However, they also highlight the structural weakness of democratic innovation in a context of the ongoing retrenchment of core services and where the local authority must make cuts in an often reactive and time-pressured way, with little prior warning or planning on the part of central government. The projects underline the potential gains of localism and the Big Society as means of countering weak support for local democratic autonomy between 1979 and the present. However, the projects also highlight the fragility of those gains in a context of insecurity of funding for those anchor institutions that have a central role in civic life. Ultimately, time-limited innovation cannot act as a substitute for stable institutions that perform a role supporting local democracy through citizen engagement, awareness raising and building connections with formal democratic arenas.

This story offers an important word of warning for advocates of a 'politics of the common good'. It suggests that democratic innovation cannot be 'contained' within a broader neoliberal attitude towards democracy and the economy that prioritises cheaper, more 'efficient', service provision. In a sense, the lesson is that you cannot fight free of neoliberal forms of politics and democracy independently of fighting free of neoliberal economics. That is not to say, however, that the funding of community sector activities by local authorities in the past has been without issue as this relationship expresses a particular balance of power between these actors. The situation therefore poses a dilemma about how stable community institutions might best be funded in the future, such that they can effectively promote democratic, egalitarian and more effective forms of local decision-making with a degree of independence from local authority hierarchies. That question is even more pressing now that we are looking to cities to lead a recovery from the COVID-19 pandemic.

One potential way forward has recently been proposed as a means of guiding the work of the North of Tyne Combined Authority, which includes Newcastle. It argues for the need to connect democratic innovation with forms of financial sustenance drawn from alternative, rather than neoliberal, economics. Community wealth building and the development of cooperative businesses are seen as means by which social assets could be developed and surplus channelled into community institutions (Driscoll, 2019; Guinan and O'Neill, 2019). Democratic businesses could, in principle, provide sufficient independence and autonomy to support a more radical community sector, as well as a revival of small- and medium-scale enterprise. However, it would be possible to pose the challenge that you cannot fight free of neoliberal economics independently of fighting free of neoliberal politics and democracy. In this sense, the politics and economics of democratic and egalitarian local decision-making are intertwined, and if headway is to be made in one area, then progress must be pursued in both. Inevitably, this is a project that requires practical and political support from community, state, social enterprise and cooperative sectors.

These suggestions have significant implications for the future of how the 'impact' agenda is understood locally within academic institutions. The experiences documented in this chapter evidence the difficulties of trying to marry the notion of a 'civic university' to community and local authority sectors where funding is scarce. Before COVID-19, it looked just about possible to continue with partnership projects of two or three years in duration, aimed at attracting impact funding. However, the political and economic consequences of the pandemic demand that we adopt a much more ambitious agenda that goes beyond merely reacting to the institutional demand for impact case studies. A proactive view of the university as an important economic entity and anchor institution in the regional economy brings with it the potential for long-term partnerships and immense political, cultural and economic change. Not only is there a strong moral case to do this, but, ironically, the opportunity to demonstrate impact here is extraordinary. Perhaps this, then, is how future university impact work might escape the economic containment of democratic innovation.

**Note**
[1]  See, for example, Vallance et al's (2019) reflections that in certain circumstances, universities have the potential to act as external suppliers of policymaking and coordination work that might traditionally have been expected to take place within local authorities.

**References**
Blond, P. (2010a) *Red Tory: How the Left and Right have Broken Britain and How We Can Fix It*, London: Faber and Faber.

Blond, P. (2010b) 'Red Tory: the future of progressive conservatism?', 6 April. Available at: www.youtube.com/watch?v=sxMdwBL0EV4

DCLG (Department for Communities and Local Government) (2010) *Decentralisation and the Localism Bill: An Essential Guide*, London: DCLG. Available at: https://assets.publishing.service.gov. uk/government/uploads/system/uploads/attachment_data/file/ 5951/1793908.pdf

DCLG (Department for Communities and Local Government) (2012) *Regeneration to Enable Growth: A Toolkit Supporting Community-Led Regeneration*, London: DCLG. Available at: https://assets.publishing. service.gov.uk/government/uploads/system/uploads/attachment_ data/file/5983/2064899.pdf

Driscoll, J. (2019) *Prosperity You Can Be Part Of: Manifesto for North of Tyne Mayor 2019*, Newcastle upon Tyne: #JD4Mayor. Available at: www.jd4mayor.com/wp-content/uploads/2019/04/manifesto.pdf

Ferdinand, J., Pearson, G., Rowe, M. and Worthington, F. (2007) 'A different kind of ethics', *Ethnography*, 8(4): 519–43.

Findlay-King, L., Nichols, G., Forbes, D. and Macfadyen, G. (2018) 'Localism and the Big Society: the asset transfer of leisure centres and libraries – fighting closures or empowering communities?', *Leisure Studies*, 37(2): 158–70.

Guinan, J. and O'Neill, M. (2019) 'From community wealth-building to system change: local roots for transformation', *IPPR Progressive Review*, 25(4): 383–93.

Hastings, A., Bailey, N., Gannon, M., Besemer, K. and Bramley, G. (2015) 'Coping with the cuts? The management of the worst financial settlement in living memory', *Local Government Studies*, 41(4): 601–21.

HM Government (2010) *Decentralisation and the Localism Bill: An Essential Guide*, London: HM Government.

Holman Jones, S.L., Adams, T.E. and Ellis, C. (eds) (2013) *Handbook of Autoethnography*, London and New York: Routledge.

Kisby, B. (2010) 'The Big Society: power to the people?', *The Political Quarterly*, 81(4): 484–91.

Levitas, R. (2012) 'The just's umbrella: austerity and the Big Society in Coalition policy and beyond', *Critical Social Policy*, 32(3): 320–42.

Miller, P. and Rose, N.S. (2008) *Governing the Present: Administering Economic, Social and Personal Life*, Cambridge: Polity.

Myers, J. (2017) 'To austerity and beyond! Third sector innovation or creeping privatization of public sector services?', *Public Money and Management*, 37(2): 97–104.

Stratton, A. (2011) 'David Cameron to end "state monopoly" in provision of public services', *The Guardian*, 21 February. Available at: www.theguardian.com/society/2011/feb/21/david-cameron-public-services

Tardiveau, A. and Mallo, D. (2014) 'Unpacking and challenging habitus: an approach to temporary urbanism as a socially engaged practice', *Journal of Urban Design*, 19(4): 456–72.

Vallance, P., Tewdwr-Jones, M. and Kempton, L. (2019) 'Facilitating spaces for place-based leadership in centralized governance systems: the case of Newcastle City Futures', *Regional Studies*, 53(12): 1723–33.

Webb, D. (2017) 'Tactical urbanism: delineating a critical praxis', *Planning Theory and Practice*, 19(1): 58–73.

Webb, D. and Greening Wingrove (2017) 'Advocacy through environmental change: developing a critical praxis'. Available at: www.ncl.ac.uk/media/wwwnclacuk/architectureplanninglandscape/files/reclaim-the-lanes.pdf

White, M. (2011) 'Muscular liberalism: Nick Clegg finds new use for an old phrase', *The Guardian*, 11 May. Available at: www.theguardian.com/global/2011/may/11/muscular-liberalism-nick-clegg-phrase

# 17

# Citizen power, the university and the North East

*Sara Bryson and Liz Todd*

## Introduction

This chapter explores community organising through the Tyne and Wear Citizens alliance in North East England and the role of the university in the alliance. Community organising has a long-established track record since the 1930s in the US and in the form of Citizens UK[1] in London since 1989 (Wills et al, 2009; Wills, 2012). It has been highly successful in London, leading to the formation of the Living Wage Foundation.[2] The economic conditions and growing inequality in the North East (see the chapter 'The North East of England') make for diverse and urgent societal needs. Given the reduction in central government funding of councils under the name of austerity and the lack of an effective industrial policy, there was interest in what community organising might be able to offer the region. Tyne and Wear Citizens was formed in 2015 when five key anchor civic institutions were willing to start to organise and pool money to fund an organiser.[3] In this chapter, Sara Bryson (the first community organiser in Tyne and Wear Citizens) and Liz Todd (one of the academics that have been leading the university membership of Tyne and Wear Citizens) tell the story of its first four years. We take a stance that is informed as insiders, yet aim to be critical and reflective. This chapter considers factors that have led to a number of achievements in relation to impacts of austerity and addresses the role of Tyne and Wear Citizens in responding to what are likely to be long-lasting societal impacts of COVID-19. The role of the university in community organising is discussed and some important critical issues are raised.

It was not clear at the start whether the methods of Citizens UK would work in North East England. Community organising relies on a strong and active civic society. Making it work would need many more organisations than the original five and would need them to work together. In the North East, civic society has been rapidly in decline (see the chapter 'The North East of England'). Trade union membership and church numbers (organisations that are often part of local alliances of Citizens UK) have fallen. Through austerity, the voluntary, community and social enterprise sector has become an agent for service delivery, a 'shadow state' (Newman and Lake, 2006), and so less able to engage in political action or citizen empowerment (Dagdeviren et al, 2019). This has been a particular problem in North East England. The fragmentation and effective privatisation of education via academisation means fewer educational establishments are truly rooted in their communities. Community divisions unleashed by the politics following the referendum to leave the EU, given that the North East voted to leave but has gained from European funding, have added substantially to pressures on civic society in the North East. Wills (2009) discusses the achievements of London Citizens despite the decline in geographical community in cities but the North East is a very different context. Wills (2009) explains the success in terms of the diverse alliance of organisations working together around a community organising methodology that enables London Citizens to capture some of the remaining diverse islands of social capital, of community, in East London. London has higher ethnic diversity and population mobility, and larger wealth inequalities, than the North East. It is also home to a higher proportion of large business headquarters and the North East has a larger proportion of small- to medium-sized businesses. However, Wills was writing at a time when political challenges were different to those today. While communities were dealing in 2008/09 with the banking crisis and youth riots, biting austerity, populism, Brexit and COVID-19 were yet to appear.

Newcastle University was one of the founding partners of Tyne and Wear Citizens. While Newcastle University has a history of civic engagement, and while local societal impact was and is university vision and strategy, it was not clear what form university involvement in Tyne and Wear Citizens would take. Many organisations have links with the university, which take varied forms for research and teaching. Would the link with Tyne and Wear Citizens be just another partnership or would it be distinctive in some way? It was not clear how any involvement in Tyne and Wear Citizens would be focused on research or on teaching, or whether staff would be involved in any jointly agreed local actions.

This chapter first relates the origin of the Citizens UK model of community organising and then describes how Tyne and Wear Citizens started. The achievements of the first four years (2016–19) in starting to tackle poverty, create safer cities and promote mental health in the North East are discussed next. We try to bring out how community organising has been used, including some underpinning ideas, as well as pointing out where the university has been involved. Final sections discuss more critical issues about using community organising in the North East, including the role of the university.

## Modern community organising

Saul Alinsky (1971), the founder of modern community organising, was focused on improving the living conditions of poor communities across the US. He began organising in disadvantaged areas of Chicago (the 'Back of the Yards') in the 1930s during the Great Depression. He focused on organising within the context of economic suffering with those who wanted change, bringing together a broad range of groups who had previously been hostile towards one another: Irish Catholics, Serbs and Croatians, Czechs and Slovaks, and Poles and Lithuanians. The way they organised and built power meant that they could advocate for the community and stabilise the neighbourhood.

In 1939, Alinsky established the Industrial Areas Foundation to bring this method of reform to other declining urban neighbourhoods. With its origins in Chicago, its most famous proponent is perhaps Barack Obama, who was himself a community organiser. As an approach, it was employed during the civil rights era, with leaders such as Rosa Parks and Martin Luther King trained in organising methodology. It has been effective in tackling gang violence, promoting affordable housing and living wages, and organising migrant workers across the US up to the present day.

The methodology is based on the theory that if you want change, you need power. This is the idea that broad-based organisations might not have certain kinds of power, such as monetary wealth or high-level corporate positions, but everyone has relational power. Civil society (institutions of faith, education and community) can consciously and deliberately work together to build relational power in order to succeed in tackling issues of social justice for the common good. This kind of power is created by building a broad and diverse alliance that is broadly representative of the community. The people and the money that Tyne and Wear Citizens has (from subscriptions from alliance organisations) are organised to take public action and win change.

Citizens UK is based on Alinsky's (1971) methods and was brought to the UK over 30 years ago. It began in East London and then spread across London. Over more recent years, chapters have emerged in Birmingham, Nottingham, Wales, Leeds, Tyne and Wear, and Manchester. Today, there are now over 5,000 real living wage employers, bringing an additional £210 million in wages and giving 180,000 low-paid workers a pay rise.[4] Other national achievements of Citizens UK have included winning caps on fees and credit on payday loans, affordable housing in London, road safety measures, ending the detention of refugees for immigration purposes, and developing safe and legal routes for refugees in response to the Syrian crisis.[5]

## Tyne and Wear Citizens: a beginning

Community organising is not about mobilising or about offering a service model or a community development approach. Instead, community organising is about building the capacity for communities to develop the power for themselves in order to make change happen. The work goes beyond the usual description of problems to win tangible changes in a relatively short timescale. Although there were people in North East England eager to give it a go, it was not clear if a community organising approach was needed and, if so, whether a chapter of Citizens UK could be formed. Eventually, enough willing organisations came forward in 2015 to fund the first community organiser.

We spent 2016 developing a broad-based, diverse and strong alliance of 25 civil society institutions, including churches, mosques, primary and secondary schools, university departments, charities, and community groups. Tyne and Wear Citizens does not take state funding in order to enable more independent action to take place on any issue or concern.

During the first year, we carried out an in-depth listening campaign. We held conversations within our member institutions, asking: 'What is putting pressure on you, your family and community?' Several thousand face-to-face conversations took place, capturing the perspectives of a diverse range of people living in Newcastle, Durham and Sunderland. Findings were shared at issues workshops. We began to realise that although many of us came from different backgrounds, our communities faced similar injustices. Member institutions came together at a delegates' assembly to decide and vote on the issues we were going to act on. Three issues were chosen: poverty, mental health and safer cities. Action teams were formed to begin strategising and organising around the issues we sought to change. The first task was a power analysis of each issue so we could identify and build relationships with key people who could make change happen, for example, transport executives were identified to talk about hate crime on the Tyne and Wear Metro and council leaders to talk about poverty.

The agenda, in terms of the specific goals of the three issues, of Tyne and Wear Citizens was officially launched in November 2017 in front of 1,000 citizens. At the event, each issue was introduced and people were invited to the stage to pledge to work to achieve the goals, for example, the communications director for the regional underground and overground train provider (Nexus Tyne and Wear Metro) pledged to bring bus and train companies together to meet with leaders about hate crime.

All Tyne and Wear Citizens events and meetings are about building power and building leaders able to act, and this was no less the case with the November 2017 launch. The process of building leaders was demonstrated when hundreds of people had a role in hosting the event, such as co-chairing, timekeeping, speaking and giving personal testimony. Many had not previously spoken at a public meeting. It felt like a significant moment in the North East, and it could be said that a different form of politics was taking shape. Action teams met following the launch, with an emphasis on taking public action together, which meant that instead of the community organiser alone attending meetings with those in power, we took a group of people from our different institutions. The term 'community leader' is used for anyone taking any part in community organising; the term does not mean a hierarchical management role in Tyne and Wear Citizens. Tyne and Wear Citizens aims for a collective form of leadership, and training is given to equip locally rooted people with the skills, knowledge and confidence to lead change themselves.

The launch event was a good start but whether Tyne and Wear Citizens would be able to win meaningful change together would be the real test of the alliance. Achievements over its first four years (2016–19) in each of the three issues are summarised in the next section, making key aspects of the community organising process more visible. While each institution in the alliance has played important and complex roles in the three issues, for the purposes of this chapter, the role of Newcastle University is highlighted and later discussed. What is distinctive and effective but also not easy in how Tyne and Wear Citizens operates is analysed. Finally, the contribution of Tyne and Wear Citizens to societal challenges such as austerity and COVID-19 is discussed.

## Making change happen

### Poverty

### *A real living wage*

Unsurprisingly, poverty was one of the issues most affecting our communities. The North East has the lowest proportion of real living wage employers in the country, the highest proportion of people on zero-hours contracts and one of the most used food banks in the UK in the West End of Newcastle. Work was often not a route out of poverty, with 72 per cent of children living in poverty having a working parent and low pay being one of the main reasons for people using food banks. This made the campaign to increase the number of real living wage employers in the North East the obvious place to start.

The poverty action team is chaired by Citizens Advice Newcastle (an organisation independent from Citizens UK that gives free advice to people with money and other problems) and includes leaders from institutions such as Newcastle University. The group began by writing to a range of employers who had strong ethical positions. Virgin Money in Newcastle became the group's first success, resulting in an uplift in pay for 500 workers. Some employers took more persuading, so Tyne and Wear Citizens carried out extensive listening exercises with low-paid workers and conducted public actions, including at St James' Park football ground. The result was by the end of 2019, the number of employers paying a real living wage had trebled from just 30 in the previous year to over 100, resulting in a pay rise for 3,000 low-paid North East workers.

In 2015, when Citizens UK came to the North East, none of the regional local authorities or universities paid the real living wage, yet all of them had and still have a strong commitment to tackling inequality. For university staff involved in the early days of Tyne and Wear Citizens, there was a growing question in the poverty action group about when the real living wage campaign spotlight would turn to Newcastle University. In 2018, Newcastle University began an extensive listening campaign to hear first-hand from staff not receiving a living wage and to find out what impact a real living wage would have on their lives. Citizens UK saw this as a bold and brave step, enabling frank and open discussions to take place across campus. This brought together cleaners, porters, catering staff, academic staff, support staff and undergraduate and postgraduate students in a unique and engaging way. Over 30 group listening sessions took place, involving many individual conversations, where over 45 staff and students listened to 220 (out of about 550) people who were not at that time being paid a real living wage. Over 80 pages of written feedback were produced by those doing the listening (data from Newcastle University's listening campaign's internal report). The difference that a real living wage would make was recorded in the feedback as to 'enable people to start a family, eat decent food', and it was documented that, at present, 'every month was a struggle to survive' and 'can't afford days out'. Tyne and Wear Citizens' listening campaign was not research or market research; its purpose was to find issues, stories and leaders. The result of the first-hand accounts, together with the production of financial models, was that the Newcastle University executive board agreed to become a real living wage employer. All in-house staff received the new pay rates from August 2019 and full accreditation (to require university contractors to pay the real living wage) followed before the end of the year. The result of using listening sessions to encourage the take-up of leadership by those being listened to was that cleaners, hospitality staff and porters became involved in either doing the listening themselves or in taking further action. There was quite a change from saying at the start of the listening campaign that they did not believe anything would change, to having the following varied reactions to the real living wage decision and the need to do more: 'over the moon', 'a starting point', 'about time', 'surprised – did well – let's crack on'.

Newcastle University staff are now continuing their work on tackling a number of fair work issues, including shift patterns and uniform supplies. One of the unintended outcomes of the listening process was the development and deepening of relationships across the university. Professors, undergraduate and postgraduate students, managers, secretaries, catering staff, cleaners, and more were working together in an action group to make further work changes. Leadership was developed as staff that had previously felt invisible and unvalued now came forward to take part in action on fair work issues. A union official attending the meeting to decide issues said that it was the most democratic meeting he had ever attended.

People's visibility was increased as managers across the university looked for ways to include those previously under-represented (such as cleaners, caterers and porters) in the posters around campus or in a range of university events. The impact was felt not only by the individuals involved, but by the university community. There are also potential economic implications for the wider region if other organisations start paying the real living wage. A Smith Institute report found that if 25 per cent of workers in the North of Tyne Combined Authority were paid the real living wage, the economy in the authority would grow by £29 million (Hunter, 2018).

## Just Change

'Just Change' became the second poverty issue. It was raised by pupils from Park View School, one of the alliance members. The discussion started with Year 10 pupils about food poverty. Jess, from Year 10, said: "You know what would make a difference to me? If I could have my change from my dinner money." When asked what she meant by that, she then explained: "Well, if I'm off school on a Monday, I still have £2.10 on a Tuesday. Where does Monday's £2.10 go?"

It became clear that while those who pay for school dinners had a credit balance that rolls forward, those on free school meals did not. Children North East's poverty-proofing audit for schools, evaluated by Newcastle University academics, including Liz (Mazzoli Smith and Todd, 2016, 2019), shows this as yet another example of how young people are treated differently based on family household income. Jess and the group went further to say that if they too could roll forward a credit balance, they could afford a breakfast and lunch the next day. Alternatively, they could save their allowance for extra food for when they had PE or an exam. The young people said that those on free school meals should be treated the same as their peers and carry over unspent monies. The young people in receipt of free school meals not only knew and understood the flaws in the system, but also knew how to fix it, another example, like the real living wage at Newcastle University, of the effect of listening before action (Todd, 2007).

It was found that free school meal change was being retained by the provider of the school meals, which might be the school itself, the local authority or a private provider. An estimated £88 million (Defeyter and Stretesky, 2019) across secondary schools nationally is taken from children on free school meals.

The Roman Catholic Diocese of Hexham and Newcastle, a strategic partner of Tyne and Wear Citizens, agreed to act. One of the Diocese schools, Carmel College in Darlington, who were the providers of their own meals, agreed to be the first to remodel and operate a Just Change approach. It cost £250 to change the school's system, leading to an estimated £17,000 returned to the poorest pupils in one year.

Leaders within Tyne and Wear Citizens, including school students and academics from Newcastle University, have since negotiated with other schools and local authorities to follow the example of Carmel

College. Just Change has been taken on as a national Citizens UK campaign for other chapters. The first few years of Tyne and Wear Citizens had unsurprisingly not solved poverty, but had seen some tangible results: a pay rise for 3,000 workers and almost £60,000 returned to children on free school meals to spend on food (four schools are now returning change to all children).

## Safer cities

Feeling unsafe and under threat came up time and time again during the listening campaign. Muslim women talked about the increasing number of verbal and physical attacks that they had been facing since the Brexit vote in the North East. People spoke of witnessing violent outbursts on public transport and not knowing how to intervene through fear for themselves. Everyone reported increasing concern as bystanders.

The action team focused on public transport as somewhere to start and as the place of many reported incidents. When incidents were reported to drivers, no action was taken. Tyne and Wear Citizens received commitment from Nexus to convene a meeting of all transport providers and the police, with the aim of developing a shared hate-crime charter. It would set a clear statement that hate crime would not be tolerated and outline the steps passengers could expect to see taken should an incident occur. The charter was delayed so it became necessary to take public action, with the press attending, to create pressure for change. In Reclaim the Metro, hundreds of people took to the metro during Hate Crime Awareness Week to clearly send a message that nobody should be scared to travel on public transport. Tyne and Wear Citizens' members of all faith and no faith were invited to wear a hijab, and roses were given out to members of the public to engage them in a conversation. As a result, the charter was published on the Wednesday before the action and the day became a celebration. Leaders are now exploring training for drivers and moving the action to supermarkets and doctors' surgeries.

The action team was led by Muslim women who had never been involved in public life before, alongside those from other communities. We found that acting alongside each other built bridges and challenged people's understandings and stereotypes of one another. Members of Newcastle University, both researchers and students, were also active participants, providing the action team with access to academic research (Hopkins, 2019; McAreavey and Krivokapic-Skoko, 2019; Najib and Hopkins, 2019a, 2019b).

## Mental health

Mental health was voted as the number one issue to tackle by the alliance, but unlike the other campaign areas, there was no clear campaign or focus for action. The issues raised were wide and varied: children's services, adult services, environmental factors, waiting to be seen – the list went on. In response, we launched a citizens' commission that met throughout 2018 with three public hearings, culminating in November 2018 in a mental health assembly attended by 500 people. This enabled a deepening of the listening, which helped to narrow the focus and for actions to emerge. Almost 400 written testimony submissions were received. A series of public commissioners were engaged, which assisted us in bringing together those with the power to act. These included a local Member of Parliament (MP), the chief executive of the NHS Mental Health Trust, the Bishop of Newcastle, those leading mental health charities and practitioners and mental health service users (including secondary school-aged young people). A total of 36 people gave verbal evidence to the commissioners and a public gallery. The mental health assembly was partly planned and organised by Newcastle University students on placements. There was a deliberate effort to involve a large number of people in organising the assembly as an opportunity for leadership development and learning about community organising.

The work of the commission was documented in a report, *Living Well*, authored by a postgraduate student who was part of Newcastle's University's Medical School's Public Health Research Institute (Barton and Spencer, 2018). Reports following commissions often contain recommendations; however, this was different in seeking firm public commitments to act on the issues raised. Actions (17 in total) included: young people redesigning a child and adolescent mental health service (CAMHS) clinic; students at Newcastle University changing the waiting-room procedures for talking to a counsellor; tackling rubbish collection on the Byker housing estate; open-door meals at Newcastle Central Mosque, with funding from Anglican churches and Quakers; and seeking legislative change in England to put it on a similar footing with Wales and Northern Ireland, so that every school has access to a school counsellor. The mental health assembly therefore demonstrated the practice of Tyne and Wear Citizens of dividing a large complex problem that it faces into winnable campaigns.

## Discussion: can Citizens UK community organising work in the North East?

There remains, of course, a long way to go to make any real impression on austerity. The achievements over the first four years have not addressed structural poverty, nor have we removed hate crime from the UK. Community organising is not unproblematic. Although actions depend on community members rather than many paid staff, the guidance of the paid community organisers is necessary and they are sometimes spread very thinly across many organisations. The funding model relies on the dues paid by alliance members, so the sustainability of organiser jobs is highly dependent on continuing membership, particularly of larger organisations. Organisations might want to be involved but might be unwilling to pay the required dues. People might want to be involved but not be part of a member organisation – though, in practice, Tyne and Wear Citizens does not turn anyone away. Faith organisations have historically been found to be attracted to membership and are central to Tyne and Wear Citizens (Wills et al, 2009); however, this deters the involvement of some who are uncomfortable in the company of faith members. Training in community organising is important but applying the practices was not easy. The practices of Tyne and Wear Citizens take time to learn. Some people do not like that it is a prescribed and particular approach.

While it is important to recognise the issues in making community organising work, it is also important to note that no approach to change is easy and that Tyne and Wear Citizens is unusual (and we would suggest unique) in the societal impact of the manner in which it achieves change and its effectiveness in successful actions. In the first four years of Tyne and Wear Citizens: the number of real living wage employers increased by 300 per cent, bringing a living wage to thousands of employees; large numbers of different communities were involved through the mental health commission in working together to bring about a number of successful actions; and a regional group of transport providers are now working with diverse citizens to address hate crime.

The 20th century saw a detachment of universities from place and 'engulfment of HE [higher education] by neoliberal doctrine' (Chubb and Watermeyer, 2017: 2368) and associated structures of marketisation, individualism and competition, with national and global league tables (Giroux, 2002; Shore, 2010; Glenna et al, 2015). Over the last decade, there has been a re-emergence of the civic university, helped by the requirement (from research funding bodies) that research should generate impact. However, the university's role in Tyne and Wear Citizens has not been easy to make work in practice. Working with Tyne and Wear Citizens requires engagement with a particular model of community organising, one that takes time to understand and use. Some aspects of the model, such as everyone seen as a community leader, may not always sit easily alongside a university's hierarchical leadership structure. Approaches taken in a listening campaign of Tyne and Wear Citizens can be very different to university staff listening practices (such as an online staff survey). Furthermore, although a good number of staff and students at every level have become involved in many different aspects of the work of Tyne and Wear Citizens, Newcastle University is a large organisation, with many people unaware of the Tyne and Wear Citizens link. Despite a firm commitment of Newcastle University to being a civic university, the core business of teaching and research, and the achievement of a particular form of excellence within both in response to market pressures, are a potential barrier to community engagement.

Despite these challenges, Newcastle University has shown itself to be a crucial member of civil society, providing a 'social foundation from which to combat injustices' (Jamoul and Wills, 2008: 2035) in multiple diverse engagements with Tyne and Wear Citizens. As a civic university, this is an expression of its tradition of working for public benefit to co-design solutions in partnership with external collaborators. It has provided principal funding, strategic leadership (students and staff leading a number of action groups) and research contributing to actions (particularly on poverty, mental health and Islamophobia). Many staff and students have played active, indeed, leading, roles in most of the action groups. Placements with Tyne and Wear Citizens have been part of students' university education. Those taking the geography module on community volunteering reported that they had gained:

> deep understanding of the work performed within the third sector and the increasing importance of this in the current context of neoliberal austerity in the UK ... Actions such as Reclaim the Metro and the mental health assembly have shown us that change powered by ordinary people within society really is possible. (McGuckin et al, 2019: 6)

University involvement with Tyne and Wear Citizens gives students and staff multiple opportunities to engage with members of their local community and work together for change, putting theory into practice in a real-life context. Many staff and students have taken the two-day training and some have been awarded a Post Graduate Certificate in Community Leadership (from Newman University), following 50 hours of practical application.

Newcastle University's engagement and place vision and strategy is to co-create knowledge in partnership with external collaborators, and its work with Tyne and Wear Citizens is a very good example of this. Co-creation assumes mutual respect for different knowledges and mutual involvement in the work of knowledge creation. Involvement in Tyne and Wear Citizens enables multiple potential entry points for deep engagement with various communities while, at the same time, having arm's length relationships with hundreds of people and many organisations (Wills, 2012). Tyne and Wear Citizens provides both university students and researchers with a powerful form of action learning in community organising. What seems to us to be particularly distinctive is the impact that community organising can have, and indeed has had, within the institution of Newcastle University in terms of building relationships, developing relational agency (Edwards, 2017) and fostering leadership across traditional hierarchies and divides.

Over the first four years of Tyne and Wear Citizens, we have demonstrated that community organising is possible in the North East and that civil society is strong enough and growing stronger all the time. However, COVID-19 has thrown society into disarray, with turbulent times ahead. There have been many generous and innovative responses from civil society at a range of scales, from weekly clapping for health workers, neighbourhood schemes to offer help to those unable to leave their houses, streaming live music performances, the use of Internet video platforms for community choirs and quiz games, and engineering firms volunteering the repurposing of their production processes to make personal protective equipment. Our communities have therefore found imaginative ways to meet some of our social and cultural needs, despite the 'lockdown', and resourceful ways to support charities.

To survive, let alone thrive, in the times ahead, society will need much more in addition to charitable contributions and imaginative community volunteering. Throughout the COVID-19 lockdown, Tyne and Wear Citizens was able to continue to organise. It took a national leadership role in relation to campaigning for a real living wage for key workers. Tyne and Wear Citizens also led one of the national responses on free school meals. What was significant was that Tyne and Wear Citizens led this within the national Citizens UK organisation based on their previous work on Just Change. The organising that had gone before enabled the COVID-19 organising to take place. People from varied organisations came together, this time using video platforms to listen to each other and commit to more listening. This provided the stories and leaders to build and win actions. In a crisis, there is not time to start from the beginning. However, if relationships and leaders already exist, then civil society is strong enough to act. Crisis has highlighted the necessity of a strong and active civil society. Given that the impact on the financial security of many civic organisations has been severely challenged by COVID-19, the practices of Tyne and Wear Citizens that foster and strengthen the ability of civil society to act through building relational power have never been more necessary. The leadership of Tyne and Wear Citizens during COVID-19 so far has demonstrated that it is in a unique position to assist people and society to navigate this changed landscape. This move towards a politics and social contract that prioritises social justice though community organising is now critical.

## Notes

[1]   For more information on Citizens UK, see: www.citizensuk.org/
[2]   The living wage is a cost of living calculation that is higher than the minimum wage and other wage calculations.
[3]   Anchor institutions are large organisations that, alongside their main function, play a significant and recognised role in a locality by making strategic contributions to the local economy. The founding partners of Tyne and Wear Citizens in 2015 were Newcastle University (Faculty of Humanities and Social Sciences Department and the Institute for Social Renewal), the Roman Catholic Diocese of Hexham and Newcastle, the Bishop of Newcastle and the Anglican Diocese of Newcastle, the Bishop of Durham and the Anglican Diocese of Durham, and Newcastle Quakers. The broad alliance also includes charities, schools and businesses.
[4]   For more information on the real living wage, see: www.livingwage.org.uk/
[5]   For more information on the refugee response of Citizens UK, see: www.safepassage.org.uk/

## References

Alinsky, S.D. (1971) 'Of means and ends', in S.D. Alinsky, *Rules for Radicals*, New York: Vintage Books, pp 24–7.

Barton, J. and Spencer, L. (2018) *Living Well: Mental Health and Public Life in the North East*, report by the Tyne and Wear Citizens Commission on Mental Health, London: Citizens UK. Available at: https://d3n8a8pro7vhmx.cloudfront.net/newcitizens/pages/3209/attachments/original/1542909839/Living_Well_Report.pdf?1542909839

Chubb, J. and Watermeyer, R. (2017) 'Artifice or integrity in the marketization of research impact? Investigating the moral economy of (pathways to) impact statements within research funding proposals in the UK and Australia', *Studies in Higher Education*, 42(12): 2360–72.

Dagdeviren, H., Donoghue, M. and Wearmouth, A. (2019) 'When rhetoric does not translate to reality: hardship, empowerment and the third sector in austerity localism', *The Sociological Review*, 67(1): 143–60.

Defeyter, G. and Stretesky, P. (2019) *Hungry for Change. Working Paper on Free School Meals*. Newcastle upon Tyne: Northumbria University. Available at: https://bit.ly/39CNeAc

Edwards, A. (ed) (2017) *Working Relationally in and across Practices: A Cultural-Historical Approach to Collaboration*, Cambridge: Cambridge University Press.

Giroux, H. (2002) 'Neoliberalism, corporate culture, and the promise of higher education: the university as democratic sphere', *Harvard Educational Review*, 72(4): 425–64.

Glenna, L., Shortall, S. and Brandl, B. (2015) 'Neoliberalism, the university, public goods and agricultural innovation', *Sociological Ruralis*, 55(4): 438–59.

Hopkins, P. (2019) 'Social geography II: Islamophobia, transphobia, and sizism', *Progress in Human Geography*, 44(3): 583–94.

Hunter, P. (2018) *The Local Living Wage Dividend: An Analysis of the Impact of the Living Wage on Ten City Regions*, London: The Smith Institute. Available at: www.smith-institute.org.uk/wp-content/uploads/2018/09/The_local-Living_Wage_dividend.pdf

Jamoul, L. and Wills, J. (2008) 'Faith in politics', *Urban Studies*, 45(10): 2035–56.

Mazzoli Smith, L. and Todd, L. (2016) *Poverty Proofing the School Day: Evaluation and Development Report*, Newcastle upon Tyne: Research Centre for Learning and Teaching, Newcastle University. Available at: https://eprint.ncl.ac.uk/file_store/production/232454/86F983AD-4159-4FE1-9F37-3B567F2182C2.pdf

Mazzoli Smith, L. and Todd, L. (2019) 'Conceptualising poverty as a barrier to learning through "poverty proofing the school day": the genesis and impacts of stigmatisation', *British Educational Research Journal*, 45(2): 356–71.

McAreavey, R. and Krivokapic-Skoko, B. (2019) 'In or out? Using boundaries as a means to understand the economic integration of transnational migrants in regional economies', *Sociologia Ruralis*, 59: 329–49.

McGuckin, L., Monaghan, A., Shattock, S. and Swain, J. (2019) *Tyne and Wear Citizens GEO3143 Collaborative Report*, Newcastle upon Tyne: Newcastle University.

Najib, K. and Hopkins, P. (2019a) 'Veiled Muslim women's strategies in response to Islamophobia in Paris', *Political Geography*, 73: 103–11.

Najib, K. and Hopkins, P. (2019b) 'Where does Islamophobia take place and who is involved? Reflections from Paris and London', *Social and Cultural Geography*, 11 January. Available at: www.tandfonline.com/doi/full/10.1080/14649365.2018.1563800

Newman, K. and Lake, R.W. (2006) 'Democracy, bureaucracy and difference in US community development politics since 1968', *Progress in Human Geography*, 30(1): 44–61.

Shore, C. (2010) 'Beyond the multiversity: neoliberalism and the rise of the schizophrenic university', *Social Anthropology*, 18(1): 15–29.

Todd, L. (2007) *Partnerships for Inclusive Education: A Critical Approach to Collaborative Working*, London: Routledge.

Wills, J. (2009) 'Identity making for action: the example of London Citizens', in M. Wetherell (ed) *Theorizing Identities and Social Action*, London: Palgrave Macmillan, pp 157–76.

Wills, J. (2012) 'The geography of community and political organisation in London today', *Political Geography*, 31(2): 114–26.

Wills, J., Datta, K., Evans, Y., Herbert, J., May, J. and McIlwaine, C. (2009) 'Religion at work: the role of faith-based organizations in the London living wage campaign', *Cambridge Journal of Regions, Economy and Society*, 2(3): 443–61.

# 18

# So what is a university in any case? A grass-roots perspective on the university and urban social justice

*Paul Benneworth*

## Introduction

Writing this critical review chapter has been made more difficult by a series of strikes paralysing many UK universities in the spring of 2020. Academic and support staff at a total of 67 universities in the UK have been taking industrial action in what are called the 'four fights': disputes between staff and managers regarding salaries, pensions, precarity and employment opportunities. The strikes reflect a feeling among many academics – repeated across blogs and social media – that the cold winds of marketisation and austerity that have blown across UK society as a whole have also severely negatively affected UK academia and urgently require addressing. A Labour government introduced a *degree* of marketisation by introducing tuition fees in 2002 but it was the 2010 Conservative–Liberal Democrat Coalition government whose reforms sought to remove any sense of social purpose from higher education.

These strikes cast into sharp relief a long-standing problem with writing about universities and their contributions to social development, social justice and social inclusion. It is tempting to write about universities through the rose-tinted lenses of their strategic orientations, their institutional visions and strategies, and their managers' aspirations and encomiums. Yet, these strikes are by staff who feel that they are being denied social justice in the workplace, fair contracts and dignified working conditions. It is the same staff that have been standing on the picket lines at universities that carry out the research, teaching and social engagement activities that interact with society and build societal capital. It is those staff who went on strike to highlight universities' own unjust approach who create the successes then claimed by management in arguing that those universities are contributing to social justice. Therein lies the contradiction: an institution may have employees who are contesting austerity and promoting social justice but the strikes make it hard to claim that universities as institutions have some kind of social justice mission when they deny basic justice to their own staff.

The case studies in this volume lie in the North East of England, and a visitor arriving in Newcastle cannot help but spot the St James Park football ground. Looming over the city as a monument to local passion, it too has become a site for contesting austerity. At the time of writing, the club is owned by the owner of a sports shopping brand whose widespread use of precarious but legal employment practices and their inept COVID-19 response saw them criticised by Parliament and the government. In recent history, Newcastle United FC was sponsored by a payday loans company who hid their Dickensian pawnbroking practices behind a clever marketing campaign. However, what most Newcastle United fans associate with St James Park is not the current owner, but a sense of attachment, what beloved manager Sir Bobby Robson famously summed up thus:

> What is a club in any case? Not the buildings or the directors or the people who are paid to represent it. It's not the television contracts, get-out clauses, marketing departments or executive boxes. It's the noise, the passion, the feeling of belonging, the pride in your city. It's a small boy clambering up stadium steps for the very first time, gripping his father's hand, gawping at that hallowed stretch of turf beneath him and, without being able to do a thing about it, falling in love. (Robson, quoted in *Evening Chronicle*, 2013)

This quotation is germane here in reminding us, when talking about universities, social justice and innovation, to pose the question: what is a university in any case? Is this its corporate interests or its knowledge workers whose knowledge praxis may drive social justice? In this chapter, the author therefore seeks to reflect on what space there remains for UK universities to develop a societal mission at the level of the institution, where social innovation is promoted because of and not despite universities' own institutional practices. We must be cautious in jumping too quickly to institutional assertions of social justice and engagement, looking instead at the extent to which institutional practices align with the agency exerted by their staff in their knowledge praxis.

## The 'modern university': freedom to micromanage towards fiduciary responsibility

The challenge of understanding the contribution of universities towards social purposes has become sharpened by what is euphemistically referred to in policy circles as the modernisation agenda for higher education (European Commission, 2011). At its core was improving higher education's efficiency by introducing market disciplines into its workings and funding universities based on producing results, such as graduate numbers, graduate salaries, PhD completions and academic publications (Kickert, 1995; Kickert et al, 1997). Creating flexible markets in higher education required changing the nature of university management to make university managers exclusively externally responsible for delivering outcomes and giving them wide-ranging internal powers to reform their institutions to best pursue these 'results'.

There are models of higher education where universities have a genuine mission to promote social development; these proliferate in Latin America, where the Cordoba Declaration of 1919 laid the basis for making universities truly developmental institutions (Tapia, 2008). Despite neoliberalism and restructuring, Latin American public higher education remains profoundly integrated into its society. The contemporary UK reality is very different, and any honest appraisal of universities' contributions to social innovation needs to accept that perspective. The last ten years have seen universities become financialised institutions, seeking to perform in quasi-markets for teaching and research, and primarily concerned with their financial stability and estate upgrading rather than in the wider well-being of their communities (Engelen et al, 2014). This has been driven by the almost total replacement of the undergraduate teaching grant with fees, the continued sharpening of the focus on excellence in the block grant for research and the use of a restrictive set of knowledge transfer metrics to reward knowledge exchange, while universities have sought to compete by unprecedented building programmes largely financed through new debt (Gore, 2018).

The notion of 'responsibility' in the contemporary university does not extend a great deal further than the idea of corporate social responsibility, what the author has elsewhere called 'munificent beneficence', in that universities may choose to do things for society but that society is denied the right to place any demands on those university choices (Benneworth, 2013). Indeed, there is a tendency that university institutional duties to their financial stakeholders drive behaviours that can only be understood as responsible from an extremely limited financial perspective on responsibility (Benneworth, 2019). Therefore, it is perhaps surprising to see all kinds of UK universities making claims that they are committed to driving a civic mission, often making reference to their past in civic movements such as mechanical engineering societies, without acknowledging the reality that the civic mission does not extend to allowing those universities to be responsive to societal demands.

## A critical reflection on the civic future for UK universities

This provides a useful lens through which to consider the examples presented in this volume, both as a cautious counterweight to more hyperbolic readings of the situation, and as providing a more critical perspective on what constitutes meaningful behaviour in the contemporary corporate university. The measure of whether a university *as an institution* contributes to social inclusion is whether its core decision-making structures provide societal partners with power to participate in co-creation activities that strengthen their own societal position (referred to in the chapter 'Realising the potential of universities for inclusive, innovation-led development' as asking what these places need from their universities). It would embody an ethos and a culture where that societal engagement is valued, in which time is made available to do it properly within the regular working week and where it is seen as being an integral part of what it means to be a 'good' academic.

It seems slightly banal at this stage to simply say that UK academia is not in a place to allow societal communities to meaningfully shape decisions, or to allow its academics to spend their work time on useful engagement activities. In the current UK environment, it would not be 'responsible' for any university to do that in the face of creditors demanding that the universities demonstrate their financial health. However, the UK higher education landscape is by no means eternal or inevitable, and this volume demonstrates some elements in place that might form a future basis for reinventing universities as genuinely civic organisations.

So, what is a civic university in any case? It is the senior professor taking time and effort to go out into the community and use their decades of experience to make a difference to people's lives. It is the junior researcher whose contact with these communities unlocks the real meaning of the hard-won knowledge and starts a journey towards more engaged research. It is the boundary-spanning researcher bringing a wealth of understanding of application contexts to help better attune research to social needs. It is the schoolchild who has their voice heard for the first time and is inspired to become an active civic advocate for their friends, families and neighbours. It is the privileged student who undertakes a community placement and learns empathy with those who lack the resources and the power to create more meaningful minds for themselves. It is the responsible company that finds ways through university–community engagement to realise their ethical desires in their own areas.

We must therefore be cautious in making 'big' claims for the emergence of the civic university on the basis of easy proclamations by managers with vested interests in validating their own strategic choices. One might even foresee a risk that 'civic-washing' is going on, with universities facing criticism for their treatment of staff and students evoking a 'civic mission' as a way of trying to respond to those criticisms without substantively addressing the factors giving rise to that mistreatment. However, this volume gives us a light of hope that there are the people around whom a more civic approach for universities could be built in the future. It is important not to underestimate the magnitude of the task given the myriad incentives for this civic knowledge community to behave and be treated instrumentally, even opportunistically, and the ways in which that opportunistic behaviour is normalised in university life. We must normalise the engaged activities depicted in this volume as an everyday part of what it means to be an academic, of the student experience and of living in a university town if we are to restore universities' rightful positions in building cohesive, caring communities.

## References

Benneworth, P.S. (2013) 'The engaged university in practice? Reinventing the social compact for the grand societal challenges', in P. Benneworth (ed) *University Engagement with Socially Excluded Communities*, Dordrecht: Springer, pp 329–43.

Benneworth, P.S. (2019) 'The modernisation agenda and university irresponsibility repertoires', in M.P. Sørensen, L. Geschwind, J. Kekäle and R. Pinheiro (eds) *The Responsible University: Exploring the Nordic Context and Beyond*, London: Palgrave Macmillan, pp 61–86.

Engelen, E., Fernandez, R. and Hendrikse, R. (2014) 'How finance penetrates its other: a cautionary tale on the financialization of a Dutch university', *Antipode*, 46(4): 1072–91.

European Commission (2011) *Supporting Growth and Jobs: An Agenda for the Modernisation of Europe's Higher Education Systems*, Luxembourg: OOPEC.

*Evening Chronicle* (2013) '"It's the noise, the passion, the feeling of belonging": what does NUFC mean to you?', *Chronicle Live*, 1 November. Available at: www.chroniclelive.co.uk/sport/football/football-news/sir-bobby-robson-quote-tell-6260751

Gore, G. (2018) 'UK universities turn to private market as debts rack up', *International Financing Review*, No. 2255, 13–19 October. Available at: www.ifre.com/story/1516984/uk-universities-turn-to-private-market-as-debts-rack-up

Kickert, W.J.M. (1995) 'Steering at a distance: a new paradigm of public governance in Dutch higher education', *Governance*, 8: 135–57.

Kickert, W.J.M., Klijn, E.H. and Koppenjan, J.F.M. (eds) (1997) *Managing Complex Networks. Strategies for the Public Sector* (1st edn), London: SAGE Publications.

Tapia, M.N. (2008) 'Service-learning in Latin America, past and present', in J.C. Kielsmeier, M. Neal, N. Schultz and T.J. Leeper (eds) *Growing to Greatness: The State of Service-Learning*, St Paul, MN: National Youth Leadership Council, pp 8–15.

# 19

# Conclusion: hope in an age of austerity and a time of anxiety

*Mark Shucksmith, Simin Davoudi, Liz Todd and Mel Steer*

## Introduction

How to thrive in today's turbulent times is a challenge for communities around the world in an age buffeted by 'rollback' and 'roll-out' neoliberalism, with governments cutting public expenditure, promoting privatisation and deregulation, and individualising social risks and responsibilities. This age of austerity has now been compounded by the anxieties of the COVID-19 pandemic, with its heavy toll of lives and livelihoods. Drawing on innovative cases and strategic initiatives from the North East of England, this book has explored multiple ways in which communities responded to neoliberalism and austerity. The aim has been to provide deeper insights into the efficacy of these approaches and their relevance and interest nationally and internationally, and to offer insights for addressing the post-pandemic challenges ahead.

This volume began by posing some difficult questions about the role of civil society in an age of austerity (see the chapter 'Islands of hope in a sea of despair'). Should we celebrate the contributions of civil society in mitigating the impacts of rolling back the state, or lament civil society's role in masking the state's abdication of its role in serving its citizens? Should we embrace the activities of civil society as resistance to austerity and neoliberalism, or criticise civil society for enabling and facilitating these? Have civil society's responses to austerity constituted real alternatives to neoliberalism (sparks of renewal), or only isolated, temporary respite (flickering candles in the wind)? Has civil society perforce become subject to, and a servant of, neoliberalising hegemony through its need for funding and for credibility? In sum, what should be our balance between hope and despair?

The opening chapter also elaborated the concepts of austerity and civil society, introducing themes that have been threaded through all the case-study chapters of this volume. The importance of place has been introduced by taking the North East of England, with its distinctive history, culture, institutions, assets and challenges (as discussed in the chapter 'The North East of England'), as a lens to explore critical social and political shifts. The case studies have offered examples of ways people in the North East, sometimes in collaboration with university staff and students, have negotiated neoliberalism and austerity during this period.

In this final chapter, these questions are reviewed in the light of the empirical accounts of social renewal in the North East, teasing out some tentative answers, as well as highlighting some crucial issues for the future. This involves not only celebrating achievements in the case studies reported here and their potential for hope, but also examining more thorny issues of power, accountability, connection and trust. This chapter starts by returning to the core concepts of neoliberalism, austerity and civil society, then turning to questions of cooperation and co-production across boundaries – a feature of the co-authored case studies in this book – and to the notion of a civic university in responding with other partners to challenges of social renewal and social innovation.

As this volume goes to press, many of these questions and challenges are being thrown into even sharper relief by the COVID-19 pandemic, with its tragic and profound impacts in the UK and across the world. The chapter ends, therefore, by asking how these case studies of social renewal might speak to society's potential to respond to the COVID-19 crisis in terms of both surviving through the crisis and rebuilding a stronger and better society thereafter. Might these offer some hope in this age of austerity and at such a time of anxiety?

## Neoliberalism, austerity and civil society

The connections between neoliberalism and austerity have already been elaborated in the chapter 'Islands of hope in a sea of despair'. The *rollback* phase of neoliberalism involves shrinking the state and the institutions of Keynesian welfarism and social collectivism through privatisation and cutting public expenditure, both core elements of austerity; while the later, emergent *roll-out* phase involves the purposeful construction and consolidation of neoliberalised state forms, modes of governance and reregulation (Peck and Tickell, 2002; Peck, 2014). These two aspects of neoliberalisation also impinge on civil society. Cuts to public expenditure (rollback) reduce the funding available to support civil society institutions, while leaving ever-larger gaps in state social provision for civil society to try and fill. Meanwhile, neoliberalised economic management (roll-out) requires voluntary and community organisations to act competitively rather than collaboratively, to seek income from the state through tenders and contracts, to pursue targets and deliverables tangential to their purpose, and, in short, to adopt the modes and practices of private business to pursue the agendas of the neoliberal state. Peck and Tickell (2002) see this asymmetrical power relationship as placing real limits on the practical potential of localised or 'bottom-up' action; however, in a later article, Peck et al (2010: 111, emphasis added) see opportunities emerging 'for the (re)mobilisation, recognition and valuation of multiple, *local* forms of development, rooted in local cultures, values and movements', which they term the 'progressively variegated economy', and that Wright (2010) has termed 'real utopias'. This more hopeful view characterises many of the North East local initiatives studied in this book.

Street activism in Newcastle (see the chapter 'The containment of democratic innovation') is perhaps one of the clearest examples of the constraint austerity places on social innovation. The authors demonstrate through their autoethnography the conditions of marketisation of the third sector, in combination with the concentration of decision-making within council structures, and the effect this has of undermining democratic innovation. Again, several of the cases do show civil society mobilising to mitigate the impacts of the state's neoliberalising policies, such as responses to food poverty (see the chapter 'Cafe society'), to digital inequality when applying for welfare benefits (see the chapter ' "Computer Says No"') and to income poverty (see the chapters 'Drive to thrive' and 'Citizen power, the university and the North East'); however, not withstanding this, the case studies also exemplify the emergence of a rather different, and more hopeful, story.

Signs of resistance to the neoliberalisation of civil society (as discussed in the chapter 'Islands of hope in a sea of despair') could include avoidance of reliance on state or corporate funding and its associated managerial technologies. Other signs could be the pursuit of public good (social purpose) or the enhancement of public space (in which deliberation occurs). Ideally, all of these elements work together, offering a goal to aim for, a means to achieve it and a framework for engaging with each other about ends and means (Edwards, 2004). The case studies demonstrate a range of such resistances, or 'flames' of social renewal, in each of these respects.

A feature of all the case studies is their pursuit of the 'public good', in some shape or form, such that they might be regarded as social innovations whose objectives address social well-being or the common good rather than private gain at the expense of others. Newcastle City Futures worked with communities and businesses to develop new citizen-led ways of providing public services (see the chapter 'Realising the potential of universities for inclusive, innovation-led development'), while Glendale Gateway Trust promoted affordable housing, employment, services and other facilities through community-led governance when state provision was rolled back (see the chapter 'Innovation outside the state'). Whether designing homes for older people (see the chapter 'Future Homes'), helping council residents avoid fuel poverty (see the chapter 'Drive to thrive'), getting children and the community to interact to solve real project-based problems (see the chapter 'The good, the bad and the disconcerting'), enabling all children in Newcastle and Gateshead to have the opportunity to engage with culture and creativity (see the chapter 'City of Dreams'), or creating more digital justice for people using a new online welfare benefits system (see the chapter '"Computer Says No"') – these initiatives' objectives were public good, not private gain. Public good is also one of the prime aims of Tyne and Wear Citizens (see the chapter 'Citizen power, the university and the North East').

Many of these initiatives have also helped to create 'public spaces' for social interaction and public deliberation, whether deliberately or incidentally, physical or digital, another element that is fundamental to social renewal and to the future of civil society. From reinventing a civic role for the cathedral in order to transform it into common ground in sacred space (see the chapter 'Reinventing a civic role for the 21st century'), to creating pocket parks in Fenham (see the chapter 'The containment of democratic innovation') or bringing people across diverse organisations together in Tyne and Wear Citizens to listen and achieve social change (see the chapter 'Citizen power, the university and the North East'), such spaces are a feature of many of the initiatives, fostering new interactions and activity. The Byker Community Trust has been developing a leadership and empowerment culture, aimed to be inclusive of all and giving tenants a voice and role in decision-making (see the chapter 'The Byker Community Trust and the "Byker Approach"'). The community cafe (see the chapter 'Cafe society') brings people into new and different social, economic, material and political relations through enabling people to access the cafe without feeling socially alienated or excluded by price.

In terms of managerial technologies, the performative culture that has moulded the English school curriculum over the last 30 years is challenged by the case study of children's project-based learning using a community curriculum (see the chapter 'The good, the bad and the disconcerting'). That the project was enjoyed by many of the students but resisted by many staff (concerned that the exam syllabus would not be covered) shows the detrimental impact of a marketised education on a more student-centred pedagogy, as well as the power of the neoliberalising and individualising framing narrative. Digital technologies that have helped drive neoliberalism and business innovation generally neglect inequalities in digital access or dangers from digital innovation – shortcomings challenged by the case study on digital inclusion and social justice (see the chapter '"Computer Says No"').

Consulting and promoting unheard voices can constitute real bottom-up political action or it can further the neoliberalist co-option of the less powerful into consumerism and responsibilisation (Whitty and Wisby, 2007; Todd, 2012). The case studies avoid the latter with innovative examples of empowerment. City of Dreams (see the chapter 'City of Dreams') finds ways that young people can be more actively engaged with organisations, including having a role in decision-making. It is listening to people's stories that develops community leaders and supports Tyne and Wear Citizens' political actions (see the chapter 'Citizen power, the university and the North East'). Consulting with the community in meaningful ways shapes thinking on digital inequalities (see the chapter '"Computer Says No"') and empowers Byker Community Trust residents (see the chapter 'The Byker Community Trust and the "Byker Approach"').

One question arising from the case studies is whether independence of civil society from the state and market matters, or whether working with the state and market on their own terms may be helpful. It is not self-evident that exclusion of the state and market from action is a necessary virtue. However, there is a danger that civil society becomes neoliberalised (as discussed in the chapter 'Islands of hope in a sea of despair') through a reliance on state funding and subjection to its managerial technologies, or through private funding serving narrow corporate interests rather than the common good. All the cases presented in this book have had to grapple with this context of power-infused austerity and neoliberal managerial technologies, promoting competition and individualism, eroding social institutions, and transferring and rescaling risk to individuals and smaller places. Yet, most of these initiatives also exhibit 'generative power', as well as negotiation of, or resistance to, 'authoritative power'; this is highly relevant to the pressing question of the state's role in social renewal.

In other words, power may be conceptualised as a matter of social production as much as social control, as 'power to' rather than 'power over' (Stone, 1989: 229). Instead of domination and subordination, we may think of the state enhancing social actors' capacity to act and to accomplish collective goals, perhaps through coming together in new forms (partnerships, alliances, networks and social movements), thereby encouraging agency, reflexivity and resistance (Healey, 2006; Todd, 2007; Shucksmith, 2010). In this way, the state can adopt the role of an 'enabling state', exercising 'generative power to stimulate action, innovation, struggle and resistance, to release potentialities, to generate new struggles, and to transform governance itself' (Shucksmith, 2010: 12). This generative role in building capacity and agency is not only the prerogative of the state, but also open to other social actors and institutions, notably, universities, as we have seen in many of the earlier chapters in this book. Indeed, the initiatives in this volume offer a range of experiences of a more transformative management of relationships with the state and market. Newcastle City Futures (see the chapter 'Realising the potential of universities for inclusive, innovation-led development') and the development of Future Homes (see the chapter 'Future Homes') both demonstrate the role of the state as enabler and supporter of social innovation (Mazzucato, 2013; Carnegie Trust, 2014; Morgan, 2016). It therefore seems appropriate to acknowledge the importance of enterprise and social enterprise to social well-being (see the chapter 'Future Homes') in the development of housing that responds to the challenges of ageing and social sustainability, and draws unheard voices into housing design. Tyne and Wear Citizens (see the chapter 'Citizen power, the university and the North East') builds a broad and diverse alliance of different kinds of organisations, and then builds the capacities of communities to take public action and win change. Moreover, these are examples of innovative methodologies for cooperation across boundaries, involving triple or quadruple helix partners (see the chapter 'Realising the potential of universities for inclusive, innovation-led development'), which bring together civil society, business, academia and the state (Etzkowitz, 2003), as discussed later. In sum, there are examples in the case studies of a generative animation of 'politics and activism that seek to transform social relations in more progressive, anti-capitalist and socially just ways' (Mackinnon and Derickson, 2012: 256), albeit alongside a wider neoliberalisation that transfers and rescales risk and responsibility onto individuals and communities while power remains centralised.

The concept of 'power as transformation' (Wainwright, 2018) has origins in grass-roots social movements, collective actions/engagement and tacit knowledge. This view proposes that change is achieved through challenging the 'power as domination' mode, where knowledge and authority are epitomised as 'the state knows best'. A case can be made for there being a number of different models emerging from the case studies of the use of power in a transformative manner. Tyne and Wear Citizens (see the chapter 'Citizen power, the university and the North East') uses and develops relational power to achieve social justice outcomes in poverty, hate crime and mental health, acting for the common good. Newcastle City Futures (see the chapter 'Realising the potential of universities for inclusive, innovation-led development') used an innovative engagement model to bring academics together with groups from policy circles, businesses and communities.

The longer-term, asset-based approach of the Glendale Gateway Trust is particularly interesting since the accumulation of community-owned assets (notably, affordable homes generating rental income) affords an independent and enduring stream of income that overcomes short-termism and enables long-term action. However, it must be remembered that Glendale Gateway Trust started accumulating its assets well before the time of austerity, when there was more funding available. Indeed, a focus on assets, in terms of social infrastructure, community organisations and community members' knowledge, networks and capacity to act, rather than a narrative of deficits, is central to all the examples.

There is, then, some optimism arising from these case studies about the role that civil society can play in resisting, and developing alternatives to, neoliberalisation and so in promoting social renewal. In many of these examples, civil society worked with university staff or students to promote change, whether informally or explicitly as partners. What can we learn about the role of academia in helping communities to thrive in turbulent times?

## Cooperation, knowledge exchange and the civic university

Earlier chapters have introduced the concept of the civic university (Goddard, 2009; Vallance, 2016), which seeks to promote the public good through strategic action and latterly through 'civic university agreements' (Civic University Commission 2019). Beyond this renewed vision of the civic university, there are good reasons on both sides for academics and civil society to cooperate, as well as many obstacles to surmount (Shucksmith, 2016; Laing et al, 2017). Civil society organisations work with academics to enhance the status and trust accorded to their work, as well as to access academics' encoded knowledge and universities' resources and networks. Similarly, academics seek to access their partners' experiential knowledge and sometimes their links with policymakers and practitioners. Fundamental to this potential for complementarity is the combination of different types of knowledge as new knowledge creation is often thought to be most dynamic at the intersections between horizontal and vertical flows of (explicit and tacit) knowledge (Lam, 2000). Such interactions may be fostered by academia and civil society working together, so long as it is recognised that both are knowledge producers and social actors.

Such partnerships have been found to be effective in promoting regional innovation (Carayannis and Campbell, 2009; Storper, 2015; Kolehmainen et al, 2016). Brewer (2013) goes further, arguing that the complex and intractable nature of many of the problems facing the world today necessitates such collaboration between universities, civil society, industry and government through the co-production of knowledge. Others criticise such a partnership approach for 'having neoliberal elements' (Glenna et al, 2014: 440), presumably because of the dangers of neoliberalisation of civil society and academia, as discussed previously. Moreover, universities are perceived by many in civil society, industry and government as uneasy partners: difficult to engage with, highly fragmented and siloed, using impenetrable jargon, and naively unaware of the policy world (Shucksmith, 2016).

Many of the initiatives reported in this volume's substantive chapters involve (and shed light on) cooperation and co-creation involving academics, sometimes in a personal capacity rather than in any formal university representative role, and all are co-authored by academics and non-academic partners. What can we learn from these co-authored accounts?

One evident feature is that most of this cooperation and co-creation derived from personal relationships, built on trust between individuals, rather than from strategic, 'top-down' initiatives from quadruple helix partners. In many instances, such as the Cathedral project, academics became involved in a personal capacity akin to volunteering or were invited in as individuals. Sometimes, after initial seed funding, these initiatives garnered institutional support. The work in Wooler was developed and conducted by the Glendale Gateway Trust (see the chapter 'Innovation outside the state'), one of whose trustees was a (very active) emeritus professor. However, some initiatives were institutional collaborations, or at least a combination of 'top-down' and 'bottom-up' initiatives. Newcastle City Futures (see the chapter 'Realising the potential of universities for inclusive, innovation-led development') began modestly as a three-week exhibition organised by another professor with a little university funding, continued as a foresight study with a small grant from the government, and then flourished with a major grant from research councils, along with university resources. Yet, its approach and its success relied on supporting and facilitating ideas emerging from individuals, entrepreneurs and voluntary, community and social enterprises (VCSEs) through a 'bottom-up' approach to open innovation. The City of Dreams (see the chapter 'City of Dreams') is a more formal, strategic, corporate partnership but it too is characterised by the commitment of the university partner and involves and supports ideas that emerge from the grass roots.

It is important that partners each gain from the cooperation, though these will be different for each partner. For instance, many of the partners in Tyne and Wear Citizens gained directly and tangibly from its campaigns for a real living wage or against hate crime, while Newcastle University's gains derived largely from the ways in which the model of community organising has fostered leadership across hierarchical staff boundaries and built relationships and respect across areas of the university that had little previous contact (see the chapter 'Citizen power, the university and the North East'). Co-creation is not each bringing and taking the same, but is the coming together of different skills and knowledges, which often leads to very different outcomes for each party.

Academic research plays a critical role in many of the cases involving university partnerships. It is not necessarily about external funding: the digital social justice project (see the chapter ' "Computer Says No"') is one of only two cases that started with a university researcher gaining external funding. The project-based learning case (see the chapter 'The good, the bad and the disconcerting') was a form of co-creation but was initiated by the university partner with the aim of creating new ways of teaching and learning in schools and the community. The research role of the university partner in City of Dreams (see the chapter 'City of Dreams') is as critical friend and supporter, giving commitment and advocacy, while helping partners interact with different subject areas in the university. Academics bring methods of research and a range of analytical lenses and concepts.

Another feature emerging from several of the chapters is the importance and value of knowledge brokers: 'agents who support interaction and engagement with the goal of encouraging knowledge exchange, supporting research use and strengthening research impact' (Lightowler and Knight, 2013: 319). In Lomas's (2007: 131) view, they link policy and practice with researchers, 'facilitating their interaction so that they are better able to understand each other's goals and professional cultures, influence each other's work, forge new partnerships, and promote the use of research-based evidence in decision-making'. This brokerage role was central to Newcastle City Futures (see the chapter 'Realising the potential of universities for inclusive, innovation-led development'), and is also mentioned explicitly as essential to project-based learning and the development of a community curriculum, where 'you need brokers working in a supportive infrastructure' (see the chapter 'The good, the bad and the disconcerting'; see also Leat and Thomas, 2018). The brokerage role of the university partner can be identified clearly in many of the other case studies (see the chapters 'Cafe society', 'City of Dreams', 'Citizen power, the university and the North East' and ' "Computer Says No"').

Knowledge brokerage functions might be performed by individuals with interlocking roles, or 'wearing different hats', in several organisations, as Sebba (2013: 397–8) suggests: 'the interlockers have multiple positions sequentially and concurrently as trustees or council members for each other's organisations, writing, speaking and being members of panels at each other's events'. Shucksmith (2016: 20) emphasises that effective knowledge brokers 'must above all be familiar with the culture and practices of all parties, from producers to users of evidence'. Some academics and their partners may have these competencies and the interest and time to play such a role but an alternative model involves the employment of specialist knowledge brokers to sit between participants and to facilitate knowledge exchange and co-creation. Unfortunately, Lightowler and Knight (2013: 318) found that 'funding models, short-term contracts, and posts combining knowledge exchange with other functions result in a transient professional group and a squeeze on knowledge brokerage, which potentially limits the effectiveness of knowledge brokers in achieving research impact'. Where established staff, such as professors, play such a brokerage role, Pohl et al (2010) found that this may disrupt the boundary between research and practice in ways that challenge the integrity of each. However, the case studies in this volume demonstrate that it is still possible to maintain critical research thinking while engaging with civic action.

Byker Community Trust (see the chapter 'The Byker Community Trust and the ' "Byker Approach"') had formalised the knowledge broker role by funding with the university a knowledge transfer partnership. The knowledge transfer partnership works with the Byker Community Trust towards a better understanding of how to improve communication with existing and potential tenants, as well as their involvement in value co-creation activities.

While the added value of university involvement in such examples of civil society action can be clearly identified, a major question hangs over their sustainability. This raises the wider issue of addressing long-term challenges with short-term actions, with many of the initiatives presented dependent on finite project funding. While Newcastle City Futures was undoubtedly an inspirational learning-by-doing initiative with valuable insights for other universities and their partners in place-based innovation, Kempton and Marlow (see the chapter 'Realising the potential of universities for inclusive, innovation-led development') are clear that 'it is unrealistic to expect short-term, low-cost pilots to develop and deliver solutions to the challenges of university contributions to inclusive future urban living. Long-term commitment and resourcing from university, place and government is important.' This is a long-standing problem for project-based and EU-funded approaches to innovation and regeneration (Shortall and Shucksmith, 1998), and one that has intensified under neoliberalism, with its penchant for competitive, time-limited project funding.

Sources of funding reflect, and, in turn, impact upon, power relations among the social actors. As noted previously, the state's funding power can be used to exert control over other social actors, not only directly, but also less visibly through funding rules, targets, audit and evaluation. For example, schools are subject to league tables of examination results, a national curriculum, Office for Standards in Education (Ofsted) inspections and possible sanctions. Local councils' autonomy and capacity to act has been diminished by substantial reductions in central government support since 2010, forcing them to cut non-statutory expenditure and, in turn, impinging on the voluntary and community sector, as elaborated by Davoudi et al (see the chapter 'Islands of hope in a sea of despair'). Civil society is often seen as 'the poor relation' in its relationships with the state because of its smaller and less secure funding base, leading to power imbalances.

Universities are not immune to roll-out neoliberalisation; they appear independent but, alongside the effects of marketisation, they too are subject to funding rules and audit, with income affected by research and teaching excellence frameworks and the insidious impact of league tables on student numbers (Collini, 2012; Davoudi, 2015; Brink 2018). Alert to the danger of boosterist propaganda, Benneworth (see the chapter 'So what is a university in any case?') provides a necessary corrective critique of universities' claims to be acting for the public good while, at the same time, perhaps treating their own staff unjustly and retaining selfish behaviours and cultures. In some cases, this may be hypocrisy; in others, it may be because the best of intentions must be pursued within a hostile, neoliberalised landscape. Brink explains that in a context of marketisation and competition to attract students and research income, the growing importance of audit and rankings:

> works against institutional diversity. Rankings are a straitjacket which universities have been keen to wear ... [However,] to any university which had been trying to tread a different path[, the growth of rankings] creates a dilemma, whether to stick to your principles and be seen as second-rate or to conform to the new model. (2018: 97–8)

He laments that, in this respect, 'universities have simply given away the power to determine their own destiny' (Brink, 2018: 99). Of course, as he argues, this presupposes that pursuit of a social purpose (the public good) is necessarily in tension with performance metrics. Truly civic universities will seek not only to reconcile these, but to demonstrate how pursuit of the public good might also offer new and different pathways towards excellence in research and teaching.

## Hope and despair through a time of anxiety

Society has been thrown into turmoil, just as this book neared completion, by the global COVID-19 pandemic. In addition to widespread anxiety, illness and loss of life, the pandemic has caused governments to close down businesses and trade, and to lock down individuals in their homes for extended periods, leading to a reduction in economic activity greater even than in the Great Depression of the 1930s. Most commentators agree that it is now inevitable that we will experience a deep global recession, a breakdown of labour markets and supply chains, and the evaporation of consumer spending. The Office for Budgetary Responsibility has forecast that extending the UK's lockdown over six months will lead to a 34 per cent decline in gross domestic product (GDP) and to 2 million unemployed, before the economy recovers strongly during 2021 thanks to the government's support measures. Tooze (2020) is less optimistic, arguing that:

> given the risk of second- and third-wave outbreaks, no one has any idea how far and fast the resumption of normal life can safely go. It seems likely, barring a dramatic medical breakthrough, that movement restrictions will need to stay in place to manage the unevenness of containment.

A protracted and halting recovery seems far more likely at
this point than a vigorous V-shaped bounce back.

Despite the government's attempts to establish a framing narrative
that we are all in this together, inequalities have been starkly visible
during the early months of the pandemic (see the chapter 'Are we
"all in this together?"'). A report by the Institute for Fiscal Studies
finds that 'low earners are seven times as likely as high earners to
have worked in a sector that is now shut down' (Joyce and Xu, 2020)
and that high earners are much more likely to be able to work from
home and so to maintain their income while minimising health risks.
The incidence of deaths from COVID-19 varies significantly by age,
ethnicity, gender and population density for reasons that are not fully
understood. Furthermore, people in social care have been treated very
poorly, as they have been through many years of government inaction
and prevarication.

Opinion is divided between those who fear for a worse future after
the crisis, those who foresee opportunities for a better world and
those who expect the status quo to be reasserted. Many view the
magnitude of these shocks as a seismic turning point in our history
that may result in very different ways in which societies and economies
are subsequently organised. For example, Davies (2020) suggests that
'Rather than view this as a crisis of capitalism, it might be better
understood as the sort of world-making event that allows for new
economic and intellectual beginnings ... as a global turning-point',
for better or worse. So, is this cause for hope or despair? And what
light, if any, do the case studies provide?

Already, some things are apparent (Unwin, 2020): years of austerity
diminished the capacity of the health service, local authorities, the
civil service and civil society to respond to the scale of the crisis, with
shortages of doctors, nurses, intensive care beds, protective clothing,
ventilators, testing kits and more. There is a renewed faith in experts
and expert knowledge, denigrated for years by populist politicians
who gained power on a ticket of people versus elites. Similarly, attacks
on core institutions such as the NHS and the BBC have ceased as
their public value is demonstrated. Key workers turn out not always
to be the most highly remunerated managers, but include nurses,
cleaners, delivery drivers, carers and similarly undervalued and often
underpaid workers.

Many of the cases of civil society action (such as using project-based
learning in schools and the Cathedral project) were paused or severely
curtailed during the COVID-19 crisis, and many civic institutions are

threatened. Indeed, the National Council for Voluntary Organisations (NCVO) warned that within three months, charities would face a £4 billion funding gap, with many closing already. However, some provided ways to continue to support communities through the crisis. For example, Citizens UK's community organising provided the means to continue to listen to people around work and food issues during the crisis. Actions could continue, albeit less visibly, online. Citizens UK saw an opportunity to campaign for the real living wage for key workers (care home staff, delivery drivers, supermarket staff and so on). Citizens UK responded to the rapidly changing policy around free school meals by listening (to schools, families and local authorities) to see what support should be offered and formed a campaign to achieve this. Anti-food waste cafes are delivering large numbers of food bags to charities for them to distribute.

Civil society's actions, including those in this volume, are important building blocks for recovery and social renewal. The lack of economic resilience following years of austerity, highlighted by food shortages during COVID-19, may prompt discussion of concepts like 'pay as you feel' (PAYF) and universal basic income, which were previously thought impossible. The mental health effects from being in lockdown without access to liveable housing will surely lead to involving more residents in decisions, as in Byker, and to the more innovative design of future homes. School exams that seemed crucial a few months ago were cancelled and pupils experienced project-based approaches to learning at home during the lockdown, perhaps offering opportunities now to rethink the future of education. Also, public spaces for social interaction and public deliberation will be crucial as we go forward, with numerous lessons emerging from the many examples among the case studies, such as the renewal of the Cathedral space, the community organising approaches of Tyne and Wear Citizens, young people's inputs to discussions around the City of Dreams and bringing business together with the public sector and civil society in Newcastle City Futures. The relationships that are at the heart of the case studies are also those that will enable further co-creation of future solutions. The digital sphere came into its own in COVID-19, offering many new possibilities but also highlighting the need to address digital injustice and exclusion, and the dangers of increased surveillance. The cases therefore provide many starting points for the debate/building blocks that will be needed as we come out of the COVID-19 crisis about what kind of social contract we need going forward in the 21st century.

Importantly for this book's conclusion, a Conservative government has discovered that there is such a thing as society, that each individual has a responsibility to everyone else and that the state does have a vital role that cannot be performed by markets or civil society organisations. In the midst of these dark times, then, there is some hope alongside the despair: hope that when we rebuild after this crisis, there is a recognition of the valuable role of the state in promoting well-being and the public good, and in sharing power and building capacity without abdicating responsibility; hope that we recognise the contribution of voluntary and community organisations, and civil society more widely, as well as investing in valued public institutions and social infrastructure; and hope that we continue to recognise the contribution of so many undervalued lower-paid workers, with better wages and a social security system that really does provide security in times of crisis.

A crucial issue, however, is which framing narrative will emerge and dominate after the crisis. Will this be one of necessary austerity, as after the banking crisis of 2008? As Tooze (2020) points out, 'when the lid comes off, politics will resume and so will the arguments about "debt burdens" and "sustainability". And given the scale of the liabilities that have already been accumulated, we should expect it to get ugly.' Will the 'thought virus' of neoliberalism (Bourdieu and Wacquant, 2001) survive COVID-19 as it survived the banking crisis? Or, will a re-energised civil society be at the heart of the changes we need in our society, 'reviving our dented democracy, rebuilding our social fabric and enabling us to address the great challenges of climate change and environmental degradation', as Unwin (2018) hopes? Will we emerge as consumers, as subjects or as citizens (Alexander, 2020)? This contest is at the heart of social renewal, and there will be a responsibility for civil society and academics to engage in this struggle, as well as in local action.

## References

Alexander, J. (2020) 'Subject, consumer or citizen: three post-COVID futures', *New Citizenship Project*, 17 April. Available at: https://medium.com/new-citizenship-project/subject-consumer-or-citizen-three-post-covid-futures-8c3cc469a984

Bourdieu, P. and Wacquant, L. (2001) 'Neoliberal speak: notes on the new planetary vulgate', *Radical Philosophy*, 105: 2–5.

Brewer, J. (2013) *The Public Value of the Social Sciences*, London: Bloomsbury.

Brink, C. (2018) *The Soul of a University: Why Excellence Is Not Enough*, Bristol: Bristol University Press.

Carayannis, E.G. and Campbell, D.F.J. (2009) '"Mode 3" and "quadruple helix": toward a 21st century fractal innovation ecosystem', *International Journal of Technology Management*, 46(3/4): 201–34.

Carnegie Trust (2014) *The Enabling State*, Dunfermline: CUKT.

Civic University Commission (2019) *Truly Civic: Strengthening the Connection Between Universities and their Places*, London: UPP Foundation. Available at: https://upp-foundation.org/wp-content/uploads/2019/02/Civic-University-Commission-Final-Report.pdf

Collini, S. (2012) *What Are Universities For?*, London: Penguin.

Davies, W. (2020) 'The 2008 crisis didn't change the world. But this one could', *The Guardian*, 24 March.

Davoudi, S. (2015) 'Research impact: should the sky be the limit?', in E. Silva, P. Healey, N. Harris and P. van den Broeck (eds) *The Routledge Handbook of Planning Research Methods*, London: Routledge, pp 405–14.

Edwards, M. (2004) *Civil Society*, Cambridge: Polity Press.

Etzkowitz, H. (2003) 'Innovation in innovation: the triple helix of university–industry–government relations', *Social Science Information*, 42(3): 293–337.

Glenna, L., Shortall, S. and Brandl, B. (2014) 'Neoliberalism, the university, public goods and agricultural innovation', *Sociologia Ruralis*, 55(4): 438–59.

Goddard, J. (2009) 'Reinventing the civic university', Provocation 12, NESTA.

Healey, P. (2006) 'Territory, integration and spatial planning', in M. Tewdwr-Jones and P. Allmendinger (eds) *Territory, Identity and Space*, Abingdon: Routledge, pp 64–80.

Joyce, R. and Xu, X. (2020) 'Sector shutdowns during the coronavirus crisis: which workers are most exposed?', briefing note, Institute for Fiscal Studies, 6 April. Available at: www.ifs.org.uk/publications/14791

Kolehmainen, J., Irvine, J., Stewart, L., Karacsonyi, Z., Szabó, T., Alarinta, J. and Norberg, A. (2016) 'Quadruple helix, innovation and the knowledge-based development: lessons from remote, rural and less-favoured regions', *Journal of the Knowledge Economy*, 7(1): 23–42.

Laing, K.L., Mazzoli Smith, L. and Todd, L. (2017) 'The impact agenda and critical social research in education: hitting the target but missing the spot?', *Policy Futures in Education*, 16(2): 169–84.

Lam, A. (2000) 'Tacit knowledge, organisational learning and societal institutions: an integrated framework', *Organisation Studies*, 21(3): 487–513.

Leat, D. and Thomas, U. (2018) 'Exploring the role of "brokers" in developing a localised curriculum', *Curriculum Journal*, 20(2): 201–18.

Lightowler, C. and Knight, C. (2013) 'Sustaining knowledge exchange and research impact in the social sciences and humanities: investing in knowledge broker roles in UK universities', *Evidence and Policy*, 9(3): 317–34.

Lomas, J. (2007) 'The in-between world of knowledge brokering', *British Medical Journal*, 334: 129–32.

Mackinnon, D. and Derickson, K.D. (2012) 'From resilience to resourcefulness: a critique of resilience policy and activism', *Progress in Human Geography*, 37(2): 253–70.

Mazzucato, M. (2013) *The Entrepreneurial State: Debunking Public vs Private Sector Myths*, London: Anthem Press.

Morgan, K. (2016) 'Speaking truth to power: the political dynamics of public sector innovation', in D. Kyriakou (ed) *Governance of Smart Specialisation*, London: Routledge.

Peck, J. (2014) 'Explaining (with) neoliberalism', *Territory, Politics, Governance*, 1(2): 132–57.

Peck, J. and Tickell, A. (2002) 'Neoliberalising space', *Antipode*, 34(3): 380–404.

Peck, J., Theodore, N. and Brenner, N. (2010) 'Postneoliberalism and its malcontents', *Antipode*, 41(1): 94–116.

Pohl, C., Rist, S., Zimmerman, A., Fry, P., Gurang, G., Schneider, F., Speranza, C., Kiterne, B., Boillat, S., Serrano, E., Hirsch Haddron, G. and Wiesman, U. (2010) 'Researchers' roles in knowledge co-production: experience from sustainability research in Kenya, Switzerland, Bolivia and Nepal', *Science and Public Policy*, 37(4): 267–81.

Sebba, J. (2013) 'An exploratory review of the role of research mediators in social science', *Evidence and Policy*, 9(3): 391–408.

Shortall, S. and Shucksmith, M. (1998) 'Integrated rural development: issues arising from the Scottish experience', *European Planning Studies*, 6(1): 73–88.

Shucksmith, M. (2010) 'Disintegrated rural development? Neo-endogenous rural development, planning and place-shaping in diffused power contexts', *Sociologia Ruralis*, 50(1): 1–14.

Shucksmith, M. (2016) *InterAction: How Can Academia and the Third Sector Work Together to Influence Policy?*, Dunfermline: Carnegie UK Trust.

Stone, C. (1989) *Regime Politics: Governing Atlanta, 1946–1988*, Lawrence, KA: University Press of Kansas.

Storper, M. (2015) *The Rise and Fall of Urban Economies*, Stanford, CA: Stanford University Press.

Todd, L. (2007) *Partnerships for Inclusive Education. A Critical Approach to Collaborative Working*, London: Routledge.

Todd, L. (2012) 'Critical dialogue, critical methodology: bridging the research gap to young people's participation in evaluating children's services', *Children's Geographies*, 10(2): 187–200.

Tooze, A. (2020) 'The normal economy is never coming back', *Foreign Policy*, 9 April. Available at: https://foreignpolicy.com/2020/04/09/unemployment-coronavirus-pandemic-normal-economy-is-never-coming-back/

Unwin, J. (2018) 'The story of our times: shifting power, bridging divides, transforming society', Civil Society Futures, November. Available at: https://civilsocietyfutures.org/wp-content/uploads/sites/6/2018/11/Civil-Society-Futures_The-Story-of-Our-Future.pdf

Unwin, J. (2020) 'Nine things I've noticed this week', blog, 20 March. Available at: www.juliaunwin.com/nine-things-ive-noticed-this-week/

Vallance, P. (2016) 'The historical roots and development of the civic university', in J. Goddard, E. Hazelkorn, L. Kempson and P. Vallance (eds) *The Civic University*, Cheltenham: Edward Elgar.

Wainwright, H. (2018) *A New Politics from the Left*, Cambridge: Polity Press.

Whitty, G. and Wisby, E. (2007) 'Whose voice? An exploration of the current policy interest in pupil involvement in school decision-making', *International Studies in Sociology of Education*, 17(3): 303–19.

Wright, E.O. (2010) *Envisioning Real Utopias*, London: Verso.

# Index

Page numbers in **bold** refer to tables and in *italics* to figures.